THE
RELENTLESS
OFFENSIVE

THE
RELENTLESS
OFFENSIVE

WAR AND BOMBER COMMAND 1939-1945

ROY IRONS

Pen & Sword
AVIATION

n Great Britain in 2009
d Sword Aviation
imprint of
Sword Books Ltd
hurch Street
Barnsley
South Yorkshire
S70 2AS

Copyright © Roy Irons, 2009

ISBN 978 1 84415 819 5

Printed in the UK by the MPG Books Group

Pen and Sword Books Ltd incorporates the imprints of
Pen and Sword Aviation, Pen and Sword Maritime, Pen and Sword
Military, Wharncliffe Local History, Pen and Sword Select,
Pen and Sword Military Classics and Leo Cooper.

For a complete list of Pen and Sword titles please contact
Pen and Sword Books Limited
47 Church Street, Barnsley, South Yorkshire, S70 2AS, England
E-mail: enquiries@pen-and-sword.co.uk
Website: www.pen-and-sword.co.uk

Contents

Foreword

The idea of researching Bomber Command began as a PhD project on tactics and technology, but due to ill health, and a consequently much reduced speed of research, the project began to lengthen and the expense of even a part time degree became unjustifiable. A book, however, gives not only more time, but enables the writer to concentrate upon the aspects of his research which he finds the most interesting, and the necessarily narrower constraints of disciplined study are, at the extremes either of age or youth, gratefully abandoned to this happy indulgence.

The campaign waged by Bomber Command between 1939 and 1945 has ever since excited admiration and horror, sometimes almost in the same breath. Much has been written, and much will continue to be written, about this campaign, its morality, its military effectiveness and its results. The casualties to civilians and crews alike are weighed in a moral balance against the savage brutalities of the regime whose fall it certainly hastened, and its contribution to that fall is the subject of an unusual moral argument, in which ethical justification depends more on judgements of its military effectiveness than on its motive, so terrible was the German regime and so destructive the campaign.

The central fact of the Bomber campaign, from which all else flows, is that the bomber was – with the exception of one type, the Mosquito, the 'speed bomber' – indefensible. A seemingly culpable inertia and a blind adherence to doctrine left it armed through most of the war with guns of rifle calibre. It was undefended by fighters until the more energetic and less doctrinaire Americans proved the case, albeit with the essential aid of Sir Wilfrid Freeman and his brainchild, the Merlin-engined Mustang fighter. It was therefore banished to the night, and even there it was always in mortal danger, yet could do little effective destruction. But the scientists had taken a hand; a thorough and very detailed analysis of the German air raids brought the opposite conclusion to that of the German attackers, who thought that they had failed. Strategic bombing was found to be worthwhile, if done properly. Brilliant minds made night bombing much more accurate, helped to cloak the bombers from prying electronic eyes, and armed the relentless offensive, not with hot revenge, not even with cold revenge, but a statistical analysis of costs and benefits, of weapons and vulnerabilities, in which civilian deaths and injury and homelessness, whether by fire or blast, were reduced to benefit formulae in a calculation of victory.

But while the unemotional mathematical clarity of great minds was bent with urgency and purpose towards the deeper exigencies of the campaign, simpler measures such as the ability to see out of a turret, to provide it with effective guns, to fill the bombs with the most effective explosives and to make the main weapon of the command – the 4 lb incendiary bomb – accurate, seem not to have been followed with comparable, or indeed with any, urgency. In a campaign in which over 55,000 crewmen died, the visions of Waterloo were darkened and obscured by the shades of Passchendaele. Of the morality of this staggering failure there can be no doubt.

My interest in Military History has been almost lifelong. It was therefore with great excitement that I took the opportunity provided by the myopial privatisation of the gas industry to take a degree in War Studies and History at King's College London. As I had to steal away to lectures during my final days at British Gas, I was restricted in my choice of subjects, and applied with some reservations for the course on 'European History since 1800', since I had had my eye on other subjects. I therefore sat in the lecture hall awaiting an opening lecture on revolutionary movements with little enthusiasm. The youngsters who filled the class were calling across to each other in loud voices, a general hubbub prevailed, and I feared that the tall white-haired man who I noticed quietly writing a book list on the blackboard would have difficulty controlling the throng. When the man turned, I saw that he was younger than I had imagined. He cleared his throat, and began to talk. There fell an immediate silence, nor was there a sound, not a cough or a whisper, for an hour, for all sat enthralled by the speaker's delivery as they were conducted through the smoky rooms and conferences, the lofty ideas and dangerous lives of the revolutionaries. This was my introduction to Professor Richard Overy. It was therefore with vast enthusiasm that I later attended his course on Germany 1914–1945, and I was not disappointed. I owe Richard a very great deal, not only for his help with this course and my previous book, but with his supervisory role in my PhD – his move to Exeter University was much regretted by many at King's, including myself. Richard has not seen this book, so although he was much involved in its genesis, he can bear no blame for the result.

My years at King's College were, of course, enlivened and informed by other very gifted tutors and other subjects. I wish I had space to mention them all, so delightful were those years, but I can only thank those who have assisted directly in this book. Firstly, Brian Bond, a military writer of great repute and a seminar chairman of great authority, charm and perspicacity, who invited me to do the daunting task of giving a talk on bomber defence to the Military History Seminar at the Institute for Historical Research. I am also grateful to Philip Sabin, not only for his lectures on ancient warfare, but for his advice on this book, and to Bill Philpott, who from his vast store of academic knowledge drew my attention to Coeman's *War and Punishment*.

Brian Riddle, the Librarian of the Royal Aeronautical Society, kindly drew my attention to Anthony Williams' article 'Cannon or Machine Gun?' in an *Aeroplane* article, and to many other publications. There seems to be no aeronautical matter mentionable which does not immediately produce a helpful smile, a verbal book list and an accurate summary of the contents.

I am most grateful to Sebastian Cox of the Air Historical Branch for his expert advice, and permission to view the Ludlow-Hewitt papers; to Hilary McEwan, Imperial College Archivist, for her help with the Tizard archive; to the staff of the Royal Air Force Museum for access to, and advice on, the Harris papers; to Elizabeth Martin and Claire Kavanagh for their help in the Cherwell Archive at Nuffield College; and to the ever helpful Julie Ash and the staff at the National Archives (Public Record Office).

My thanks are due to an old schoolfriend, the late David Sawyer, for his help and technical advice, in particular for sending me a copy of David Robertson's article on Alec Reeves in the *IEE Journal*.

I am indebted to Mr Fraser Mitchell, of the Handley Page Society, for his advice, and great kindness in sending me a copy of George Volkert's paper.

I have to thank two ex-Purchasing managers of British Gas for their help. Firstly, Geoff Johnson, who read through the book and offered many always helpful comments, including calling my attention to my inclusion of some otherwise interesting, but utterly irrelevant, material and for judicious warnings when he observed me straying from my intended thematic approach. Secondly, to Albert Foot, for his always astute and valuable comments on the philosophy of the last chapter.

My thanks are due to Peter Coles and Ting Baker at Pen and Sword; to Peter for his patience, and to Ting for her unerring detection and sympathetic indication of many textual inconsistencies.

I have long valued the friendship of Harry Winter, and thank him for permission to include his experiences. The story of his career at Bomber Command in the Appendix illustrates in his own words the quiet and matter of fact approach to the most hair raising emergencies which seems to typify the men of the Command, while his very variable experiences of captivity illustrate that all 'nations' are composed of individuals, who when acting as individuals are capable of great humanity towards a helpless enemy prisoner.

I must thank many people for their encouragement. My long time friend Joanna White, of Melbourne, has encouraged me not only directly, but by the example of her dedication to her musical compositions. My twin brother Ken I have known even longer – as long as it's possible for me to know anyone – and his encouragement has always been great, although I cannot persuade him in turn to market his own literary works more assiduously. My daughter Rebecca has always been helpful, always warm, always enlivening; and her advice, especially on computer matters, invaluable.

Lastly, Erica, my wife; always my *sine qua non*.

Prologue

Walking along the Victoria Embankment in London, the curious traveller might come across an obelisk, erected originally by the imperious pride of the great Egyptian Pharaoh Thutmose III, removed to a Roman temple in Alexandria by the Emperor Augustus, and in 1878 erected on the banks of the Thames, amid the applause of the people of the capital city, in celebration of heroes of a more extensive Empire, secure and invulnerable behind the great guns of her ironclad fleets. Sphinxes were cast, and placed on either side. One of these sphinxes is gouged and scarred, and an explanatory plaque bears witness to an event just thirty-nine years after their erection which ushered in a new era – the first bombing of London by a fleet of German aeroplanes on 4 June 1917.

The deep shock of this event, which would have been incredible to those who had witnessed the erection of 'Cleopatra's Needle', exploded all the old certainties, and blew in a new era of insecurity and terror. As the power and payload of the aeroplane increased, the destruction of cities by explosives and fire and poison gas, and the ruin of civilisation itself, were foreseen in lurid and terrible visions of a future war. Some thought salvation lay in disarmament and the destruction of all military aeroplanes; some in a League of Nations, which would police the world. The Royal Air Force, created amid the bloodshed of the Great War, saw salvation in the doctrine of a relentless offensive by a bomber force which would sail over trench lines to the enemy cities and annihilate the ability of the enemy to wage war, thus promising a peace of terrors, or a war of horrors.

This book gives a view of how that doctrine, clothed with fire and explosives, driven by courage and coldly sharpened by scientists, brought those visions to reality.

CHAPTER ONE

The Doctrine

...This method, conclusions first, reasons afterwards, has always
been in high favour with the human race: you write down at
the outset the answer to the sum; then you proceed to fabricate,
not for use but for exhibition to the public, the ciphering by
which you pretend to have arrived at it...

AE Housman[1]

The doctrine first took root and flourished in the mind of a very
extraordinary man. Hugh Montague Trenchard was born in 1873, the
son of a Captain in the King's Own Yorkshire Light Infantry. Powerful
in both mind and voice – his later nickname was 'Boom' – he always found
difficulty in communicating his thoughts clearly, being both inarticulate
and almost illegible, and after several examination failures, he finally
entered the Army via the militia, being commissioned into the Royal Scots
Fusiliers. He fought in the Great Boer War, serving in the 1st Imperial
Yeomanry Bushman Corps, and later, the Canadian Scouts. Dangerously
wounded in the autumn of 1900, Trenchard was to serve again in the war
in the mounted infantry, and in subsequent years gave distinguished
service in Nigeria. By February 1912 Trenchard, a man, in Vincent Orange's
memorable phrase,[2] 'impatient of all orders except his own', was casting
around for new fields, applying to the colonial defence forces of Australia,
New Zealand and South Africa, and in May of that year to the Macedonian
Gendarmerie. While these applications were under consideration at the
War Office, the newly formed Royal Flying Corps (RFC) attracted his
attention, and with just ten days left before he would be considered by the
War Office as too old to fly, he applied himself to learn. A model pupil, he
passed within a week, little realising, perhaps, that this achievement would
be of some significance in the history of the Air Force, and of the world.

As an indication of the remarkable skill and personality which Major
Trenchard possessed, having passed on 13 August 1912, by 1 October he
was appointed an instructor, and on 23 September 1913 he became
assistant commandant. On 7 August, three days after the United Kingdom
declared war on Germany, Lieutenant Colonel Trenchard applied himself

with boundless energy to the task of expansion, recruiting pilots and mechanics and scouring the country for aircraft. On 18 November 1914, he was appointed to command the First Wing at St Omer, and in August 1915 to command the RFC in France, continuing until 1918, when he was briefly Chief of the Air Staff, then commander of the Independent Bombing force, before finally becoming Chief of the Air Staff again, a position he would hold until his retirement in 1929, when he was appointed Commissioner of the Metropolitan Police.

In September 1916 Major General Trenchard elaborated the doctrine in a memorandum entitled 'Future Policy in the Air'. He began by pointing out that the air operations in the Somme offensive had been fought mainly over the enemy's lines, and speculated on the action which should be taken were the enemy to become more aggressive. Because the 'moral effect of an aeroplane is out of all proportion to the damage it can inflict' (a recurring theme for the next three decades) there would be a temptation to detach aeroplanes from offence to defence. But because the sky was so large, vision so uncertain in the air, wind and cloud so unpredictable, this was a mistaken policy – some aeroplanes would always get through, even with unlimited defenders, and feints would force the defenders into guarding everything. There followed a statement of the central core of the doctrine: 'The aeroplane is not a defence against the aeroplane.' The aeroplane was an offensive weapon, not a defensive one. The considerable moral effect of aeroplanes, said Trenchard, should be exploited by attacking with them, and not allowing the enemy to exploit their moral effect upon you. If the enemy still attacked you, then you should extend the attack to the enemy's homeland, to his industries and communications. In the air, attack was the only defence.[3]

On the Western Front, the offensive maintained by the RFC had been expensive in blood and aeroplanes, but it had, to an extent, been dictated by the early course of the war. Defeated on the Marne in 1914 and falling back, the Germans had skilfully selected every advantage of ground on which to stand on the defensive. The British positions were overlooked, while the Germans generally occupied the high ground, and the Army was therefore reliant upon the use of both kite balloons and aircraft for observation purposes. Reliance upon defence under these circumstances meant accepting a severe disadvantage in intelligence for the Army.

From reconnaissance had grown fighting and ground attack, both with bombs and machine guns. The aeroplane also became essential for artillery spotting and aerial photography, which gave a constantly updated mosaic of the German positions. The Royal Naval Air Service (RNAS) had in 1916 begun a strategic bombing attack on Germany from its base at Luxeuil les

Bains in Belgium which, although the targets were mostly naval industries, had caused a 30% drop in output at some of the factories in the Saar and caused the Germans to detach squadrons and guns for home defence. Paradoxically, the RFC objected to this, as it wanted all available aircraft to support the Flanders offensive, although the Navy's offensive was doctrinally agreeable, in drawing off German forces by a relentless attack. The call to the strategic offensive was, however, shortly to be renewed by the dramatic event of a German daylight air raid on the capital.

The great shock of the German daylight air raids of 1917 led the cabinet on 2 July 1917 to order a vast expansion of the Air Force from 108 to 200 squadrons, the majority of the additions to be used for bombing Germany. The alarming failure of the defences also led the Prime Minister, David Lloyd George, to form a committee to consider 'the defence arrangements for home defence against air raids', and the 'air organisation generally and the direction of aerial operations.' The Committee consisted of himself as chairman, and Lieutenant General Smuts, a militarily gifted leader of the Boers some fifteen years before, and now visiting London after his recent conquest of German South West Africa. General Smuts was empowered to consult the leaders of the Army and Navy. His first report dealt with the organisation of the defence of the United Kingdom, and with the great diversion of forces which even a single bombing squadron could provoke.[4]

His second report, dated 17 August 1917, included the following passage.

> …Essentially, the Air Service is as subordinated to military and naval direction and conception of policy as the artillery is, and as long as that state of affairs lasts, it is useless for the Air Board to embark on a policy of its own, which it could neither originate nor execute under present conditions.

> The time is, however, rapidly approaching when the subordination of the Air Board and the Air Service can no longer be justified. Essentially the position of an Air Service is quite different from that of the artillery arm, to pursue our comparison; artillery could never be used in war except as a weapon in military or naval or air operations. It is a weapon, an instrument ancillary to a service, but could not be an independent service itself. Air Service on the contrary can be used as an independent means of war operations. Nobody that witnessed the attack on London on 11th July could have any doubt on that point. Unlike artillery an air fleet can conduct extensive operations far from, and independently of, both army and navy. As far as can at present be foreseen there is absolutely no limit to the scale of its future independent war use. And the day may not be far off when

aerial operations with their devastation of enemy lands and destruction of industrial and populous centres on a vast scale may become the principal operations of war, to which the older forms of military and naval operations may become secondary and subordinate...

The report went on to recommend an independent Air Ministry which would look after the surplus of aircraft for 'independent' operations which the recent vast increases in production would yield, even after deducting all that the Army and Navy might require. Neither of the old services was felt to be competent to do this. General Smuts wrote:

It requires some imagination, to realise that next summer, while our Western Front may be moving forward at a snail's pace in Belgium and France, the air battle front will be far behind on the Rhine... and may form an important factor in bringing about peace. The enemy is no doubt making vast plans to deal with us in London if we do not succeed in beating him in the air and carrying the war to the heart of his country.

Smuts then went on to forecast that air power might not only triumph in a strategic role, but also in a tactical, theatre role, such as Palestine, wresting 'victory and peace' by 'cutting... precarious and limited railway communications' and preventing the enemy from concentrating their forces against an advance. In the event, General Maude's victories at Megiddo in 1918 would be turned into catastrophe for the Turkish forces by air attack on the narrow mountain passes through which their defeated armies were attempting to retreat.

The German aeroplane raids seemed to confirm and enlarge the Trenchard doctrine, for defence had been difficult and had indeed entailed a great diversion of forces. The real defence against German raids was to be sought in the creation of a very large strategic bombing force, not only to divert enemy forces, but to ruin his industry.

The Smuts report was accepted, and the RAF replaced and amalgamated the Army's RFC and the Navy's Royal Naval Air Service on 1 April 1918. Ten days earlier, General Smuts' forecast for the Western Front had been proved to be utterly mistaken, for the front exploded into activity in the first of three huge German offensives. After a hurricane preliminary bombardment that had cut telephone lines and hit machine guns and artillery, storm troopers had penetrated the British line and sent the Army reeling back. They had been supported by a strong concentration of the German Air Force, flying ground attack missions and protected by two layers of aircraft above them. The German forces were eventually contained, and after a further two offensives, Germany had shot her bolt. She had lost some 800,000 men. Air power played no small part in the defeat of these offensives, as a cautionary German document of July 1918 reveals. It stated that in the recent offensives, 'losses through the action of enemy aviators has proved to be extraordinarily high'. It called on the troops, even in training and in rear areas, to avoid main roads, to dig zigzag trenches, to keep a close lookout for aircraft, to avoid crowding and blocks in roads, to shelter horses under the cover of trees when stopped and to disperse vehicles. Anti-aircraft machine guns were to become essential equipment for artillery, for troops on the move, and even for troops in training behind the lines.

In the great emergency of the German 1918 offensives, the Allies agreed on a *generalissimo* – Marshal Foch of France – who now orchestrated a series of attacks on the German lines, each one broken off before momentum was lost. In these attacks, the British Army played a major part. The Air Force, as well as protecting the British kite balloons, protecting observation aircraft and artillery spotting, was heavily engaged in ground attack, targeting the highly effective and dangerous German anti-tank guns, bombing and machine-gunning troops and machine gun nests and calling artillery fire down on exposed German forces. So formidably accurate had artillery become, that this was virtually a death sentence to troops in the open.[5]

Yet these were not the only influences of the RAF on the defeat of Germany in 1918. In May of that year, the decision was taken to form an Independent Force, under Major General Trenchard, for the bombardment of Germany.[6] The attacks of the RNAS Luxeuil Wing, which were noted above as having been suspended at the request of the Army, were renewed after the bombing of London by the 'small and makeshift'[7] forces of the 41st Wing, later called the 8th Brigade, of the RFC. The Allied air raids on Germany delivered 14,208 bombs, 229 by day and 446 by night, 37% of the total in 1917 and 50% in 1918. German casualties were 746 killed and 1,843 injured, and the cost £1.2 million.

In 1928, Major Grosskreutz, writing in *Die Luftwacht*, made the following comment:

> The direct destructive effect of the enemy air raids did not correspond with the resources expended for this purpose. On the other hand, the indirect effect, namely, falling off in production of war industries, and also the breaking down of the moral resistance of the nation, cannot be too seriously estimated.

In assessing the role of air power in the Great War, the central fact must always be that victory had come on the Western Front by the direct application of military power. The war had lasted for so long, and been so bloody, not because of trenches or artillery or machine guns, important as these were. The central fact had been that the German Army, five million men, imbued with pride, with the iron Prussian discipline, with competent leaders and an incomparable organisation, faced superior forces which it proved incapable of defeating. That great nation, of 'nearly seventy million souls, constituting the most industrious, tractable, fierce and martial race in the world'[8] could not be defeated until its army had been defeated in the field. This the Allies accomplished in 1918, the British Army bearing the brunt of the offensive. The British Army had grown, by 1918, to be the equal, if not the superior, of the German. This was achieved by a perfect combination of all arms, of artillery, of ground attack and artillery spotting and bombing and mapping and fighting aircraft, of machine gun barrages and infantry attacks supported by tanks, all co-ordinated by a first class communications system. When the German Army had been defeated in the West, her allies, Austria–Hungary, Turkey, Bulgaria – collapsed. Finally, Germany collapsed, in revolution, strikes, mutinies and chaos. The primary role of air power had been intimately connected with the army, and air power had been a very essential part of that army's victory, and in the victories of the French and American armies.

But the analysis of the defeat of Germany was complicated and obfuscated by the German moral collapse and revolution. As an analogy, consider the destructive testing of a sample of steel. Put into the test apparatus, sufficient force is applied until the metal cracks. Scientists then examine the metal to see *how* the break occurred. But there is no science necessary in determining *why* – the metal cracked because overwhelming force was applied. Similarly, Germany cracked because overwhelming force was applied – defeat in the field, blockade and hunger, the realisation that defeat was inevitable. *How* did she crack? In revolution, precipitated by the failure of nerve of General Ludendorff, the German Chief of Staff and effective army commander. Ludendorff, having become convinced that victory was no longer possible, arranged a meeting with Germany's political leaders. On 29 September 1918 he seems to have suffered a fit, brought on by the successful British attack on the Hindenburg line. Recovering, his will broken, he decided that it was necessary to appeal at once for an armistice. On 1 October, he told the horrified German Government, precipitating a moral collapse. For Germany, *how* the war ended was in a complete breakdown of the home front, in mutiny and civil war, revolution and bloodshed, precipitated by

Ludendorff's catastrophic failure of nerve. Irresistible force was applied to the structure, and this was how it collapsed. In the midst of revolution and mutiny, she was forced to accept armistice terms which precluded any possibility of continuing the war, which she might otherwise have continued into 1919.

All this would be used by Hitler and the German right to argue, not that defeat had caused revolution, but that revolution had caused defeat. The involvement of Jewish intellectuals in the revolutions would be highlighted by the right, while the role of the many thousands of German Jews who would lie forever in German war graves was disgracefully forgotten. Even now, with the centenary of these events a little over eleven years away, a discussion of the role of the German revolution and the undoubted and understandable indignation of the soldiers who fought bravely on, some of whom regarded it as a 'stab in the back', arouses fears of a seeming justification of the nightmare of the slaughter of the innocents which afflicted Europe, and which that continent will rightly remember for centuries. But in any long drawn out conflict, divisions will arise between those who see peace without victory as a betrayal of the dead, and those who see war without end as a betrayal of the living. British soldiers would feel 'stabbed in the back' in the Great War – Guy Gibson, born in 1918 and a Bomber Command pilot of quite extraordinary skill and heroism, would write:

> I had read books on the last war and knew that apart from the many lives lost and the chaos, misery and devastation it caused, new, evil and unknown things blighted the country, such as inflation, racketeers and industrial money grabbers. I hoped that this would not happen in this war and, if it did, there would be the severest punishment for such individuals.[9]

Germany had its share of these, and defeat vastly increased and sharpened the bitterness. But they did not *cause* the defeat. The inescapable truth was, the 'stab in the back' perceived by many Germans was irrelevant to the conflict; they had been battered to death from the front. The defeat was in the field, and was brought about chiefly by the British Army, with the lessons of four years' failed offensives behind it, in a brilliant campaign in which air power, artillery, machine gun barrages, infantry attacks and armoured support had been combined. Yet, the German revolution *had* occurred, and it *had* shortened the war. The Official Historian put the bombing contribution to the revolution thus:

> It was the allied aeroplanes that carried the war into Germany, and when hopes of a military victory on the Western front had been

shattered the outlook of the people was such that the maximum moral effect was assured for aircraft bombing.[10]

Thus the revolution may have been a factor in the consideration that, in any future bombing war between Germany and Britain, Germany would crack first. The morale factor was supported by highly dubious anecdotes to show the terrible effects of strategic bombing. A captured letter concerning air raids on Mannheim, stated:

> My eyes won't keep open while I am writing. In the night, twice into the cellar, and again this morning. One feels as if one were no longer a human being. One air raid after another. In my opinion this is no longer war, but murder. Finally in time one becomes horribly cold, and one is daily, nay hourly, prepared for the worst.

Even those who tried to plan a practical campaign against German industry were very conscious that morale factors supported and underpinned all their efforts. Lieutenant Commander Lord Tiverton of the RNAS in Paris, writing to Captain Vyvyan of the Air Board Office in London on 3 September 1917, pointed out that concentration was of vital importance, both materially and for its effect on morale. Day bombing was preferable to night bombing both for its accuracy and for navigation and for morale, since at night the people were 'in their own houses where they have at any rate got a roof over their heads, a fact which gives a considerable moral sense of safety and a considerable practical factor of safety against stray shells from anti-aircraft guns'. Tiverton also recognised the vital factor of concentration, both for material damage and morale, suggesting that if Mannheim were attacked by 100 squadrons and 'if Frankfurt were attacked later in a similar way it is quite possible that Cologne would create such trouble that the German Government might be forced to suggest terms before the town was attacked.'[11]

(Paradoxically, on 18 September, Captain Vyvyan told Tiverton that 'The Army at last I think have grasped the fact that aeroplanes are long-range artillery and seem anxious to make up the leeway'. This is an interesting observation, in view of General Smuts' comment in his second report dated 17 August that 'artillery could never be used in war except as a weapon in military or naval or air operations…').

All this may seem an irrelevance to the history of Bomber Command and its doctrine, but the cracking of *morale* lay at the heart of the doctrine of strategic bombing. It had been obvious that the material damage caused by strategic bombing to the gigantic power of German industry had been very little. It had been intended in 1919 to attack Germany with the new four-engined bomber, the Handley Page V/1500, which, with its crew of six, could carry thirty 250 lb bombs to Berlin. The British Government had ordered 255 of these formidable machines, and three had been delivered prior to the Armistice. But Germany had cracked first. The great essential of the offensive strategic doctrine was its effect on morale, and the very essential fact that, in any future bombing war between Britain and Germany, Germany would crack. The other essential was, of course, that Britain would *not* crack, so any analysis of the effect of bombing on British morale would need to tread a fine line between emphasising the great moral effect of bombing *and* a superior British resilience.

In March 1922 a report on the 'General Effect of German Air Raids on Industry during the Late War'[12] was issued to the Committee of Imperial Defence by the Air Ministry.

The first section consisted of an interview with Sir Herbert Walker KCB of the London and South Western Railway. It also contained extracts from the official publication *British Railways in the Great War, Part V*, which made the point that the system of air raid alarms for railways had been 'altogether defective', noting that a raid on Sheerness had resulted in a stoppage of all trains in the whole London area. Some 4,000 people had been left at London Victoria Station, and had a bomb landed among them, the result would have been catastrophic.

On the London Underground (tube) railways the official policy had been that people who were in the streets when the alarm sounded might take shelter in the stations below. However, it was noted that, in an air raid on London, which had resulted in fifteen deaths and seventy injuries, 'the rush to the tubes was so great that that the number of people who sought refuge in them was estimated at 100,000'. On the following night, another raid brought 120,000 shelterers.

> On September 26th and on September 27th [1917], people began to flock into the tubes as early in the evening as half past five, without waiting for any warning. On neither of these two nights, in fact, was there an air raid at all.

The report went on to say that:

> On the very rumour of a raid being expected – and even as a result of what had become a matter of almost nightly routine – thousands of people, *mostly belonging to the poorer type of aliens in the east end or in the north east of London* [italics added], left their homes and went to the tubes, where they proceeded to camp out until such time as the danger, real or imaginary, was over. They not only went there in entire families, diminutive girls or boys carrying the latest baby, but they took with them supplies of provisions, pillows and bedding, on small

carts or otherwise, together with their cat and their dog, their parrot or their pet canary. They established themselves on the stairs, along the passages, or on the platforms; though in the latter case they aimed at keeping as near to the exits as possible – resisting all attempts on the part of the railway officials to distribute them better – their aim being to make sure they would be among the first to leave when the 'all clear' message came. Should that message be late in coming, they had still made all possible provision for spending the night in the tubes with such comfort as they could expect. During the raid of February 1918, a total of 300,000 persons took shelter in the tubes.

A section of the report was drawn from the Home Office, and made the point that the decision to continue working the railways during alarms had, at first, 'occasioned some difficulty and protest both among railwaymen themselves and munition workers'. However, it noted that 'these difficulties …appear to have been overcome when the reasons for the policy adopted were fully explained to the men concerned'. In the North, great stoppages of work had occurred over wide areas due to alarms of Zeppelin raids, loss of production had been caused to ironworks due to shutting down blast furnaces on the orders of GHQ Home Forces, and the raids had 'a very bad effect upon the men', resulting in grave absenteeism. With the defeat of the Zeppelin raids, the 'Industrial Districts of the centre and North of England enjoyed immunity from air attack for the remainder of the war'.

A Mr HM Selby, Managing Director of Schneiders and Son, the largest clothing manufacturers in England, reported that the effect of air raids on production had been serious. In September 1917, the raids caused a reduction in output from 40,000 suits per factory to under 5,000. Mr Selby felt that this effect was so marked, because 90% of the employees were women, 'easily frightened and liable to panic'. The other 10% were *'alien Jews, who were even more liable to panic than the women'* (italics added). [Whether or not under 'alien Jews' they would have included a son of German Jewish immigrants to Melbourne is unknown; the cream of the British Army in the Great War were undoubtedly the Australians, and on the Western front they were led by the brilliant Monash, possessor of degrees in the arts, in law and in engineering, who could discourse expertly on medicine, on Beethoven, on history or on German military doctrine, who was mentioned three times in despatches at Gallipoli, a man who was the central figure in Ludendorff's 'black day' of 8 August 1918, and was a practising Jew who exactly fitted this description! No doubt also the Jewish Captain Stanley Lewis Tuck, formerly of the Royal West Surreys during the Great War, and his wife Ethel, might have been surprised had they read this; their son Wing Commander Roland Stanford Tuck, the famous Battle of Britain fighter pilot, no less so.] However, Mr Selby reported that the factories were on the direct line of approach of the bombers, and 'offered no shelter, being largely constructed of glass by reason of the necessity for light'. For poorly paid staff to remain sewing and cutting quietly for their wealthy employer in a factory made of glass under the flight path of aeroplanes dropping high explosive bombs might be considered behaviour more appropriate to a Buster Keaton film than to the real world.

However, the clothing manufacturers reported that production would cease anywhere in any trade in the East End, due to the *enormous preponderance of Jewish aliens about whom they spoke in no measured terms*'. But the report noted that Messrs Schneider, Jacobs, and others who voiced this opinion, 'appeared only to be separated from the class they so vigorously denounced by the narrow margin of wealth.'

This peculiar report ended with a statement by the Chief of the Air Staff himself. Sir Hugh Trenchard said that 70% of the clothing of 'the British Army, the Dominions, and of certain allied armies' was made in London and that as a result of air raids '80% of the workers…were continually leaving London'.

'Again,' said Sir Hugh, 'I remember a certain big manufacturer stating that one air raid alarm so upset the working arrangements of his factory that the works did nor recover their normal output for two months.' He made reference to the diversion of squadrons of fighters from the front in France for Home Defence. Needless to say, no reference was made to the diversion of aircraft from the front, where Germany had been defeated, for strategic bombing.

John Coteworth Slessor, another great and influential airman, spoke in a similar vein. Slessor was born in India on 3 June 1897, and entered the RFC in 1915. After the Great War, Slessor would enter the RAF Staff College, become Director of Plans at the Air Ministry, command a bomber group, lead Coastal Command and eventually become Chief of the Air Staff. While at the Staff College in 1925 he recalled, in a lecture, his experiences of October 1915, after a Zeppelin night raid on London. While driving through east London with spare parts for his crashed aircraft, he recounted that:

> …I had a special permit to use full headlights owing to the urgency
> of the duty on which I was employed. Coming through the east end
> of London we were practically mobbed by a crowd, and had finally to
> station a policemen on each side of the step in front to get along at

all. The people were certainly very frightened indeed. …

I was however very much impressed at the time with the very genuine state of funk, bordering clearly on panic, which seemed to possess the bulk of the population east of the Temple Bar after what was an inconsiderable dose of bombing compared to what we might expect in a future war. *It should be remembered that it is not the Englishman which we have to consider, so much as the aliens of all nationalities who constitute a respectable part of the population of greater London…* [italics added]

Slessor ended with the somewhat enigmatic comment that 'However, this whole question is now receiving attention in the proper quarters and there is nothing to be gained by discussing it further now.'

Thus was *strategic* air power justified by its terrible morale effect on cities, and its hint of panic and chaos, and social breakdown and disorder. What escaped mention was a German *tactical* raid on Calais on the night of 11 August 1918. Just nine aeroplanes were involved. Spare parts for 6,497 motor cars and ambulances, for 12,270 lorries and 799 tractors were destroyed. These figures represented about 55% of all motor cars and ambulances on service with the British armies on the Western front, 40 per cent of all lorries and 93 per cent of tractors. About 26,000 inner tubes and 16,000 tyres also disappeared. The monetary value of the goods destroyed amounted to one and a quarter million pounds sterling. '*It may be noted, in passing*', wrote the official historian, '*that this compares with an estimated monetary value of £1,434,526 for the damage caused by all of the fifty-two day and night aeroplane raids on London.*'[13] (italics added)

As a result of this raid, the transport position of the British Army on the Western front became immediately grave. An order was sent to home manufacturers giving 'absolute priority' to all outstanding orders for transport. Units in the field and in the UK had to surrender their spares. The British offensive in Macedonia was severely hindered by a lack of motor spares.

And in four successive night raids in May 1918 12,500 tons of munitions were destroyed by German bombers. The German 1918 offensives had compressed the British supply dumps into a small area, 'a situation so favourable to air action that the German air service, had it been strong enough to take advantage of the situation, might possibly have changed the course of the war.'[14]

So why, when tactical bombing of supply dumps had proved to be so successful on both sides, was so much emphasis in the new, post-war RAF placed on strategic, city, industrial area bombing? Why had an offensive doctrine, born of the struggle between the fighters[15] and partly if not mostly justified by German occupation of the high ground on the Western front, been extended to a strategic offensive? Trenchard's Independent Force itself had been used often on supply dumps, rail junctions and bridges, at the request of Field Marshal Haig, and with Trenchard's approbation. Indeed, Trenchard had himself been opposed to reprisal bombing at first, for the Germans 'would always beat us at reprisals unless we put forth our whole energy and this would seriously interfere with the supply of the machines necessary for artillery work.'[16] However, he did report his view that 'the German population is more easily moved by having their own country touched than the English population', although providing no evidence for this statement. Perhaps the German revolution provided a background justification.

The answer seems to be that Field Marshal Smuts' second report justified an independent Air Force by its ability to carry the war directly to the enemy, over trenches and fleets; and after the war, the older services demanded the return of their air arms. An independent Air Force could be justified best by strategic bombing. If the Army, as Captain Vyvyan hinted, had argued that strategic air power was 'long range artillery', Trenchard might have been in a more difficult position!

The RAF thus depended for its survival on strategic bombing, a form of war 'to which the older forms of military and naval operations may become secondary and subordinate'. Unfortunately, ground attack, army co-operation, the naval air arm, anti-submarine work and, almost to the last moment, fighter defence, became subordinated to the doctrine. Even a brilliant little *army* operation against Kurdish 'rebels' in Iraq, which received the maximum air support because the RAF were in supreme command, was, by a clever inversion, considered as an *air* operation with army support.[17]

The RAF was also preserved by what was almost a Dutch auction, Sir Hugh Trenchard's minimalist vision of (in his own inimitable style) 'building the foundations for a castle which may be built at some later date but in the meantime building a cottage upon those foundations' being preferred to the more militarily sound, but expensive and therefore politically offensive Imperial Air Force of the existing Chief of the Air Staff, Major General Frederick H Sykes CMG. The 188 operational squadrons became thirty-three. The strategic bomber force was disbanded. The doctrine survived.

Notes

1 Introductory lecture as professor of Latin at University College, London, in 1892, from http://www.chiark.greenend.org.uk/

2 Vincent Orange, *Slessor: Bomber Champion*, Grub Street, London 2006, 31.

3 When corps commanders in the British Second Army complained of enemy air attacks on their trenches, Field Marshal Haig agreed with Trenchard that there was *'no* other way of stopping them' than to bomb and attack more than the enemy. See diary entry for 2 Friday November 1917 in *Douglas Haig: War Diaries and Letters 1914–1918*, Weidenfeld & Nicholson, London, 2005.

4 PRO Air 41/39.

5 See Paddy Griffith, *Battle Tactics of the Western Front*, Yale University Press, London, 1994, p41 for an account of cavalry caught in a German 'box' barrage at Monchy Le Preux in 1917.

6 The cabinet had decided against a German proposal (received via the King of Spain) to mutually agree to halt the bombardment of open cities. This proposal would have effectively confined aerial bombardment to towns within twenty miles of the front line – all of which lay in France or Belgium! Born of the 'severe moral shock' caused by Allied bombing, this suggestion might even have weighed in favour of the Independent Force.

7 PRO Air 41/39.

8 Winston Churchill, 'Hitler and his Choice', in *Great Contemporaries*, Fontana Books, 1937 (4th impression 1972), 216.

9 Guy Gibson, VC, *Enemy Coast Ahead*, Pan Books, 3rd imp (London, 1955), 28.

10 HA Jones, *The War in the Air*, Naval and Military Press, London (originally published 1937).

11 PRO Air1/462/15/312/12.

12 PRO Air1/2132/207/121/1.

13 HA Jones, *The War in the Air*, Naval and Military Press, London, (originally published 1937), 429–30.

14 HA Jones, *The War in the Air*, Naval and Military Press, London (originally published 1937), 423.

15 PRO Air41/39.

16 PRO Air41/39.

17 See PRO Air1/2132/207/121/1 for Air Vice Marshal Sir John Salmond's despatch on operations in Iraq. Salmond's strategy was masterly. But see also Air5/292, Col Vincent's report on ops by 'Koicol' against the Kurdish rebels in the mountains 10–28 April, the success of which he attributed to the skill and experience of his 3 Btns of British and Sikh troops, the 3.7" Howitzer, and the *assistance* of the RAF.

CHAPTER TWO

Enter the Scientist

...one of the most hideous forms of sentimentalism which
has ever supported evil upon earth – the attachment of the
professional soldier to cruel and obsolete killing machines...
JBS Haldane, *In Defence of Chemical Weapons*

By mid 1944, every raid by Bomber Command was meticulously planned, the target selected by coldly analytical minds after careful research and aerial photography, and the precise weapons, weapon mixes, aiming points, bomb tonnages and bombing approaches selected with a literally mathematical precision. The backward looking National Socialist German war ethos, with its cult of the warrior, dark age myths and heroic oratory extolling the glories of battle, was countered and, to an extent, rendered helpless by the application of modern businesslike scientific demolition techniques. Some regret this method of warfare, though they are seldom to be numbered among those who would otherwise have had to descend into the Wagnerian arena and meet the warriors hand to hand. But science and Bomber Command had not always been so well and closely connected. Indeed, until 1924 there had been no department or individual in the Air Ministry whose task it was to devote himself *exclusively* to scientific research.

The need for science in bombing was foreseen by Winston Churchill when, as Minister of Munitions, he wrote a paper on 'Munitions Possibilities of 1918'.[1] He noted in typical Churchillian fashion that 'War proceeds by slaughter and manoeuvre'; the possibilities of manoeuvre had been constrained by the trench system across France, leaving manoeuvre to the sea and the air (although by no means banishing slaughter from those elements). Churchill noted that the German submarine campaign had forced Britain, in order to contain it, to divert fifteen or twenty times the effort expended by the Germans. Strangely, Churchill, not always prescient, had in a memorandum of 1 January 1914[2] rejected a suggestion by Admiral 'Jackie' Fisher that submarines would sink unarmed merchant vessels as 'an unthinkable proposition' that would never be carried out by 'a civilised power'. Against a power 'vile enough to adopt systematically such methods, it would be justified and indeed necessary, to employ the extreme resources of science against them', including the poisoning of water supplies. Churchill, however, did not propose, even under the circumstances of an unrestricted submarine warfare which was now only too apparent, that cities should be bombed for morale purposes, writing that 'it is not reasonable to speak of an air offensive as if it were going to finish the war by itself,' feeling that it was 'improbable that any terrorization of the civil population' would 'compel the Government of a great nation to surrender'. He noted, however, that injuries to the civil population by attacks 'on bases and communications' must be regarded as 'incidental and inevitable'.

These air attacks on bases and communications might, however, in conjunction with an army offensive, be decisive. Noting that some had decried the accuracy of bombing, he noted that others 'claimed that aerial warfare had never been tried except in miniature', and that 'bombing has never been studied as a science'. He also noted that 'the hitting of objects from great heights by day or night is worthy of as intense a volume of scientific study as, for instance, is brought to bear upon perfecting the gunnery of the Fleet.' But this was not pursued with any great vigour, and the science of aerial navigation and bombing, of bomb and bombsight design and performance, slumbered fitfully on until new aeroplanes, a new commander and the imminence of a new war awoke Bomber Command to the terrible truth, that its bombs, and how to find a target and to drop them accurately onto it – the sole reason for its existence – were in urgent need of the support of the scientist.

Sir Hugh Trenchard, Churchill's choice as Chief of the Air Staff, had fully realised the value of science to the RAF, but in the stringent financial circumstances after the war, it was not until 1924 that, on the suggestion of Air Marshal Salmond (and at the instigation of Henry Tizard, a brilliant scientist who we shall meet formally later on) a Director of Scientific Research (DSR) was appointed. There already existed an Aeronautical Research Committee (ARC) of eminent aeronautical scientists, which was purely an advisory body. This ARC controlled the Air Ministry Section of the National Physical Laboratory, and had 'considerable influence'[3] over the Royal Aircraft Establishment. The DSR now sat on the ARC, together with a new Director of Technical Development (DTD), jointly referred to as the Joint Directorate of Scientific Research. Deputy Directors were added in 1926. The first Director of Scientific Research was HE Wimperis, and he, with his Deputy, was to have a considerable influence upon Bomber

Command. Wimperis, who had served in the Royal Naval Air Service (RNAS) and the RAF as an Experimental Officer in the Great War, had later set up a small Air Ministry Laboratory at Imperial College. He was a friend of Tizard from his wartime days.[4]

The DSR aimed to improve the condition and status of scientists in the Air Ministry, so as to attract recruits of high quality, wishing to 'break down the barrier between the Air Ministry and the scientific world generally'. It was agreed with the universities that theses on confidential matters would be accepted by them for higher degrees. Air Ministry scientists were encouraged by a subsidy to attend meetings of scientific bodies in London, and Mr Wimperis also invited leading scientists to attend conferences organised by him. His Deputy, Dr Pye, would visit heads of university departments 'to arouse their interest and…encourage new graduates to turn towards the services'.

Obviously, the DSR kept in close touch with research at the ARC and the RAE, the National Physical Laboratory (NPL), the universities, the Aeroplane and Armament Experimental Establishment and the Ballistics Research Station at Orfordness. This close liaison with the scientific world generally was soon to bear fruit in a remarkable way. But great events in the wider world, in which old terrors and menaces seemed to loom ever closer, must first provide an increasingly fearful background.

In 1923, French action in the Ruhr led Britain to contemplate the extreme disparity in air power between the French, with their hundreds of bombers – 'a force 15 or 20 times as numerous as the *Englandgeschwader* had ever been and based within an even shorter range of London'[5] and the RAF – which, although the thought of war between the two nations was patently ludicrous, did not aid British diplomacy. It was decided to increase the RAF to, as a first stage, fifty-two squadrons (although this was not met), comprising thirty-five bombers and seventeen fighter squadrons. Trenchard had decided that the bombers would have to be self-defending, for otherwise the proportion of bombers to fighters would have had to have been lowered. However, all were under the organisation called 'Air *Defence* of Great Britain' (ADGB) – the only real defence was attack. The aeroplane was not a defence against the aeroplane.

In 1924, Ramsay MacDonald, the first Labour Prime Minister, appointed an Air Raid Precautions Sub Committee of the Committee of Imperial Defence to 'examine the whole question of the protection of the civil population against air attack'. On 23 July 1929, a 'policy' sub committee met for the first time under the chairmanship of Sir John Anderson, who would later give his name to the famous Anderson pre-fabricated garden shelter, and be given responsibility for 'Tube Alloys', the British atomic bomb project. Anderson, then Permanent Under Secretary of State at the Home Office, made clear how much the 'advent of the air arm had altered profoundly the whole aspect of war in the future'. He pointed out that in the Great War 300 tons of bombs had been dropped on England, and that the Air Ministry's view was, that in the event of a war with a first class European power, a *minimum* of 200 tons might be dropped on London on the first *day*, falling to 150 tons for the next day, and 100 tons every day thereafter.

The chairman noted that going down as low into the earth as possible was the most effective passive defence against high explosive blast and fragments, yet the worst possible action for avoiding poison gas; it was a dilemma reminiscent of that faced by the Britons 1,600 years before – 'The barbarians drive us to the sea, and the sea drives us to the barbarians'.

The natural question was, could the fighting services defend Britain in a better way? The Air Ministry explained that:

> ...whatever the state of efficiency of the defence it was quite certain that a proportion of the enemy would penetrate to the objective. On further consideration Sir John Anderson thought it could hardly be otherwise, since attack in 3 dimensions was being considered.

It was 'the considered opinion of the officers responsible for active defence arrangements, that the only way that relief could be obtained would be the launching of repeated counter attacks against the enemy...' Indeed, tactical exercises held later, in 1930, had resulted in the bombers getting through, the 'indifferent success' of the fighters being due to 'the superior speed of the bombers'.[6]

The gas problem, however, was rated as secondary to that of high explosive bombs, due to 'the almost universal ratification of the Geneva Gas Protocol', which outlawed its use. But this protocol, of course, had been ratified by the civilised, if ineffective, government of the German Weimar Republic. What reliance could be placed on the collection of gangsters, mystics, thugs and racial jingoists who had seized that great nation in 1933? On 12 December 1933, an appraisal of London's passive defence needs in the event of war noted that incendiary bombs would have to be *added* to the minimum of 200 tons of high explosive to be faced on the first day – and additionally estimated that 1,120 areas would be contaminated with gas every day, which would require 240 six-man decontamination squads and a *weekly* production of 20,000 tons of bleaching powder, the only agent known to destroy the very persistent mustard gas.

On 10 November 1932, the Lord President of the Council, Stanley Baldwin, [Prime Minister from 1923–4, 1924–9 and to be Prime Minister again from 1935–7] rose to address the House of Commons in words that have now become famous – even infamous.

> What the world suffers from – and I have said this before – is a sense of fear, a want of confidence, and it is a fear held instinctively and without knowledge very often. But in my view, and I have slowly and deliberately come to this conclusion, there is no one thing more responsible for that fear – I am speaking now of what the Hon. Gentleman the member for Limehouse [Clement Atlee, Deputy Prime Minister in Winston Churchill's war cabinet, and Prime Minister from 1945 to 1951] called the common people of whom I am chief – there is no greater cause of that fear than the fear of the air…I think it well for the man in the street to realise that there is no power on earth that can protect him from being bombed. Whatever people may tell him, *the bomber will always get through*, and it is very easy to understand that, if you realise the area of space…Now imagine a hundred cubic miles covered with cloud and fog, and you can calculate how many aeroplanes you would have to throw into that to have much chance of catching odd aeroplanes as they fly through it… *The only means of defence is offence*, which means that you have to kill more women and children more quickly than the enemy if you want to save yourselves…We remember in the last war areas where munitions were made. They now play a part in war that they never played in previous wars, and it is essential for an enemy to knock these areas out. *So long as they can be knocked out by bombing and no other way, you will never in the practice of war stop that form of bombing*…[italics added][7]

It is difficult to understand the extent of the uproar this caused, since Sir Hugh Trenchard could not have put it better himself. Indeed, he or his successor may have had a hand in the content.[8] But the world was changing politically, and not for the better.

In 1931, the Japanese Kwantung Army had provoked an incident, and seized Manchuria, which action was later ratified by the Japanese politicians, in constant fear of assassination. China, long the world's greatest and most civilised nation, had been for the previous century humiliated by both Europeans and Japanese, and protected only by their mutual jealousies and greed. She now entered a nightmare of suffering, from which she has only just awoken to a new dawn and a resumption of her natural place at the forefront of the nations. The League of Nations, the hope of the world, objected to the Japanese seizure. Japan, in martial pride, withdrew from it, showing the League's impotence to the world.

All this had been preceded by the great crash on the stock exchanges of 1929. This seminal event, followed by the Great Depression, hit Germany hardest of all, struggling as that nation was to repay the cost of the Great War to the victorious Allies. Germany had also borrowed heavily from America in order to rationalise her industry. The parliamentary parties signally failed to alleviate the unemployment and distress which followed, leaving hope to lie with the Communists and Nazis, who both promised comprehensive, radical solutions and a return to order. Hitler gained huge popular support. The German conservatives, thinking that they could use him to defeat the communists and socialists, invited him to be Chancellor. This dark genius of manipulation and violent intimidation, fired by fierce resentments and a pseudo scientific 'racial' mysticism, then seized power.

Whatever the view of these events which might be taken in Britain, whether to seek some arrangement, some *modus vivendi*, or to oppose the menace and nip it in the bud, it seemed prudent to increase armaments, especially in the air. The doctrine that the bomber will always get through, and that the only defence is therefore attack, loomed even larger and ever more fearfully in the minds of governments and people. British defence policy had, for the years of hope which followed the Great War, been based on a 'ten-year rule'.[9] In 1919, Lloyd George's cabinet decreed that the Admiralty, War Office and Air Ministry should base their estimates upon the presumption that the British Empire would not be involved in a major war during the next ten years. The rule applied only to that year, and to the finite period ending in 1930.

In February 1925 the rule was reaffirmed by a decision that the Admiralty might presume that no war with Japan would take place in the next ten years. In December of that year this was applied to the RAF by a postponement of the implementation of the fifty-two squadron ideal of 1923 until 1935/6. In July 1927 the Army was told to presume that no European war would take place within the ten years ending 1937. These restrictions were not 'rolling' ones, and applied to the Navy for the Far East and the Army and RAF for Europe.

But in July 1928, the Chancellor of the Exchequer, Winston Churchill, decreed that the forces should presume that no major war would take place within ten years, but on a 'rolling' basis, although this was to be reconsidered each year. This rolling ten-year rule was reaffirmed by the cabinet in 1929, 1930 and 1931, and was to have an effect on the RAF and its ability to conduct exercises, which will be recounted in the next chapter. The implementation of the rule meant that the RAF's expansion to fifty-two squadrons was postponed until 1938. But in 1932 the rule was withdrawn, and on 15 February 1933 the Cabinet directed that a start should be made on defensive preparations, with a priority for the Far East. In 1934 Parliament approved what is known as RAF expansion scheme 'A', which involved an increase in strength from the projected fifty-two to seventy-five squadrons, of which twenty-five were to be fighters.

Harold Macmillan, briefly Chief of the Air Staff in 1945 and Prime Minister from 1957–61, was to write that'we thought of air warfare in 1938 rather as people think of nuclear warfare today'.[10] In *The Shadow of the Bomber*,[11] Uri Bialer has detailed the impact of this fear on British politics between 1932 and 1939, and the hopes which were placed on disarmament, notably air disarmament, which also inhibited bomber development. That fear would cast its shadow over the Munich negotiations of 1938.[12] It is customary now, in the light of knowledge of the actual results from Second World War bombing, to suggest that the apocalyptic view of bombing taken by the Government and public in Britain was misplaced. Perhaps it was not. The great difference between the fear and the actuality was to lie in the dread of poison gas. Gas masks were available, but these were unpleasant and restricting to wear for long periods, and the view of the world provided through a gas mask in an air raid shelter or a cellar would be a most unpleasant and isolating one, particularly in view of the very lingering and persistent effect of mustard gas. Poisonous smokes could penetrate gas masks. As it transpired, the new German gases sarin and tabun would penetrate masks and be fatal if droplets touched the skin. The horrors were not overstated. In the event they were considerably reduced by the banning of the use of poison gas in the Geneva protocols of 1925. But who could say that this would *prevent* their use? Churchill himself, in fear of the flying bomb, proposed its use in 1944, although this was perhaps a petulant outburst at his own sidelining by the war professionals. Murder is *forbidden* by law, but is not *prevented* by it, and all else being equal, crime increases as the sanctions – retaliation by the law – are gradually relaxed. The sanction against poison gas was retaliation, and the bomber force was essential for this.

But the march of science and technology were now to swing the balance towards the fighter aeroplane. Great minds had applied themselves to the problems and mathematics of flight, of lift and drag, among them Professor B Melville Jones, who we shall encounter again later. Jones wrote *The Streamline Aeroplane* in 1929, and 'from this time onwards, the various components of drag and their relationship to each other began to receive detailed attention from designers, and aircraft performances improved out of all proportion to the extra power of the latest aero engines.'[13] The high drag biplane was replaced in the next decade by the low drag all metal stressed skin cantilever wing (ie not supported by struts) monoplane with a retractable undercarriage – and performance leapt forward year by year, for both fighters and bombers. Thicker aeroplane wings enabled machine guns to be mounted in them, without needing interrupter gear to fire through the propeller, which reduced the performance of both gun and engine. The fighter aeroplane began to gain major advantages over the bomber in both speed and firepower. *But it could not find the bomber.* During exercises in the summer of 1934, both the Houses of Parliament and the Air Ministry were 'destroyed'. Only two out of five bombers were intercepted.

A very great scientist, and a vigorous and very ambitious politician now took a hand in the debate. The great scientist was Frederick Alexander Lindemann (from 1941 Lord Cherwell) – and the politician the ubiquitous Winston Churchill. Lindemann was the son of an aristocratic Alsatian father (who left Alsace when Germany took it from France in 1871 and became a naturalised British citizen) and an American mother of Scottish descent. Although his name had German Jewish connotations, he denied Jewish ancestry,[14] and regarded himself as completely English. His birthplace, however, was Baden Baden in Germany, where his mother was staying at the time, a fact that seemed to some to qualify his claim to be British, and denied him a commission in the Great War. He was brought up in Devon, and after prep school in Scotland, he was educated in Darmstadt and then at the University of Berlin, where he studied under Nernst. His brilliance and all round scientific knowledge led Einstein, a lifelong friend, to describe him as 'the last of the great Florentines'. He was an accomplished pianist, had won the Swedish tennis championships and played at Wimbledon, and was also expert at squash, golf and skating. He was a very strict vegetarian and restricted himself to a very limited diet. He inherited great wealth and did not hide the fact, turning up for meetings in a chauffeur-driven Rolls-Royce.[15]

Professor Lindemann was employed in 1915 as a civilian researcher in the Royal Aircraft Establishment (RAE) at Farnborough, and applied himself to discover the mathematics involved when aircraft went into a spin, which at the time was usually fatal to the pilot. He then learnt to fly to put his work to the test, not wishing to risk the life of a pilot in the process. However, JBS Haldane, an anti-establishment scientific and mathematical genius who also gained a first class honours degree in classics at Oxford, and who had risked his life in experiments with poison gas during the Great War (in which he had been an extraordinarily daring soldier), later criticised Lindemann's arrogance and contempt for those who disagreed with him. 'I suspect that he was happy not only when risking his own life in the air, but when risking all our lives – and losing a great many – by impracticable schemes. Such people take to rock climbing.'[16] 'JBS' himself, however, was not noted for exceptional humility.

Lindemann was quintessentially English, even wearing a bowler hat and dark suit to fly, 'leaving his [carefully] folded coat, hat and umbrella in the plane before pulling on his flying suit and getting on board'.[17] Although very reserved, and of a political position described by Thomas Wilson[18] as 'marginally to the right – of Genghis Khan', he was to those who knew him best a charming man of quiet humanity and unobtrusive charity. He occupied the chair of experimental physics at Oxford.

Professor Lindemann had met Churchill in 1921, and they became friends for the rest of their lives. Churchill relied on Lindemann for scientific advice, and both men rejected the current acceptance of the defencelessness of cities. Professor Lindemann now wrote to *The Times*, in a letter published on 8 August 1934 and headlined 'Science and Air Bombing'. He wrote:

> Sir,
>
> In the debate in the House of Commons on Monday on the proposed expansion of our Air Forces, it seems to be taken for granted on all sides that there is, and can be, no defence against bombing aeroplanes and that we must rely entirely on counter – attack and reprisals. That there is at present no means of preventing hostile bombers from depositing their loads of explosives, incendiary materials, gases and bacteria upon their objectives I believe to be true; that no method can be devised to safeguard great centres of population from such a fate appears to me to be profoundly improbable…It seems not too much to say that bombing aeroplanes in the hands of gangster Governments might jeopardise the future of our whole Western civilisation…
>
> To adopt a defeatist attitude in the face of such a threat is inexcusable until it has definitely been shown that all the resources of science and invention have been exhausted. The problem is far too important and urgent to be left to the usual endeavours of individuals and departments. The whole weight and influence of the Government should be thrown into the scale to endeavour to find a solution. All decent men and all honourable Governments are equally concerned to obtain security against attacks from the air, and to achieve it no effort and no sacrifice is too great.[19]

At that time, the primary role in the detection of the approach of hostile aircraft lay with the War Office, fighter aircraft being considered a second line of defence to anti-aircraft guns. The Air Ministry, in their belief that the aeroplane was not a defence against the aeroplane, were, of course, committed to what was considered to be the real defence – the attack of enemy cities and airfields, industry and administration. But sound locators, the principal means of detection, were approaching the end of their usefulness, due to the rapidly increasing speed of aircraft.

However, despite the War Office's responsibility for the matter, at the Air Ministry, Dr AP Rowe, who, it will be remembered, was the Assistant Director of Scientific Research, proposed to the Director, HE Wimperis, that he should warn the Secretary of State for Air (Lord Londonderry) in a sinister reverse of the ten-year coin, that unless science evolved some new method of aiding air defence, Britain was likely to lose the next war if it started within ten years.

Mr Wimperis decided to approach the head of the Radio Department at the National Physical Laboratory, a Mr Watson Watt, to ask him his opinion on the use of radiant energy to directly disable aircraft and their occupants – the death ray beloved of inventors, cranks and fraudsters at the time. Mr Wimperis also discussed the matter over lunch at the Athenaeum with Professor AV Hill, a physiologist and Professor of Biophysics at University College London, who had been director of the Anti-Aircraft Experimental Section in the Great War, and who had 'helped to devise the rudiments of what was later called operational research'.[20] He minuted both the Secretary of State for Air and the Chief of the Air Staff, Sir Edward Ellington, suggesting that a committee should be formed under the chairmanship of Henry Tizard, comprising himself, and Professors PMS Blackett and AV Hill, to 'consider how far recent advances in science and technology can be used to strengthen the present means of defence against hostile aircraft'. The 'Committee for the Scientific Survey of Air Defence' was duly formed, and met for the first time on 28 January 1935. At that first meeting, a memorandum was submitted by Watson Watt, stating that a death ray was impracticable. However, it might be possible, the memorandum carried on, to detect an aircraft by means of radio waves.

At this point we should formally introduce the chairman, since he figures largely in any history or analysis of the bombing campaign in the Second World War. Henry Tizard (later Sir Henry) was born in 1885 at Gillingham in Kent, the son of Captain Thomas Henry Tizard RN, who traced his ancestry back to the Huguenots, and of a mother descended from a great family of civil engineers. He was, like Lindemann, quintessentially English – 'with a name like mine', he wrote, 'you have to be.' Henry Tizard appears to have enjoyed, again like Lindemann, an

Arcadian childhood. However, the fly which entered his left eye as a child, and partially blinded him, ended all hopes of following his father into the Navy, but his great mathematical abilities pointed to an academic career, and enabled him to enter Westminster School, from where he progressed with distinction to Magdalen College Oxford. Gaining a First in Chemistry, he went to Berlin for postgraduate research with the great Nernst, and there he met and befriended Lindemann. Frederick Alexander Lindemann was, as we have seen, a most accomplished sportsman, and detested being beaten by men of his own age. Henry Tizard kept fit at a Berlin gymnasium run by a former English lightweight champion, from whom, despite his defect of vision, he seems to have absorbed more than the rudiments of the noble art. He persuaded Lindemann to join him in the ring. Tizard, more fleet of limb, outclassed his inexperienced opponent, who lost his temper. Tizard, for this reason, declined to renew the contest on other occasions. 'I don't think he ever forgave me for that,' wrote Tizard. 'Still, we remained close friends for 25 years, but after 1936 he became my bitter enemy.'[21]

Tizard was no stranger to air force matters, for having enlisted in the Royal Garrison Artillery in 1914, he was given the task of training a platoon of Territorials in anti-aircraft gunnery. He was then invited by other scientists to the Central Flying School at Upavon in Wiltshire, where he worked on a bombsight. Checking the accuracy of bombing on the Western Front, he realised that the chance of gaining a hit using the current methods was small, and concluded that accurately gauging the performance of the aircraft itself was a necessity if bombing were to be accurate. Returning to Upavon, he learned to fly, and this experience stood him in good stead for the future, for he could always see things from the pilot's point of view, and so gained the trust of service personnel. Tizard had been offered the post of Director of Scientific Research at the Air Ministry in 1924, a post which we have seen he was instrumental in establishing. He commented later on the post – 'He [the Director of Scientific Research] had no responsibility, for instance, for radio research; was only partly concerned with Armament research and development; and had no scientific control over large scale trials, under conditions simulating that of war, of weapons and tactics of offence'.[22]

Tizard had said in a talk at the Royal Aeronautical Society in 1924:

Our little aeronautical world has tended to be divided into so called scientists (a small, slightly troublesome, and wholly incomprehensible sect) and practical men (who do the work). Placed on close but parallel lines, they meet only at infinity…[23]

This great understanding of the worlds of the scientist and the man of action was to be of vast use to his country.

On 26 February 1936 a successful test of radiolocation was conducted, which Rowe, the Committee's secretary, called RDF (Radio Direction Finding) as a cover, for although the existence of the target had been shown, its direction had not! Needless to say, this problem was soon solved, and thanks to Tizard's gifts and his energy, a system of air defence using radar and centrally controlled fighters was implemented in time for the Battle of Britain in 1940.

All this, of course, was not good news for the bomber since, given Germany's scientific and technical excellence, it could hardly be supposed that she would fail to develop radar herself. Indeed, in May 1934 a German researcher, Kuhnhold, obtained radar reflections from the research ship *Grille* at 2,100 metres, and by March 1936 a Junkers W-34 aeroplane was detected at 30 km.[24] By 1939 the German Air Force and Navy possessed radar which was equal, if not superior, to the British; but largely thanks to Tizard, their fighter control *system*, of which radar was an essential part, was inferior. 'Imagine a hundred cubic miles covered with cloud and fog,' Baldwin had said, 'and you can calculate how many aeroplanes you would have to throw into that to have much chance of catching odd aeroplanes as they fly through it.' That cloud and fog could now be seen through from the ground, and so could the darkest night; however, the bombers possessed a small consolation, for they could not be seen in fog by the fighter itself until the fighters carried airborne radar sets. But on cloudless nights, they could be seen only too often, when their hunters had been guided towards them.

But the 'Tizard Committee' was to be invaded, for unaware of the existence of the Committee for the Scientific Survey of Air Defence, Professor Lindemann and Churchill pressed for action on air defence. The failure of the defences in the 1934 exercises had led to the formation of a committee of RAF officers under Sir Robert Brook-Popham, who was in charge of air defence, and to this committee Lindemann gave evidence. But where Tizard had a genius for working with people to find solutions, Lindemann did not, and was unimpressed by the committee – perhaps by all departmental committees. He therefore wrote to Stanley Baldwin, asking that a *non-departmental* committee, with direct access to the Prime Minister (Ramsay MacDonald) be considered. He also approached Lord Londonderry, who suggested that he contact Tizard. But Lindemann, with no faith in this departmental committee, invoked Winston Churchill and involved Austen Chamberlain. These now approached Ramsay MacDonald. It was decided to form a sub-committee of the Committee of

Imperial Defence – the Air Defence Research Sub Committee – which would in any case regularise the position, since the 'Tizard Committee' was an Air Ministry Committee, and the question of the location of enemy aircraft had been, as we have seen, primarily the concern of the War Office. The 'Tizard Committee' was now made a sub-committee of the new committee. Tizard was a member of both. Churchill arranged that both he and Lindemann, as his indispensable advisor, should sit on the new committee.

Lindemann and the older 'Tizard Committee' now collided, not so much due to a clash of personalities as of ideas and, much more, of methods. Lindemann's ideas for air defence consisted of infrared detection and the use of aerial mines attached to parachutes or balloons [the 'Short Aerial Mine' will be met later]. Lindemann believed in direct political action. Tizard believed in adapting the system in which he found himself, by seeing people's points of view and working with them. Lindemann dismissed the staff at the research stations as being bound to be unhelpful; Tizard engaged their support.

Churchill, ever impatient, on hearing from Lindemann that his aerial mine project was not being pressed (it had been to some extent been dealt with before Lindemann's involvement) clashed with Tizard at the CID sub-committee (known as the 'Swinton Committee' from Lord Swinton, the capable Air Minister and chairman), saying that the matter should have been pressed. Tizard then wrote to Lindemann, politely but firmly deprecating Lindemann's action. Churchill wrote to Swinton, regretting Tizard's 'very offensive' letter to Lindemann.

Lindemann now took direct action, announcing that he would stand as a conservative for one of the University seats at the forthcoming parliamentary elections – and few could doubt that air defence would be one of his platforms. Blackett, Hill and Tizard now resigned. The 'Tizard Committee' was dissolved, and then re-constituted without Lindemann. The rift between the two was now complete, and it had very great consequences for Bomber Command and its doctrine. As Tizard's biographer, Ronald W Clark, wrote:

> Had Lindemann been 'in' rather that 'out' during the crucial period between September 1936 and the autumn of 1938, it is likely that Bomber Command would have entered the war less ludicrously ill equipped for the task in hand. But unless he had sprouted a hitherto concealed genius for marrying up the scientific and the operational, radar would hardly have been integrated into Fighter Command in time for the trial of 1940. Without that, the Battle of Britain would have been lost.[25]

Meanwhile, the RAF was expanding rapidly, and with the RAF expansion programmes came a new organisation. The Metropolitan Air Force had been organised as the 'Air Defence of Great Britain' and had been divided into three bombing areas and a fighting area, consisted of Fighting Area HQ, and under that, 'Fighting Squadrons' and 'Ground Defence HQ', which controlled the ground troops. In the expansion that followed, the creation of new bombing and fighting areas led to a fear that the Commander in Chief of the Air Defence of Great Britain would spend too much time on co-ordinating the activities of all these bombing and fighting groups, for his *main* task, in air defence, was the *offensive*, the bombing force. In July 1936, the system was reorganised into commands, the chief being Bomber Command, Fighter Command and Coastal Command. These were administrative, not doctrinal, changes, for the rise of the modern fighter and of radio detection had not affected the doctrine. They had, however, raised serious questions about the defence of the bomber, which were also linked closely to the type of bomber which would be required, and this again was closely linked to the expansion programme and bomber parity with Germany. In the next chapter, therefore, the very rapid expansion of Bomber Command will be recounted, and the problems of bomber defence – which alone of the technical and scientific problems confronting the 'ludicrously ill equipped' Bomber Command were never properly resolved – will be traced until the doctrine has finally sent 55,000 bomber men to their Maker, and the war is won.

Notes

1 HA Jones, *The War in the Air*, Vol 7, 18–21.
2 Ed by Nicholas Lambert, *The Submarine Service 1900–1918*, The Navy Records Society/Ashgate Publishing, Aldershot 2001, 232.
3 PRO Avia/46/158.
4 In Ronald W Clark, *Tizard*, Methuen & Co., London, 1965, 66–7.
5 PRO Air41/39.
6 PRO Air41/39.
7 Official Report, 5th series, Parliamentary debates, Commons, 1931–32, Vol. 270, 7 Nov to 17 Nov.
8 Thomas Wilson, *Churchill and the Prof*, Cassell, London 1995, 32.
9 All the following information on the ten-year rule was taken from the summary written by the Air Historical Branch in PRO Air41/39.
10 Jonathan Falconer, *Bomber Command Handbook*, Sutton Publishing, Stroud, 2003, 2–3.
11 Uri Bialer, *The Shadow of the Bomber*, London, Royal Historical Society, 1980.
12 In a letter about the Munich settlement dated 14 October 1938 to Lord Tweedsmuir, Gov. Gen. of Canada, Lord Cherwell would write 'If only we had developed the defence against aircraft, for which I have called for so many years, our position might well be very different...' CA A32/F4.
13 Christopher Chant, *Aviation*, Book Club Associates/Orbis Publishing, Novara, 1978, 117.
14 CA A30/F1.
15 Thomas Wilson, *Churchill and the Prof*, Cassell, London, 1995, 13.

16 Ronald Clark, *JBS: The Life and Work of JBS Haldane*, Hodder & Stoughton, London, 1968, 58.

17 Thomas Wilson, *Churchill and the Prof*, Cassell, London, 1995, 2–9.

18 Thomas Wilson, *Churchill and the Prof*, Cassell, London, 1995, 2–9.

19 CA E28/1.

20 Ronald W Clark, *Tizard*, Methuen & Co., London, 1965, 108–9.

21 Ronald W Clark, *Tizard*, Methuen & Co., London, 1965, 19–17.

22 Ronald W Clark, *Tizard*, Methuen & Co., London, 1965, 71.

23 Ronald W Clark, *Tizard*, Methuen & Co., London, 1965, 70.

24 Harry Von Kroge, *Gema: Birthplace of German Radar & Sonar*, Institute of Physics Publishing, Bristol, 2000, 23.

25 Ronald W Clark, *Tizard*, Methuen & Co., London, 1965, 148.

CHAPTER THREE

Bomber Defence – The Speed Bomber

...And everyone said, who saw them go,
'O won't they soon be upset, you know!
For the sky is dark, and the voyage is long,
And happen what may, it's extremely wrong
In a sieve to sail so fast!'…

Edward Lear

The formation of Bomber Command in July 1936, although an act of 'administrative convenience',[1] was also in harmony with the increasing specialisation of aircraft, which had now rendered bombers useless as fighters. For bombing, an increasing emphasis was placed on speed and bombload, whereas a reconnaissance aircraft needed all round vision above all else, and a Coastal Command aircraft range, vision and an ability to detect and attack submarines and surface craft. Above all, the use of RDF (radar) and the increased power and speed of the fighter meant that the bomber was inch by inch losing its place as the main defence, since fighters might reduce the enemy bomber offensive by a heavy attrition of his forces. But the separation of Bomber and Fighter Commands was to make cooperation between them difficult, and this would bear fruit when fighter escorts, or fighter intruder operations, were called for.

When it became apparent that the enemy to be planned against was again to be the great and warlike German state with its vast industrial power, high science, superb engineering and brave and martial population, governed by a determined, vengeful and fanatic visionary, the perception of the air danger by both the public and the Government grew rapidly. And in addition to the obviously expansionist and aggressive policy of Japan in the Far East, in 1935 Mussolini's Italy, seeking both expansion and revenge for the catastrophic defeat of an Italian Army at Adowa by the Emperor Menelek II of Abyssinia in 1896, conquered the pre-industrial empire, using air power to deliver poison gas, a violation of the Geneva protocols and a sinister reminder of the terrible dangers to civilisation to be expected from the new warfare. The modern liberal might presume that gas was used on the Ethiopians because they were non European; a better deduction might be that it was used because they were unable to retaliate in kind, possessing no air power, a dreadful reminder of the need either universally to disarm, or to possess a potent striking force. Hailie Selassie, the Ethiopian Emperor, appeared in person at the League of Nations, and gained trade sanctions against Italy. Having failed to defend China from Japan, and Abyssinia from Italy, from thenceforth the League sank into contempt. Mussolini, irked by sanctions, turned to Germany, and in November 1936 the Rome–Berlin Axis was proclaimed. Three days later, Japan and the Axis Powers signed the Anti-Comintern Pact which, although obviously directed against the Soviet Union and its tame international arm, signalled Japan's position to the world. And in 1936 German forces re-entered the Rhineland, in a direct violation of the Treaty of Versailles. The British Army's forces available to respond to this were two divisions which could have been moved to the continent in three weeks, but which were without air defence, tanks, anti-tank weapons and mortars. The RAF could have provided seven squadrons of fighter aircraft, three of the fighter squadrons possessing obsolescent aircraft and two being incapable of operating at night. The bomber squadrons were capable of dropping 25 tons of bombs on the Rhineland for a short period. Of more import to diplomacy, only a third of the ground defences of London could be manned, and *none* could be manned elsewhere.[2]

The fear of the 'knock out blow' to London, which animated Government and people alike, was the most potent factor in the expansion of the RAF. By March 1933 even the Prime Minister, Ramsay MacDonald, had despaired of air disarmament, and by October of that year, when Germany withdrew from the Disarmament Conference, the need to re-arm became obvious, although Britain did not give up *all* hope of disarmament until 1939.[3] The fear of the air shaped the rearmament as well. The problem was that London was too large and too close to the continent. A German air force occupying the Low Countries would not need to travel very far to London, while the distance to Berlin was 650 miles, and even to the Ruhr was 350 miles. So Britain could not, therefore, conduct a war safely from the island itself, shielded by the

Royal Navy, as in former times. It might be thought that Britain ought to have ensured that Germany did not occupy the Low Countries, and so create a large expeditionary force with a large air component which would, by the side of the French, defeat Germany as she had been defeated in 1918 – by overwhelming her army. But Britain did not wish to send over to the continent a great army as she had twenty years before, and engage in a military slogging match with that most martial of peoples. The memory of the horrors involved was still fresh, and fortified daily by the war memorials with their long lists of names inscribed, which seemed to mourn silently from every hamlet, every borough, every city in the land. Many in power had served in the Great War, and those who had not, like Neville Chamberlain, seemed to dread war even more; the fear of the mass casualties which would be *inevitable* in *any* conflict with a great and brave and skilful army, trenches or no trenches, was widespread and paramount. So the RAF's promise of a new warfare, in which a bomber force would destroy Germany's will and ability to resist, while a small army operated on the left of the French line, protected to some extent by bombers striking at the German Army's lines of supply, seemed attractive. Not so much, of course, to the Army and Navy – but the consideration of the knock out blow overrode all else. It lay in the public mind, and in the mind of Government. Needless to say, the Air Ministry were unlikely to disagree with their own doctrine, which had not only secured their independence in the years 1919–23, but now placed them in the forefront for defence expenditure. Indeed, in October 1934, Ramsay MacDonald compared the air hysteria to the battleship hysteria before the Great War.[4] Conflicting reports of the size of Germany's Air Force added to the insecurity, for if Germany were to gain a lead in aircraft numbers, her huge industrial potential would mean that Britain could not catch up. The naval hysteria prior to 1914 had been about the production of battleships and battlecruisers of a known type. But aircraft were developing much more rapidly, and were even now being changed radically – just what aircraft should Britain's industry produce?

The Air Ministry were wisely not in favour of a simple, all out expansion straight away, which would merely fill the RAF with obsolete and obsolescent aircraft (as actually happened to the French Air Force). The years of financial stringency and the ten-year rule had meant that the most economical bomber was the light, two-seater machine, almost indistinguishable from a fighter. The Metropolitan Air Force (the air force based in the UK) had also been expected to provide a general reserve for the age old problem of the defence of Afghanistan and India in the event of an attack by the Soviet Union, some twenty-four squadrons being allocated for this purpose. This was fatal to any attempt at the employment of a specialised bomber. The bomber force had had this secondary role in the defence of India – but did not have a primary role, since no clearly identifiable enemy existed in Europe. This emphasis on the light bomber had also inhibited the development of more powerful engines, and of larger bombs. The light bomber – cheap, easy to build and maintain, requiring no particularly expensive runways or hangars, was the ideal bomber for the Treasury.

The light bomber also satisfied the RAF's desire for a high-speed high performance aircraft. But the light bomber did not have the range for a war with Germany, and against the modern fighter, it carried insufficient defensive firepower. The Air Ministry concluded that:

> ...bombers, in spite of improvements in speed, climb, and ability to fly through cloud and bad visibility, must expect to be engaged [by fighters], perhaps more often than not, in the course of their missions.[5]

If this were the case, they would need defensive armament. It was impossible, given the high speed of the new monoplanes, to operate guns from the cockpit, and gun turrets were being developed which could be fitted into the fuselage without creating too much drag. However, if turrets were to be fitted to a light bomber its size would need to be increased to such an extent that it became a medium bomber anyway. Furthermore, if a light bomber could fly so high that it evaded the fighter, it would be faced with serious problems of navigation and target location; and if it flew at low level, it would run into anti-aircraft machine guns and cannon with their very high rate of fire. In addition, bombing from this height would also not allow the bombs sufficient time to gain the terminal velocity necessary to penetrate a hard target. And such specialised tactics did not put so great a strain upon the enemy defences as would a bomber capable of bombing from any height. As if this were not enough, the crisis over the Italian attack on Ethiopia drew the need for an adequate range into a sharper focus.[6]

On 8 November 1935, the Chief of the Air Staff, Sir Edward Ellington, circulated a discussion minute on the composition of the bomber force, based upon defence, man power, finance and maintenance, which was seen by the historian of the Air Historical Branch as marking the beginning of the search for the 'ideal bomber'.[7] The comments from his staff were unfavourable to the light bomber in terms of defensive firepower and bombload and economy. Perhaps the most decisive comment came from the Deputy Director of Plans, a Group Captain Harris, a man who was to be of a vast significance in the Second World War.

Arthur Travers Harris was born in 1892. His father was a civil engineer, the consulting architect to the Government of Madras and the Maharajah of Gwalior, and his mother a daughter of a surgeon in the Madras cavalry. At the age of eighteen he emigrated to Rhodesia and became a farm manager – 'for the rest of his life Harris would think of himself primarily as a Rhodesian'.[8] On the outbreak of the Great War in August 1914 Harris enlisted in the 1st Rhodesia Regiment as a bugler and campaigned with them in German South West Africa. After a short break he went back to England, determined to enlist in a unit where he could remain seated, his hard marching in South West Africa having provoked a lifelong aversion to walking if a vehicular alternative presented itself. There being no vacancies in the cavalry or artillery, Harris enlisted in the RFC. He was soon engaged on Zeppelin interception, thereby gaining experience of both strategic bombing and night flying. His qualities of leadership, energy and thought were such that he was appointed as a squadron leader after only ten months' service. Transferring to France, he flew patrols over Ypres, and over the long and bloody slog forward at Passchendaele.

After the war, Harris elected to stay in the RAF, and served with distinction in India and Iraq, where he demonstrated both his high abilities and his impatience with blinkered high-ranking military officers.[9] He attracted the attention of both Trenchard and his successor, Marshal of the Royal Air Force Sir John Salmond, and after commanding a squadron of 'heavy' bombers was placed on a two-year course at the military college at Camberley in Surrey. After a further tour in the Middle East, he took charge of a flying boat squadron, where he impressed all with his night flying ability. In 1933 he was called to the Air Ministry, promoted to the rank of group captain, and appointed Deputy Director of Plans.

Harris, in his reply to the discussion minute circulated by Sir Edward Ellington, suggested that 'Germany's effort to compress the maximum range and hitting power within a given numerical total of aircraft has eliminated even the medium bomber class'.[10] In this he was completely wrong, for the German Air Force was building only light and medium bombers.[11] Harris thought that Britain would have to eventually have a force composed of heavies only, since only this type possessed the range to hit targets deep in Germany. He wrote:

> ...it is in fact, a matter of urgency to place ourselves on a level with our potential enemies by adopting a policy of the maximum range

and/or bomb carrying capacity obtainable within the limits of our first-line numerical strength. As a corollary, it seems apparent that even the medium bomber will tend to disappear...

But perhaps the really decisive influence on the development of the heavy bomber lay with Britain's limited industrial capacity. Peacetime Britain simply could not match Germany's bomber force without a full-scale mobilisation of industry, and that, it was thought, would lead, if the effort were prolonged, to financial ruin. But if she could not match bomber for bomber, she could match, or overtake, bomb for bomb, since building larger aircraft allowed space for more men to work on it in the factory, and was also more economical, ton for ton, on trained fitters. It also allowed space for an 'astrodome' so that the navigator might observe the stars, and for machine gun turrets.

On 29 January 1937 the Chief of the Air Staff agreed that the future bomber force should be composed of medium and heavy bombers. This force was to be capable of bombing by night as well as by day. Two bomber specifications had been issued in 1936, B12/36 and P13/36. The B12/36 four-engine heavy bomber was specified to carry eight machine guns in power operated turrets, two in the nose, two amidships and four in the rear. Its top speed would be 245 mph, its bombload 2,000 lbs and its range 1,500 miles. Out of this grew the Short Stirling. The P13/36 specification twin-engine medium bomber would carry 1,000 lbs for 1,500 miles. It would have two turrets, the nose turret carrying two machine guns and the rear carrying four. It would cruise at 275 mph, and have a top speed of 317 mph. Out of this, paradoxically, grew the Halifax and the Lancaster four-engine heavy bombers.[12]

But how was the bomber, which would be needed, if not for an immediate all out offensive, then at the very least to attack the German Navy and Army, to be defended from the fighter? A battery of .303 machine guns in a power operated rear turret had been chosen, as we have seen, for the new heavy bombers, although many attempts would later be made to uprate them. Yet, there were several other strategies, apart from heavy defensive firepower from gun turrets, that the bomber could adopt to defeat the fighter. One of these strategies was speed – to design a bomber so fast that it could outrun the fighter, or to be fast enough to allow the fighter such a small a margin of speed over the bomber that interception was difficult, if not impossible. A further advantage of speed lay in the fact that it reduced the time the bomber spent in the danger area over enemy territory. Could such a bomber be built?

The search for the 'speed bomber' was linked to the need for a big bomber, which was not only enabled by its size to carry a heavy defensive armament; as has been seen, it was thought to be capable of a high speed because it *was* big.

In 1935 the Royal Aircraft Establishment circulated a specification, B1/35, for a high-speed wooden bomber able to operate by day, powered by two Rolls-Royce Merlin engines, capable of a speed of 330 mph, and armed with three machine guns,[13] but the idea was not taken up, since there was a very considerable pressure on design staffs. In 1936, twelve new designs were proposed, including the heavy bomber design. However, there were only sixty-eight design staff in the fourteen independent aircraft companies, and these had forty-five designs under way with a further thirteen still to be issued for 1935. They could tackle no more than ten new designs in 1936, while the design staff at the Directorate of Technical Development could manage no more than eight, and were pushed to achieve this. It was only when the Admiralty decided that it could manage with two, instead of its originally planned four, new designs that the heavy bombers themselves could squeezed into the design programme.[14] Britain was very close to a flat out expansion of its air power, and could only have increased its effort by a full peacetime mobilisation of industry, a measure which the Treasury considered to be unsustainable and which they thought would produce a financial disaster.

But the speed bomber still retained its appeal to certain influential RAF officers, among them Sir William Freeman, the Air Member for Research and Development, and Sir Edgar Ludlow-Hewitt, the Air Officer Commanding Bomber Command. That such a bomber would ultimately be needed was first suggested by Air Commodore JA Chamier, the Director of Technical Development, in 1928, although the bombload envisaged was to be no more than the armament load of a fighter, thus assuring a comparable speed.[15] Yet it was presumed in 1937 that the B12/36 bomber, one of the requirements for which was a top speed of 275 mph at 15,000 feet, might almost reach 330 mph, although in actual fact, in trials during 1941, the top speed attained was only 218 mph.[16] This presumption of a high speed as well as heavy armament for the big bomber was to act as a damper on the perception of the need for a special high-speed bomber.

In 1934 the De Havilland Company designed and produced 'in a few months'[17] an airliner, the Comet, which had 'a large load carrying capacity and a performance so high that only the latest fighter then in service could catch it',[18] although Colin Sinnott reports that it was 'considerably faster than the fastest fighter then in RAF service'.[19] However, the Air Staff comforted themselves that this was solely due to the incorporation in the Comet of the most modern features up to 1933, a year in which several novel and important features of design simultaneously reached a culminating point in development. The RAF fighters, however, they reasoned, were bound by 'the most stringent economy'[20] and they simply could not afford to design and produce a new fighter every time an improvement presented itself. They had been designed with the knowledge available in 1929. The latest design features, when incorporated, would give a speed advantage of some 40 mph over the Comet. The lesson the Air Staff drew was that a 'close and alert watch' must be kept on technical progress, and the speed of the procedure for producing new designs 'must be so rapid that an enemy cannot steal a march on us in this way'.[21]

Despite this explaining away of the phenomenal performance of the Comet, the logic of the unarmed, high-speed bomber could not simply be banished from consideration. In May 1937, George Volkert, Chief Designer at Handley Page, proposed a very fast, unarmed bomber design to meet the P13/36 specification. In 'A Memorandum on Bombing Policy and its Influence on Design',[22] Volkert argued that 'a drastic revision of present ideas is essential if the utmost performance and destructive power is to be obtained, combined with the maximum economy in the use of highly trained personnel and highly expensive and delicate equipment.' He saw that the bomber's need for 'complete defence from attack in every possible direction' had led to the installation of nose and tail turrets, which 'very adversely' affected performance. He observed that the higher the speed, the more adverse would this effect on performance grow – and the specially curved material of turrets also reduced visibility through 'fracture, misting, icing up and distortion', and further, needed a highly vulnerable hydraulic system to operate them. He estimated that for a 2,000-mile range, without turrets, and therefore also without the weight of guns, gunners and ammunition, the total weight of the aeroplane would be reduced from 32,131 lbs to 30,966 lbs, and its cruising speed would increase from 275 to 297 mph. Further, by reducing the wing area, and thereby enabling smaller tail surfaces and a shorter fuselage to be incorporated, a cruising speed of 327 mph and a maximum of 380 mph could be attained. Volkert submitted his memorandum to the Royal Aircraft Establishment and to the Air Ministry, the former thinking the speeds unattainable and the latter believing that the latest bomber design to which they aspired would not only be of greater speed, but would be armed with *eight* 20 mm cannon!

However, Volkert's paper had not simply been about a speed bomber, but about bombing *policy*. Here, he strayed onto ground which it was impolitic to tread – from the quicksands and mires which lay in the road which led from the killing of civilians as an inevitable result of destroying the war-making potential of an enemy, to the inevitable destruction of the war-making potential of an enemy by the policy of killing and frightening civilians. Volkert wrote:

> Modern science and invention has made war so utterly ruthless that any country which can hope to repel an invader must be prepared to retaliate at once…with little or no regard for pacts and international agreements…

Volkert adduced as reasons the 'prohibitive' cost of war with modern weapons, the rapid and devastating progress of air raids, the terrorising of civilians, the inability to combat gas and incendiary bombs, and – most impolitic of all – he wrote that 'Adherence to "precision" bombing calls for greater elaboration and perfection of equipment and far more skill than dropping bombs at random.' The most efficient bomber, thought Volkert, was 'the one that can carry out the greatest destruction with the smallest crew and the simplest equipment'. He noted that the supply of 'highly trained pilots, navigators, gunners and bomb aimers' would be impossible to replace rapidly, nor would it be possible to manufacture and maintain 'in perfect working order' much of the equipment. Volkert, unaware of the trials, or even the existence, of radar, then referred like Baldwin, to the cloud and mist which prevailed most of the time over Europe, and which would hide the bombers and their deadly cargoes. He noted that a future war would 'revise all previously accepted opinion in regard to the relative danger incurred by combatants and non combatants'; this, however, was not to decry the killing of civilians, but rather to suggest that the concern over the safety of pilots and crew might be reduced – after all, pilots had not, in the early days of the Great War, possessed parachutes!

Once the commitment to precision bombing was abandoned, it did not matter so much how accurately the bombs fell upon their release, and therefore they might be stowed more economically in the bomb bay, and bombs could be especially designed to fit into the aeroplane. This curious concept of weapons and weapon carriers, that the weapon should be designed to suit the carrier, was one that was more widespread than might be imagined, as we shall see.

It was not to be imagined that the Air Staff would take kindly to the idea of a speed bomber designed for nothing less than area bombing, and their higher echelons would no doubt be aware of the progress of radar and its integration with Fighter Command and the air defence system. But the speed bomber was a persistent idea, and its champion, Sir Edgar Ludlow-Hewitt, a persistent and very able man. Described as 'a hopeless bungler and fuddler'[23] by one officer, who wrote 'I have never served with anyone as indecisive as Ludlow-Hewitt', Harris thought him 'by far and away the most brilliant officer I have ever met in any of the three services…I vividly remember the wave of black despair which overwhelmed me when …he told me…that he was leaving…'[24] Harris understood the reason to be his insistence on using front-line aircrew in operational training units. 'Ludlow-Hewitt saved the situation', wrote Harris, 'and the war, at his own expense.' His only fault, if he had one, felt Harris, was too much attention to detail. However, the reader may conclude that the Relentless Offensive was *conceived* (*planned* might imply too much detailed thought) with too *little* attention to detail. There are few people whose actions and ideas attract unanimous praise or blame; many were those convinced by the nonsense of Adolf Hitler or Roy Jenkins, and many were those who refuted the wisdom of Jesus or Mohammed, despite close contact. At this distance, I *feel* Ludlow-Hewitt to have been a very great commander.

In May 1938 Ludlow-Hewitt noted that it would be undesirable to standardise on one type of aircraft, and to thereby put 'too many eggs in one basket'. He 'did not wish the speed bomber to be lost sight of'. In July of that year he wrote to the Air Ministry, suggesting that the speed bomber was needed for a 'harassing' role against morale. The standard bomber, thought Ludlow-Hewitt, had as its 'main characteristic' an ability 'to carry a great load of bombs with sufficient speed to give it, when operating in formation, a reasonable chance of fulfilling its mission in the face of a strong defence'.[25] But harassing bombing could not be carried out by a large formation of aircraft, and its accuracy need only be sufficient to 'ensure air raid precautions'. This, however, sounded far less bloodcurdling and indiscriminate than Volkert's memo! But Ludlow-Hewitt felt that 'It must, however, carry sufficient armament to keep enemy fighters from closing into decisive ranges without themselves running considerable risk in doing so'.

The need which Ludlow-Hewitt foresaw for at least some armament was understandable, for he felt strongly that crew morale would surely suffer otherwise. It needed great nerve and great faith to sail through the skies unarmed, relying on your speed against fighters which were not only heavily armed, but very fast indeed. The psychological bridge to be crossed seemed to him insuperable. Suppose you had to cross a belt of land in which roamed some large and savage dogs. Should you plod across clad in the heaviest leather and armed with a heavy cudgel, or should you, if you could perhaps outpace the dogs thereby, sprint across clad only in light running shoes? Even if a biologist and mathematician of some repute were to assure you that you were safest when naked, there would be a very strong and natural temptation to don at least a stout pair of underpants, and to clench a small stick tightly in the hand.

Ludlow-Hewitt was shown a copy of Volkert's paper, and on 23 April, commented that he was glad to have been given the opportunity, usually discouraged by the Air Ministry, to comment on it, since 'it would do no harm, and a great deal of good if C in Cs were given more opportunity of giving their views on important Air Ministry subjects'. He wrote that:

> …2. Mr Volkert marshals his arguments in favour of the unarmed bomber with considerable ability and his paper is interesting and convincing as far as it goes. There are, however, two factors which must be taken into account before we make up our minds about the Volkert type of unarmed bomber. The first is the confession implicit in the production of bombing aircraft incapable of precise bombing, that we definitely intend to employ indiscriminate bombing of the civilian population in war. Secondly, the moral effect on the crew of an aircraft being entirely unarmed. Both these objections can, I think, be overcome without prejudicing the principles underlying Mr Volkert's arguments.
>
> 3. The term 'unarmed' is, I think, a misnomer. It is not an unarmed bomber that we require but a *speed* bomber. It is not necessarily true that some measure of armament or protection is irreconcilable with speed. The modern fighter proves that the two are more or less reconcilable.
>
> 4. To deal first with the role of the speed bomber. Bombing in war falls into two main categories, (a) destructive bombardment and (b) harassing bombardment. The first requires attacks not necessarily sustained but repeated until the object is achieved. The object of the latter is to impose upon the enemy the necessity of constantly applying all the restrictions of its air raid precaution schemes thereby causing constant delays and interruptions in all forms of activity, particularly in munitions work in the factories and in the control and operation of traffic on the railways…[26]

Ludlow-Hewitt had indeed been perceived by the Air Ministry as endorsing indiscriminate bombing. On 23 September 1938 he wrote to Air

Vice Marshal Peirse, Deputy Chief of the Air Staff, saying that:

> When I was in your office a few days ago, we discussed shortly my proposals for a speed bomber. You said you did not agree with my letter on the subject because I proposed to use the speed bomber for the indiscriminate bombing of civilian populations from above the clouds. I assured you that I was certain no such suggestion was included in the letter.

Commenting that, in his letter of 19 July 1938 he had again advocated a speed bomber for 'harassing' bombing, he went on…

> …Against a factory I cannot destroy all the factories all the time, and, moreover, we know from past experience that it takes a tremendous amount of heavy bombing to destroy anything. The factories still continued to operate in Barcelona in spite of many heavy attacks. The most economical way of dealing with a factory is to send over a heavy destructive attack to do as much destruction as possible and to frighten the workers, and then follow it up by sustained attacks, if possible by single aircraft at irregular intervals. A fully sustained attack would stop the factory, and not only the factory, but all other factories and activities in the neighbourhood. That is what is meant by harassing bombing, and I think you must admit there is nothing in my letter suggesting the frightfulness which I would be the last to approve.

On 3 December 1938 Ludlow-Hewitt wrote to Air Chief Marshal Sir Cyril Newall, Chief of the Air Staff, again hammering the points about the advantages of a speed bomber. Noting that 'many designers and aircraft manufacturers are itching to be given the task of producing a speed bomber', he pointed out that:

> Every meeting of the Air Fighting Committee and of the Bombing Committee brings out in one way or another the great advantage that our single seat fighters now have over the bomber. It has been established that our .303 weapons are practically ineffective against the single seat fighter, and can be made more so by the disposition of a small amount of armour in the fighter. It appears also that the difficulties of fitting larger calibre guns to any of the '36 or '37 class bombers may prove insuperable, and in any event may seriously affect their performance. Further, the problem of providing armour in bombers cannot be satisfactorily solved as it can only be made effective against single seat fighters armed with .303 guns attacking from astern.

Ludlow-Hewitt went on to say that the big bombers under order were 'frightfully expensive' but might 'prove unable to defend themselves successfully against determined attacks by modern fighters.' He went on:

> With no other strings to our bow, therefore, we may find our striking force disappointingly weak in penetrative power over enemy territory. The Germans, on the other hand, appear to be concentrating on the speed bomber and, according to all accounts are producing a Junkers bomber of phenomenal high speed, which our best fighters may find extremely difficult to overhaul.

The aircraft to which Ludlow-Hewitt referred was the Junkers 88, the fifth prototype of which had in March 1939 attained a speed of 321 mph with a 4,400 lb bombload.[27] However, the provision of a fourth crew member and additional defence meant that the aircraft later doubled in weight and its speed dropped to 286 mph.[28] This, but for the vision of Sir Wilfrid Freeman, could easily have been the fate of the British speed bomber, the Mosquito, as we shall see. However the Junkers 88, like the Mosquito, was to prove to be a formidable night fighter.

Ludlow-Hewitt went on to say that, if the heavy bomber proved too vulnerable in the first few weeks of war:

> We may easily find ourselves with a huge force of bombers unable to reach the Ruhr, while the Germans, concentrating on high speeds, may be able to sustain attacks on, say, the London docks or other vital and exposed centres with comparative impunity owing to the difficulty of catching them. These attacks may not be of very great weight, but it is easily possible to attach too much importance to the weight of bombs dropped. All our experience in the past has proved that it is the nuisance value of bombing, the interruption and delay caused by bombing, which is the most effective characteristic of air bombardment against a highly organised nation. The demoralizing, delaying and disorganizing effect of relatively light but sustained attack may well prove again to be of more value in the aggregate than the destructive effect of heavy air bombardment even at its best. Given that you can have both, so much the better; the attempt to combine both in one aircraft may result in our getting neither.

Ludlow-Hewitt then went on to point out that Britain had no fighters which could be used as escorts overseas. He foresaw four uses for the speed bomber – as a fast bomber for harassment, for sporadic attacks beyond the penetration of the heavies, for reconnaissance and as a long-distance fighter. 'It would, I imagine, be a large twin', he wrote, and he pressed Newall for a prototype 'at the earliest possible moment'.

Again, on 7 August 1939, Ludlow-Hewitt, in reply to a paper on the light bomber sent by the Air Ministry, wrote:

> I am strongly of the opinion that the development of the fastest possible type of bomber, whatever its size, is a project which ought to be put in hand so that we should have a prototype of this kind of bomber should the need arise. We are very much in the dark, and will remain so until we have actual war experience, as to the ability of existing types of bombers to reach their objectives in the face of modern defences and it is very probable that we shall find ourselves vitally in need of a speed bomber type for evasive methods or as an alternative to reliance upon breaking our way through with heavily armed relatively slow bombers. Apart from the uses to which a speed bomber could certainly be put, the probability that such a bomber might prove essential in war is at least sufficiently high to justify the experimental development of the type.

Ludlow-Hewitt next gave an advantage of the speed bomber which was the very opposite of that which he seemed to have endorsed in Volkert's idea. He now proposed that, due to the difficulties of hitting small targets from high altitudes, the ease of interception from these heights and the low clouds which frequently beset northern Europe, that the speed bomber could evade fighters and attack from low level, which could be done in all weathers save for fog on the ground. Further, he pointed out that such accuracy would obviate the need for a large bombload, 2,000 lbs being 'quite adequate' for all purposes, and that 1,000 lbs 'should be sufficient to produce excellent results'. He asked again for the 'highest possible priority' for such a development.

The reply from the Assistant Chief of the Air Staff (ACAS), Air Vice Marshal Sholto Douglas, was that the light bomber paper would be amended and discussed at the next meeting of the Bombing Committee. Eventually, a full conference would be held on 12 December 1939, after three months of war, with Air Vice Marshal Sholto Douglas in the chair and the Director General of Research and Development, Sir Wilfred Freeman, also present.

The chairman began by saying that they had met to discuss proposals put forward in varying forms by Ludlow-Hewitt. Douglas said:

> All analyses of such concrete suggestions as had been received from Bomber Command had led to the conclusion that the resultant

aircraft would be a bad compromise as, in an endless endeavour to combine exceptionally high speed with modern armament and other requirements, neither would be attained.

In the light of these concerns, Sir Wilfred Freeman asked Ludlow-Hewitt if Bomber Command would be prepared to sacrifice armament if aircraft could outrun contemporary fighters, and Ludlow-Hewitt suggested that such an aircraft could always be used for reconnaissance duties, 'when the enemy had little warning to prepare for interception'. However, since the high-speed bomber would be needed for 'harassing bombing' following a major raid, interfering with firefighting and damage repair, it would be expected by the enemy, and such a bomber needed 'sufficient defensive armament to give the crew confidence they had a fighting chance'.

The Director General of Research and Development, Air Vice Marshal Tedder, pointed out that were the aircraft to be armed, it would 'lead to the same indifferent compromise which had resulted in additional armament for the Blenheim, ie ineffective defence and insufficient speed'.

Tedder went on to say that, '…once an aircraft was designed with guns it was not possible to achieve very much extra speed by the simple expedient of taking them out'. He also made the significant point that a bomber with sufficient speed need not fear attack from below, since the fighter would be unable to catch it while climbing.

Another significant advantage was pointed out by the Deputy Director of General Production, who stated that a wooden aircraft supplied by a firm such as de Havilland would avoid 'dislocating existing production arrangements by making heavy demands on skilled labour'. Indeed, de Havilland had already pointed this out to Air Marshal Freeman in September 1939, explaining the advantages that would accrue from their projected wooden speed bomber – its products would use labour 'outside and additional to that used in the main aircraft production'. It used wood rather than scarce aluminium, which meant that 'minimum time and man hours would be spent on making jigs etc.', and even the timber itself would be of 'mixed grades' – spruce, birch ply and balsa.

Eventually, it was agreed that two designs should be pursued, a wooden aircraft 'on the lines of the de Havilland project already discussed between Geoffrey de Havilland and Sir Wilfrid Freeman', together with a very large high-speed bomber on the basis of the Manchester. It was indeed fortunate that the latter was not pursued at the expense of the former, since the Avro Manchester was a great disappointment, and even the Lancaster, which was a stretched and more powerful Manchester, could only manage a top speed of 287 mph.

On 7 January 1940 Ludlow-Hewitt wrote to the Under Secretary of State at the Air Ministry,[29] referring to the meeting on 12 December and once again calling for the need for a good rearward view for the speed bomber in case it was caught at cruising speed by a fighter coming from behind and above at top speed, but acknowledging that the unarmed bomber was accepted 'as an interim measure because no other alternative is available'.

He also added that 'the future of the heavy bomber needs thoroughly reviewing', adding that 'it is very evident that our thought should be concentrated upon making the heavy bomber as invulnerable to attack as possible'.

The Bomber Command Commander in Chief then referred to the need for a long-range fighter to co-operate with bombers. 'The advantage of the long-range fighter, given that they have performance, is that the bombers provide them with the means of making contact with enemy fighters under terms which may be favourable to our own fighters.' He added the comment that 'though they may not be able to prevent losses to our bombers, they will make the operation more expensive to the enemy by causing greater casualties to his fighters'.

Ludlow-Hewitt ended on an even more prophetic note:

> Finally, we may be compelled by the prowess of the modern fighter to use our bombers mainly for night bombing, and we should therefore devote our attention to the development of that form of operation and particularly to enable precision bombing to be used at night. *So long as night bombing virtually means indiscriminate bombing, it will be a relatively weak form of attack* [italics added] but if by some means we can obtain greater accuracy at night, which requires the identification of targets, then we can without great loss abandon day bombing in favour of night bombing. This is a problem which our scientists should be asked to solve as a most urgent requirement.

Ludlow-Hewitt added that, largely due to the prohibition in the use of flares in wartime over the UK, very little night flying development work had been done. He ended with the comment that:

> ...as things are, very little progress has been made, and yet it seems certain that the future will compel us for a time to revert more to night bombing than to day bombing, at least during those periods when the fighters may establish decisive superiority over the bomber by day.

On 7 April 1940, exactly three months after Ludlow-Hewitt's letter to the

Under Secretary of State at the Air Ministry, the Commander in Chief Bomber Command received a reply signed by JB Abraham. After commenting on the speed bomber and agreeing that all round view was of great importance to it, the letter went on to say that 'the importance of increasing the armament and armour protection of the heavy bomber is fully appreciated and efforts are continually being made to improve them'. Armour protection was increased for the Stirling, Manchester and Halifax, and a new servo fed gun turret provided for later models of the Wellington. 'The gun defences of the Blenheim are being multiplied by three and may possibly be increased by four.' [David Mondey would say of the Blenheim that 'Undoubtedly the skill of their crews and the aircraft's ability to absorb a great deal of punishment were the primary reasons for their survival, for high speed and heavy firepower were certainly not their forte.']³⁰

On precision bombing at night, Mr Abraham wrote that 'The [Air] Council entirely agree with your remarks on the necessity of improving the techniques of night bombing' and were prepared, with approval from the War Office and after notice to Fighter Command, to approve the use of flares.

On fighter escort, the Air Council letter referred to the Beaufighter as 'very well suited for long range fighting', superior to the Me110 in offensive armament. However, the Beaufighter was not an escort fighter, since with its slow speed and lack of manoeuvrability it could not contend with the Me109 by day, although it proved a superb night fighter as well as heavy attack aircraft.

However, as we have already seen, Ludlow-Hewitt was replaced as Commander in Chief on 4 April, three days before the letter was signed. Perhaps the Air Ministry were relieved that the author of such a seemingly pessimistic letter had been finally removed. They would find, however, that it was not pessimism but prophecy.

Yet the Air Ministry moved with unusual speed in ordering the DH98 – the Mosquito, as it would later become known. The specification was written quickly, the requirements were all speeded up, and the Director of Aircraft Contracts at the Air Ministry had placed an order for fifty on 27 January 1940. The first six to be produced were to be used as prototypes to save time.

The Mosquito first flew on 25 November 1940. It reached 388 mph at 22,000 feet – faster than the Spitfire!³¹

In October 1940 Sir Charles Portal was promoted to the position of Chief of the Air Staff, an office he would hold until the end of the war. His successor as Commander in Chief at Bomber Command was Air Marshal Sir Richard EC Peirse, who we have already met in connection with his condemnation of indiscriminate bombing when Ludlow-Hewitt was proposing the urgent need for a speed bomber years before. Peirse had certainly been converted to belief in the speed bomber, for on 13 February 1941 he wrote to the Under Secretary of State at the Air Ministry seeking to retain the Mosquito as a speed bomber, as he thought that it had begun to be thought of as a reconnaissance and long-range fighter aircraft only.

His letter was replied to on 7 March 1941 by none other than Air Vice Marshal Arthur Travers Harris, now Deputy Chief of the Air Staff. Harris pointed out that the change in the strategical situation caused by the fall of France and the enemy's advance to the Channel coast made it appear unlikely that this aeroplane, in small numbers, without defensive armament and with a very small bombload, would fulfil the purposes for which it was designed. He pointed out that it had therefore been decided that twenty of the first fifty aeroplanes made would be allocated to Photographic Reconnaissance, which required no modification from the bomber specification, followed by thirty fighters. A new order had been placed for 150 of the fighter version, equipped for night interception. Harris therefore suggested that it would be wise to evaluate the Photo Reconnaissance version, before deciding whether the bomber version was required.

There were always voices to be heard prophesying doom over the lack of rear armament of the speed bomber, and in file notes both Peirse and Saundby, his SASO, averred that it was quite unnecessary to give the Mosquito rear defence, pointing out that the Photo Reconnaissance version (which was also the bomber version) was faster than the Spitfire fighter. Surprisingly, perhaps the last man to be convinced of the virtues of the Mosquito was Harris himself. On 10 April 1942, as Commander in Chief of Bomber Command, he wrote to Wilfred Freeman, the Air Member for Development and Production, and the father of the Mosquito if anyone was (it was called 'Freeman's folly') saying that:

> The Mosquito is now so delayed that it must inevitably suffer a still grimmer fate than has always been the lot of such naïve attempts to produce an aeroplane much faster than anything the enemy possesses that it needs no armament. It will go down in history as a second 'Battle' as far as its bombing role is concerned.

Freeman replied on 12 April – 'I have received your unhelpful letter …dated 10th April…Thank you…I hope you will prove to be wrong.'

Harris was, and comprehensively so. The Mosquito was perhaps the most successful aeroplane design of the Second World War. As a bomber it was always used in the forefront of the attack; as a night fighter intruder it would give absolutely invaluable assistance to Bomber Command, and severely unsettle the German night fighter crews; as a Photo Reconnaissance aeroplane it was, until the advent of the German jet fighters, secure. The bombers would sometimes visit Berlin twice in a night. It was the only Allied aeroplane mentioned by type in the diaries of Dr Goebbels, the German Minister of Propaganda; and that very astute man bore witness to the nerve rending quality of the seemingly unceasing harassment by Ludlow-Hewitt's speed bomber.

But surely the ultimate accolade came from Harris himself. In the last months of the campaign, and on the very day of the attack on Dresden, Harris wrote to Donald Bennett, the Air Officer Commanding No. 8 Group, and the youngest Air Vice Marshal in the RAF's history, saying:

> The term 'Light Night Striking Force' is not to be used in connection with the Mosquitos under your command.
>
> The Mosquito carries to Berlin a load equivalent to the Flying Fortress [it carried a 4000 lb bomb] …The word 'Mosquito' itself has a similar effect, being connected in the minds of the public with an insect which produces an irritating but normally not particularly effective sting.
>
> For some time this HQ has endeavoured to impress upon [the] public generally that Mosquito raids are most serious matters for the enemy…

The production of Mosquitos was limited; because it relied on highly skilled woodworkers, it could never have been produced on a scale sufficient to replace the heavy bombers, although output was at a maximum for three or four years in the UK, and they were also produced in Canada and Australia. The speed bomber could therefore be only a partial solution to the problem of bomber defence.

Notes

1 PRO Air41/39.
2 PRO Air41/39.
3 Uri Bialer, *The Shadow of the Bomber*, Royal Historical Society, London, 1980, 41–2.
4 Uri Bialer, *The Shadow of the Bomber*, 69.
5 Papers prepared for Lord Weir June–July 1935, in AHB narrative Air41/39.
6 PRO Air41/39.
7 PRO Air41/39.
8 Henry Probert, *Bomber Harris: His Life and Times*, Greenhill Books, London, 2001, 32.
9 Henry Probert, *Bomber Harris: His Life and Times*, Greenhill Books, London, 2001, 48–9.
10 PRO Air41/39.
11 General Wever, who had favoured the development of heavy, long-range strategic bombers, was killed

in an accident in 1936. The German Air Force was mainly dedicated to army co-operation – see Richard Overy, *The Air War*.

12 PRO Air41/39.

13 Colin Sinnott, *The RAF and Aircraft Design*, 204.

14 PRO Air41/39.

15 Colin Sinnott, *The RAF and Aircraft Design*, 54–8.

16 Colin Sinnott, *The RAF and Aircraft Design*, 49–50.

17 PRO Air41/39.

18 PRO Air 41/39.

19 Colin Sinnott, 203.

20 PRO Air41/39.

21 PRO Air41/39.

22 I am deeply indebted to Mr Fraser Mitchell of the Handley Page Society for his great kindness in giving me a copy of this, and for his invaluable advice.

23 See Denis Richards, *The Hardest Victory*, Coronet Books, London, 1994, 53–4.

24 Sir Arthur Harris, *Bomber Offensive*, Greenhill Books, London, 1998, 35–6.

25 PRO Air14/151.

26 PRO Air14/251.

27 David Mondey, *The Concise Guide to Axis Aircraft of World War II*, Chancellor Press, London, 1996, 119.

28 ER Hooton, in Putnam's *History of Aircraft, Aircraft of the Second World War*

29 PRO Air14/251.

30 David Mondey, *The Hamlyn Concise Guide to British Aircraft of World War Two*, 56.

31 Buttler, 80.

CHAPTER FOUR

Defensive Armament, Guns and Turrets – Before the War

But mousie, thou art no thy lane,
In proving foresight may be vain;
The best laid schemes o' mice an' men
Gang aft agley,
An' lea'e us nought but grief an' pain,
For promis'd joy!

Robert Burns

O f crucial importance to the defence of the bomber was the type of armament which was to be installed. Three main types of gun were considered.

The first was the Mark II Browning, of .303" calibre, which fired a solid projectile weighing 0.025 lbs at a muzzle velocity of 2,400 feet per second and at a rate of some 1,100 rounds per minute. The complete cartridge weighed 0.056 lbs and the gun itself 22 lbs.

The second was the M2 Browning, of 0.5" calibre, which fired a solid projectile weighing 0.11 lbs at a muzzle velocity of 2,600 feet per second and at a rate of 750 rounds per minute. The complete cartridge weighed around 0.186 lbs, and the gun 53 lbs.

The last weapon was the formidable 20 mm (.78") Hispano cannon, which fired an explosive projectile weighing 0.276 lbs at a muzzle velocity of 2,820 feet per second at a rate of around 620 rounds per minute. The complete cartridge weighed 0.54 lbs. The gun weighed around 109 lbs.

In an RAF Staff College lecture in 1925, it was stated that 'The aircraft gun is not likely to be required to penetrate armour, and a couple of .5" bullets in a pilot will incapacitate him as much as the fragment of a one and a half pound shell. On the other hand a .303" bullet has but little effect on any aeroplane.' The .303" was the standard infantry rifle calibre. Yet the .303" was chosen as the defensive weapon of the heavy bomber, and for 'unsound' reasons.

In his book *The RAF and Aircraft Design 1923–1939*,[1] Colin Sinnott details the reasons for this decision, which was of momentous importance to the whole bombing campaign. The Chief of the Air Staff, Sir Edward Ellington, looking at the Air Staff requirements for the B12/36 heavy bomber, and no doubt reflecting on the inadequacy of the .303" calibre, and that larger weapons had been one of the chief advantages of the heavy over the light bomber, suggested that the 20 mm cannon should be considered as the armament. 'The Air Staff advised that this neither possible nor necessary', wrote Sinnott, who noted that 'their reasoning was unsound'.

The reasons advanced for this decision by Wing Commander RF Oxland, who had been the head of the newly created Operational Requirements section since 1934, were that *four* 20 mm cannon in the rear turret would present centre of gravity problems, a strange assertion, as Sinnott pointed out, since the aircraft had not yet been designed! As can be seen, four 20 mm cannon, at 436 lbs, were a considerable increase over four .303" guns, which would weigh just 88 lbs. Yet just *two* 20 mm cannon, at 218 lbs, would give a weight of fire per minute of more than three times the .303", since the cannon round weighed some eleven times that of the .303" round, and this was a weight of *explosive* shells at a higher velocity and much longer range. Taking the admittedly great weight of four cannon as an example, therefore, seems like an attempt to rule out the cannon for other reasons. One of these reasons seems to have been that the recoil of a cannon would present 'grave' problems, except for firing astern. And the ammunition load would be an unacceptable detraction from the weight of bombs carried. This latter view was later repudiated by Ludlow-Hewitt, the Commander in Chief of Bomber Command, who (although writing of armour protection) thought the survival rate more crucial than the bombload:

> It is much more important to halve the risk of losing the aircraft and its crew than to double or even treble the bombload. It is the size of the casualty rate in our fighting forces which will lose the war...[Italics added.][2]

The argument that guns or armour unnecessarily detracted from the bombload will be found resurfacing later, although – unsurprisingly – not by those who would fly in the bombers.

Perhaps the most unusual reason adduced by Operational

Requirements against the necessity of increasing the defensive armament of the new heavy bombers was the following, which would bedevil discussions on bomber armament for the critical and decisive years. At the fourth meeting of the Air Fighting Committee, which was held at the Air Ministry on 12 December 1935, Group Captain MacLean, the Officer Commanding the Air Fighting Development Establishment at Northolt, pointed out that the high speeds of modern aircraft raised questions of relative bullets speeds – and the fighter was coming towards the bomber's bullets, whereas the bomber was receding from the fighter's. He is recorded as saying:

> As aircraft speeds were now reaching a figure which was an appreciable percentage of bullet velocities [ie up to 20%], we must think in terms of relative bullet speeds as well as relative aeroplane speeds.

The tendency seemed to be to consider one aspect of the problem by itself, ie that of the fighter and to ignore the bomber except in the role of a target.

> If one actually considers what was actually happening to the two bullets, that of the bomber and that of the fighter, one would realise that the bomber bullet was going to work under more advantageous conditions.

On this account he:

> …was of the opinion that in the straight behind form of attack by the fighter, the bomber will be in the position of advantage and would be able to engage the fighter earlier than the fighter would be prepared to engage the bomber, ie the fighter would probably be compelled to open fire long before the bomber has closed to 400 yards.
>
> It was a question of accuracy of fire. Assuming the bomber's speed to be 280 mph and the fighter's 315 mph, the bomber is able to engage the fighter sooner than the fighter could engage the bomber, as at 600 yards the bomber bullet would only travel $^2/_3$ of the distance of that of the fighter, and would hit the fighter .13 of a second earlier than the fighter would hit the bomber.

He felt that if, for the above reasons, the bomber was able to shoot more accurately than the fighter, the question of firepower was being somewhat overstressed, and accuracy of aim ignored.

The minutes noted, however, that 'the above view did not meet with general acceptance…'

It was also stated at the meeting that it had been 'found by tests' that the bomber's gun, mounted on a Scarff ring, was 10% more accurate than the fixed gun of the fighter when fired at ground targets. In a paper dated March 1939, however, Operational Requirements would note that 'trials at Northolt had proved that the aiming of fire from the bomber is *less steady*' [italics added], and this was another perceived advantage of the bomber which would prove to be illusory.

Operational Requirements noted that:

> ...the defence of the bomber relies on improvements in speed, coupled in some instances with tail turrets, and in general a rather inadequate armament of machine guns when compared to the modern fighter.[3]

However, since the speed of the latest aircraft now approached 20% that of the speed of a bullet (which travelled at 2,400 feet per second) the question of their relative speeds raised other issues, perhaps hopes. Group Captain MacLean's theory was that, as the fighter approaching astern of the bomber was moving *towards* the bomber at, say, 450 feet per second, and the bomber was moving *away* from the fighter at, say, 400 feet per second, the bomber's bullets did not have to travel as far to meet the approaching fighter as the fighter's bullets did to meet the receding bomber. If fighter and bomber were 200 yards apart, the fighter's bullet would have to travel 230 yards, while the bomber's bullet would only travel 160 yards. Operational Research when considering the absolutely vital question of the required armament of the new heavy bombers suggested that:

> If there is anything in the theory that as speed increases the bomber is firing at increasingly shorter range *the necessity for the bomber to adopt long range weapons of larger calibre than a machine gun is not so great...This shortening of the range in favour of the bomber would avoid the great difficulties and disadvantages attendant on installing guns of the 20 mm or similar variety with adequate fields of fire, together with sufficient ammunition supply.*[italics added][4]

On being shown Group Captain MacLean's paper, which had detailed his theory at length, Professor Lindemann made the comment that 'Thinking in terms of distance however may lead to hopeless confusion. It is not the distance travelled, but the time during which the bullet is travelling which is important...' Professor Lindemann noted that the great advantage to the bomber lay in air resistance, suggesting that:

> ...the bomber bullet starts on its travel up the barrel with a negative velocity according to the speed of the aircraft, let us say, of 400 feet

per second [270 mph]. The fighter bullet starts up the barrel with a positive velocity of, say, 450 feet per second, ie the actual velocity for the two bullets when they meet in the air is 2000 against 2900 approximately, and I believe it is a fact that somewhere about 2800 to 3000 feet per second is a critical speed at which the resistance to the bullet begins to rise from, as the square of the velocity to, as the cube of the velocity. If this is the case it is valueless to give the fighter a high velocity gun, while as regards the bomber it will pay every time to boost the velocity up to whatever may be the critical figure.[5]

The use of the high-velocity gun (ie a gun firing a very high-speed bullet) was considered in a paper (AFC42) dated 5 October 1937 written by the Armament Group at Eastchurch. This paper was itself in reply to a paper (AFC37) dated September 1937, which investigated the possibility of developing guns with a higher *rate* of fire (ie firing more rounds per minute). This latter paper had concluded that, for the bomber, a higher rate of fire might enable turrets with two guns to be carried instead of turrets with four guns, which would give speed advantages by a reduction of air resistance through the bomber being able to carry smaller turrets. However, it was concluded in this latter paper that, since guns would need stripping and cleaning after 2,000 rounds, this would make guns unreliable. 'If 2 guns jam or break in an 8 gun fighter we still have 75% of our firepower left; whereas if we replace a 4 gun turret by a 2 gun turret and 1 gun fails we lose 50% of our fire power.' The possibility of arming the bomber with *four* rapid fire guns seems to have been ignored by the Operational Research Section.

In the answering paper on high velocity guns, the Eastchurch armament group noted that Operational Requirements had sought to increase the *range* of guns by doubling the number of rounds fired to 2,000 per minute, ie enabling the same number of hits to be made on the target, but at a greater distance. It noted that this carried a weight penalty, due to extra ammunition, of 170 lbs for the fighter. All these extra rounds, it was argued, would produce 1.4 hits for every one hit before over a 20 foot circle. However, this increase in *lethal density* was just one aspect of range – you also had to get the centre of the 20 foot circle on the target! This essential was made easier, it was stated, by increasing the muzzle velocity of the bullet. At 800 yards range, at a height of 15,000 feet, firing from a stationary gun at a target moving at 300 mph, a bullet with a muzzle velocity of 4,000 feet per second would take .74 seconds and would drop (due to gravity) just 8.9 feet, compared with 1.58 seconds travel and a *39.8 feet gravity drop* for the bullet fired at 2,000 feet per second. At 300 mph, the target would have moved 327.5 feet from the higher velocity bullet, and 694.2 feet from the slower. The faster bullet would strike at 2,630 feet per second, the slower a 1,195 feet per second, a very considerable increase in the force of impact – as effective in increased force and impact as an increase in calibre.

In complete contradiction to Professor Lindemann's calculations, the Eastchurch group had calculated that air resistance, which increased as the square of the speed at 2,000 feet per second, would increase by the velocity to the power of 1.4 at the higher speeds. (Modern experience seems to show that this power increases very greatly at around the speed of sound – roughly 1,100 feet per second – but falls when above it.)

It can thus be seen that 'range' can be seen in two aspects, both of which have validity: the number of hits which you can get within a circle at a distance, which is obviously, all else being equal, a function of the number of rounds you can fire in a given time, usually two seconds; and the velocity (and weight) of the round itself, which will enable the bullet to travel a greater absolute distance and with a flatter trajectory, which makes sighting calculations easier as the bullet drops less. A further factor, dependent on both the impact velocity and the weight of the bullet, and whether it is armour-piercing or incendiary or explosive, is the vulnerable area of the target. This last, vital, factor seems often to have been overlooked by the proponents of the .303". Obviously a 20 mm round would damage almost any part of the aircraft, whereas the parts vulnerable to the rifle calibre .303" round would be considerably less, with the area of the aeroplane vulnerable to .5" ammunition being somewhere between the two. A .303" calibre weapon will fire at a greater rate, but with less impact and less velocity, and with greater bullet drop. A 20 mm cannon has a higher velocity and impact and less gravity drop, but a reduced rate of fire. It may be thought, however, that inertia and wishful thinking might have also been on the side of the more rapid fire and the .303" bullet. Yet here was a paper which suggested that *both* the rapidity of fire *and* the weight advantages of the .303" gun *and* the power of the impact and increased vulnerable area and sighting advantages of higher calibre weapons could be had in just one high velocity weapon, as the speed of the bullet multiplied the force of the impact. The paper noted that 'there would be no difficulty in applying high velocity guns to bomber aircraft'.

Both the high-speed and the high-velocity guns were discussed at the eleventh meeting of the Air Fighting Committee on 4 November 1937. It was noted that the high-speed gun (high rate of fire) would be heavier, eight high-speed guns weighing some 170 lbs more than eight guns of normal speed. An extraordinary example of the disadvantage of ammunition wastage was also advanced against the high-speed gun:

…a stable aircraft might continue on a straight course for some seconds after the pilot had been killed, and it should therefore be taken into account that the wastage of ammunition caused by the fighter continuing to fire, not knowing that his aim had been achieved, would naturally be greater with guns firing at ultra high speeds.

Dowding, the Commander in Chief of Fighter Command, felt that the gun would be less reliable, but the Director of Armament Development, Group Captain G Baker, felt that reliability would increase with development, 'and in any case would be considerably greater than that to be expected from a higher velocity gun'.

The Eastchurch armament group, who had produced the paper on the high-velocity gun, now admitted that 'the technical difficulties might be greater than had been visualised' when the paper was written. Group Captain Baker confirmed that even the use of an existing cartridge, which produced a muzzle velocity of 2,700 feet per second, 'would probably necessitate redesigning the gun'. If the muzzle velocity were doubled, the cartridge weight would be four times that at present, the cartridge case would be larger, and the size, weight and length of travel of the moving parts would all increase. He confirmed that experiments were being carried out at Woolwich on high-velocity rifles, but these were 'only in an early stage'. When the fact that the higher velocity gun might have a reduced rate of fire was broached by the head of the Air Fighting development Unit at Northolt, Group Captain Drummond, Mr RS Capon pointed out that 'a good working rule was that, to achieve the same advantage as doubling the muzzle velocity, the rate of fire would have to be quadrupled'. This quiet comment seems to have pointed out a major advantage of the high-velocity gun over the high-speed gun – and indeed, of the ordinary gun. However, it seemed to carry little weight, as Baker felt that the development period would be too long, pointing out that Gebauer, a Hungarian who had produced a high-speed gun, had been fifteen years in the process. However, the Bomber Command representative, Wing Commander Lowe, thought that 'the arguments in favour of a higher muzzle velocity gun were so strong that he considered a full investigation should be made as to its practicability'.

The Committee recommended that trials of the high speed gun be pushed forward, and that the problem of the high velocity gun be studied in detail by D.Arm.D. – who had seemed to suggest it might take fifteen years to develop!

The ability to carry larger calibre higher velocity weapons had been seen to be an advantage of the big bomber, and there was also some faith in its superior speed, Slessor's note of August 1937 commenting that 'Owing to its mass the big aircraft, by putting its nose down, can increase its speed very rapidly and will probably be able to get away from any fighter'.

By December 1938 another Air Staff note on the advantages of size for bomber aircraft ran:

> As regards vulnerability to enemy fighter attack, the larger bomber not only has a higher speed but, with more guns and better turrets, must always be better than the smaller class in its ability to defend itself; and moreover, although the Stirling was not so designed, the larger type of bomber can be armed with 'cannon' guns firing high explosive shells at relatively long range whereas it is impracticable to install in the smaller aircraft heavier weapons than machine guns. The great importance of this lies in the fact that fighter aircraft carrying 'cannon' guns are already in existence in foreign air forces and, since the 'cannon' gun fighter could outfight the machine gun of a bomber, the bomber would be very seriously handicapped unless it was also armed with the 'cannon' gun... It seems certain that the fitting of 'cannon' gun turrets will be essential in future types of bombers and this is not practicable in the smaller classes...[6]
> [Underlined in the original.]

But the Manchester (from which grew the Lancaster), Stirling and Halifax bombers designed to meet the B12/36 and P13/36 Air Ministry specifications, however armed, would not be available for some years to come. The aircraft types that would bear the brunt of the doctrine in the first years were the Fairey Battle, the Armstrong Whitworth Whitley, the Bristol Blenheim, the Vickers Wellington and the Handley Page Hampden. All first flew in 1936. The Battle was built to a 1932 specification (P27/32, the second two figures indicating the year of the specification), the Whitley to B3/34, the Blenheim to B28/35 (although it was an adaption of a pre-existing Bristol light transport aircraft), the Hampden to B9/32 and the Wellington to B9/32.

But the defensive armament of these aircraft was weak, particularly that of the Battle, as Ludlow-Hewitt pointed out in a memorandum to the Air Ministry of September 1938:

> ...the existing armament of the Blenheim and Battle, both of which consist only of one Lewis gun for rear defence, has become very inadiquate (sic) and it seems more than doubtful whether even strong forces of these bombers will be able to repulse determined attacks by modern fighters. It is, therefore, of the utmost importance

that everything possible should be done to improve the rear defence of all our bomber squadrons, but in particular those operating by day, namely the Blenheims and Battles…[7]

Ludlow-Hewitt wanted 'K' guns (.303" calibre) put in place of the Lewis guns, two being required for the rear of the Blenheim, although it was doubtful if the Battle could be so armed. This was not all. 'I am anxious about the weakness of the rear armament of the Hampden,' he wrote, 'and trust that everything possible is being done to find means to improve this.'

The Commander in Chief also suggested that the Blenheims, re-armed with forward-firing guns, might operate as fighters at times when 'it might be difficult to find a suitable offensive bombing role' for this type.[8]

But, in December 1938 it was the Operational Requirements Section who noted, in a paper on mounting cannon in a fixed gun fighter, that not only was the Blenheim vulnerable from behind, but from astern and below. All bombers obviously present a larger target than a fighter, but the target area of a bomber increased from astern and below, that of a Blenheim offering a target of 127 square feet from dead astern, 259 square feet from astern and 12 degrees below, and 389 square feet from astern and 25 degrees below. The fighter, climbing towards the bomber from astern at this angle, presented the minimum target.[9]

By March 1939 the Operational Requirements Section, having argued against the arming of bombers with 20 mm cannon guns when in the design stage (and *for* the arming of fighters with 20 mm cannon) now, in March 1939, produced a paper on gun calibres[10] which must have added to Ludlow-Hewitt's anxiety. It noted, firstly, that the .303" armed bomber gunner aimed to bring down the fighter by killing the pilot or damaging the petrol tanks, engine or controls. It noted, however, that the target was small and that one hit was not likely to be lethal, save on the pilot. It was necessary therefore 'to produce a very high density of fire in order to attain the aim', which had led to the 'introduction of multi gun installations of high speed guns together with the largest practicable supply of ammunition'.

However, in the next paragraph a 'very serious limitation of the Browning .303" gun' was related – its 'inability to fire a burst of more than about 250 rounds without overheating'. After a burst of this length it required a period of several minutes in order to cool down. 'This cannot be obviated', it warned, 'except by a very large re-design of the gun which would take a very long time to do.' A burst of 250 rounds at 1,150 rounds per minute would last some thirteen seconds, an incredibly long time for a continuous burst, given that the eight .303" guns of the Spitfire and Hurricane were designed to destroy a bomber with a two-second burst –

about 300 rounds in all – which meant that the bomber in all probability had no more than this amount of time to destroy the fighter.

Then came further ominous forecasts for the defence of the bomber:

Bomber aircraft armed with .303" guns, when attacked by a fixed gun fighter from astern, labour under three disadvantages:-

(i) The fire power which an individual bomber can develop directly astern is, and is likely to remain, less than that of the fixed gun fighter.

(ii)Trials at Northolt have proved that the aiming of fire from the bomber is *less* steady. [Italics added.]

(iii)The vital target in the fighter, ie the pilot, already largely protected from injury by his engine, can be given *practical immunity from .303 fire* [italics added] by a quite small addition to the all up weight of the aircraft.

There then followed, in intended mitigation of the bomber's plight, and perhaps of their own mistakes, two fallacious arguments; the first, discussed above, was that the *effective* range from the bomber to the fighter is shorter than that from the fighter to the bomber. The second was a corollary, that the bomber's bullets strike the fighter with a higher velocity than the fighter's strike the bomber.[11] It did, however, make a valid point, that 'the effect of cross fire from other aircraft in a bomber formation may reduce the protection afforded to a fighter pilot by his engine and armour'. However, 'Should complete armour protection be fitted to the fixed gun fighter, covering engine tanks and pilot (which is by no means an impracticable proposition) the bomber's .303 guns will become ineffective'.

There was one glimmer of hope for the bomber in all this, however, but as we shall see it was to be excluded by RAF doctrine. That the fighter could be armed and armoured so as to be almost invulnerable to the bomber could not be denied. However, in doing so it slowly ceased to become a fighter and became a bomber destroyer, itself vulnerable to a 'pure' fighter, analogous to the twin engine Me110 'Zerstörer' which proved so vulnerable to the Spitfire and Hurricane during the Battle of Britain. A clearer example will be given in the chapter on fighter escorts below, when the effect of a group of especially heavily armoured FW 190 fighters on the 'Liberator' bomber, and their vulnerability to the American escort fighters, was seen written full clear in one amazing day of aerial carnage. But the American bombers were armed with the 0.5" Browning, a very much heavier weapon as we have seen, and one which demanded much heavier armour than the .303" – and RAF doctrine excluded escort fighters as a detraction from the offensive, and as ineffective.

In summarising the position of the .303" armed bomber, the conclusion reached in the paper was that '.303" armament is fairly effective against an unarmoured fixed gun fighter but will not be effective if the fighter is fitted with armour'– this despite even an unarmoured .303" armed fighter being a smaller target, having double the rate of fire, firing more accurately and being protected by the mass of the engine!

Then came a summary of the 0.5" gun, in which it was noted that this calibre, although used 'to a limited extent' in the USA and Italy, had not been used in the United Kingdom for the following reasons:

(i) Weight of gun and ammunition is greater.

(ii) Comparatively slow rate of fire. [Vickers .5" was 550 rounds per minute.]

(iii) The difficulty of producing a satisfactory explosive bullet. [This was a disadvantage against the cannon gun, not the .303", where an explosive bullet was virtually impossible!]

(iv) The structural damage caused by a .5" bullet is rarely greater than that caused by a .303" bullet, and the effect of explosive .5" ammunition is very limited owing to the small charge carried.

(v) Although heavier than the .303" ammunition, armour protection against astern attack is possible against ammunition of this calibre. The relative weights are 20 lbs per square foot with the plate inclined at 30 degrees at a range of 200 yards for the .5" compared with 6.5 lbs per square foot for the .303". [In the appendix, it was stated that to keep out .303" the armour thickness required was 4 mm, and to keep out .5" was 11 mm.]

It was then stated that the figures given were for the .5" Vickers gun, 'which is somewhat out of date', and noted that 'the performance of guns of more modern design found abroad is probably superior in the matter of rate of fire and penetrative performance'.

After noting, however, that it would take 'some time' to modernise the gun and ammunition, which would need different mountings and turrets, the conclusion reached was that the .5" calibre was 'likely to be rendered obsolete by weapons of still larger calibre and by armour protection', although, of course, weapons of still larger calibre would be of still larger sizes and weights!

Now, having rejected the 20 mm cannon at the design stage of the heavy bombers in 1936, it was pointed out that 'complete protection by armour against 20 mm projectiles is out of the question' on weight grounds, but it was noted that 'a 4 mm plate is of value in protecting personnel, tanks etc. against *splinters*' [italics added]. It went on to say that:

> Recent trials indicate that although solid shot of a 20 mm calibre is more effective than bullets of smaller calibre [from the weights given in the appendix, the projectile was over ten times the weight of the .303" bullet], explosive shell is *vastly more damaging* owing to the distribution of large quantities of high velocity fragments which not only kill the crew but cut controls and vital services. In addition the explosive shell has a potential incendiary value which is not possessed by solid shot. [Italics added.]

A firing trial had been held with a Blenheim as the target, and the paper noted that, firing from astern:

> ...with the target nose down at 45 degrees, 4 out of 17 hits with 20 mm high explosive shell proved immediately lethal, and a further 6 would have prevented the aircraft from returning home, 4 other rounds so damaged flap gear, brakes and a tyre that the aircraft would probably crashed on landing. All members of the crew, wireless and fixed gun [would have been] put out of action.

The paper grimly went on:

> Notwithstanding, therefore, several limitations, the fighter armed with fixed 20 mm guns renders attempts to protect the bomber largely ineffective, and should therefore be a valuable weapon.

As if this were not enough, in turning to the bomber it noted that 'It is impracticable to fit guns of this calibre to give a useful field of fire in any bomber aircraft now in service'. However, it hinted at a possible relief for Bomber Command in the future, suggesting that:

> In view of the development abroad of fighters armed with 20 or 23 mm guns, steps have been taken to develop turrets for the Stirling, Halifax and Manchester to carry 20 mm guns. It is hoped to accommodate 2 guns in each upper and lower amidships turrets with 300 rounds of ammunition per gun as a normal load, and more ammunition can of course be carried with a reduced load of bombs or fuel. The fuselages of these 3 aircraft will have to be re-designed to carry these turrets. ...Once the fighter adopts armour protection the bomber's .303" machine guns become relatively ineffective and the adoption of a heavier calibre is urgently necessary.

The conclusion reached by Operational Requirements was that the 20 mm cannon should be adopted for both fighters and bombers, noting for the future, however, that:

> The trend of development seems to be that armour defeats the .303" machine gun, and that the 37 mm or 40 mm gun will probably defeat the 20 mm gun, by enabling a more effective shell to be employed *with greater accuracy at longer ranges.* [Italics added.] This development is so far ahead that we are justified in adopting a more powerful machine gun, such as the 20 mm Hispano…The adoption of a lower calibre such as 12.7 mm (.5") or 15 mm cannot be justified, as a long development period must elapse before a satisfactory weapon is available, and even then it seems that it would not be as efficient as the 20 mm Hispano gun.

Thus by early 1939 it had been recognised not only that the existing bombers, particularly the Battle, Blenheim and Hampden, were ill armed to meet German fighter opposition, but that the new heavy bombers' armament would be out of date without a re-design. The bomber presented a larger target than the fighter. Its purpose was to carry bombs, and its defensive firepower detracted from this, and had to be spread between nose, upper and lower amidships, and rear, while the fighter was designed to bring down other aircraft and all its weight of fire was concentrated forward. The fighter had a considerable advantage in speed, and could attack when, and from whatever angle, it chose. It could carry much larger calibre weapons than the bomber. The fire of a fixed gun fighter was more accurate than that of the turret fire from a bomber. All this was known to Bomber Command by March 1939. Experience in the Great War had shown that the strategic bomber was vulnerable to the fighter, even without the fighter possessing the very great advantage in speed which it had now attained, and without the electronic eyes of radar with which the defence could search the cloud and the night, and which a nation so technically and scientifically advanced as Germany might be presumed to possess. Experience in the Spanish Civil War had also shown the great advantages possessed by the fighter, especially when the Germans had introduced the very formidable Bf (Messerschmitt) 109, which had taken the world speed record in 1937, and which was armed with 20 mm cannon as well as machine guns. What chance would the bomber have?

The RAF were now faced with a dilemma. Their doctrine of the offensive, their very *raison d'être*, was that of the strategic offensive, the aeroplane being an offensive weapon, and not to be considered as a defence against the aeroplane. Yet the bombers themselves, the jaws of the offensive, with their teeth of high explosive and breath of fire and poison gas, rather than always getting through, were increasingly seen as vulnerable. They would have to fight their way through, rather than materialising like harpies from the clouds to terrify citizens and obliterate civilisation. The fighters were faster, with larger jaws and could now be guided to the bombers by the use of invisible rays. Hope might be on the horizon in the shape of the Stirlings and Halifaxes and Manchesters, but these aircraft, with their heavier defensive armament, would not be available until 1940 or 1941, and the offensive, if war came before then, would have to be carried on by the indefensible Blenheims and Battles, the Hampdens and Whitleys and Wellingtons.

Salvation from this dilemma into which their rigid belief in the doctrine of the now seemingly impracticable relentless offensive had led them came to the RAF in two unlikely shapes. The first came from that very fear of the air which had given the doctrine its credibility. The fear of the bomber had been at the centre of British Government policy for many years, and its abolition keenly desired. London, easily identifiable, easily found by following the estuary of the Thames upriver until the world's largest city lay helplessly below, close to the continent, a great centre of finance and of industry containing the Government and almost a fifth of the population, might be blasted and burnt and poisoned early on by a knock out blow – even, perhaps, before a declaration of war. Britain, therefore, had every interest in banning the bomber and banning the bombing of cities, and most certainly, in not commencing a war of city bombing. Not only did it seem morally undesirable and militarily foolish, but an unprovoked offensive against the enemy civil population would have alienated opinion in the United States. Furthermore, the bombing of cities and civilians was contrary, it was thought, to international law. Two sets of plans were therefore devised for RAF Bomber Command – a 'legal' war against clearly identifiable military objectives, and a war 'with the gloves off' against the enemy nation as a whole. The 'legal' plans were considered by Neville Chamberlain at the time of the Munich crisis to be that it was illegal to bomb a civil population, that targets must be clearly identifiable as military objectives and that care must be taken, in bombing these, that no 'collateral' (to use a modern term) damage to civilians was caused. Bomber Command was virtually restricted to an attack on the German Navy, and German Army lines of communication.

The second salvation of the RAF from its dilemma came from the even more unlikely direction of a strategic evaluation provided by a civil servant. It had been recognised by all of the Chiefs of Staff that any future war would have to be conducted on land and sea and air alike, despite Mr Chamberlain's hopes that the bomber force would make a British Expeditionary Force to the continent unnecessary. The Government therefore in July 1937 asked the three services what would be required to complete their respective programmes. The Air Ministry accordingly submitted expansion scheme 'J', which took account of hostilities with Germany, Italy and Japan together. A force of 203 squadrons was proposed – forty-five for overseas, four for trade defence, and 154 squadrons for the Metropolitan Air Force, backed by war reserves of 225% of this first line strength. Of the metropolitan squadrons, thirty-eight would be fighters and ninety bombers, and the rest general reconnaissance (nine), flying boats (six) and army co-operation (eleven). The ninety bomber squadrons were, by 1943, to be all heavy, although by this definition twenty-two squadrons of Hampdens and Wellingtons were included.

These proposals were scrutinised by Sir Thomas Inskip, the Minister for the Co-ordination of Defence. He pointed out to the Air Ministry that defeat at sea would be fatal, whereas if the bomber force were to be inferior to Germany's it would involve discomfort – but that the onslaught of the enemy bombers would be better blunted by the close defence provided by the increasingly effective fighter force, than by any counterstroke.[12]

Needless to say, this reversal of the policy of the relentless offensive caused consternation to the Air Staff. It availed them little. The new scheme 'K' which replaced scheme 'J' 'marked a virtual revolution in air policy'.[13] The all out offensive was abandoned – or rather, postponed – the planned reserves of the bomber force were reduced to a level where the offensive could not be maintained, and the bomber force 'rolled up' and conserved. The planned reserves of fighter aircraft – much easier to manufacture anyway – were maintained in full. Trenchard's relentless offensive gave way – for a time – to a close defence provided by the new Hurricane, Spitfire and Defiant fighters guided by radar and by Dowding's and Tizard's fighter control system, and heavily seconded by the Army's battery of anti-aircraft guns. The all out offensive would wait until such a time as the new bombers came through in quantity – and until it became, after a catastrophe in France and a defensive victory by Fighter Command, the only offensive option which remained.

Perhaps the greatest hope which lay in the minds of the planners was a belief in the defensive power of flying in formation, which threatened the fighter with the combined firepower of all the aircraft in the formation, should he stray within range. However, trials were held between Spitfires and formations of Blenheims at Wyton in April 1939. The conclusions were not encouraging to Bomber Command. It was thought from the trials that large formations of Blenheims 'should be dispersed on as wide a front as other considerations allow, in order to keep an effective look out, particularly underneath each other'. If attacked, however, the maximum volume of fire could be obtained by a formation with a narrow front and shallow depth. But if large numbers of fighters were involved, 'the depth should be greater'. A flat vic (a 'V' formation) of 120 degrees was thought to be the simplest formation to provide some sort of supporting fire and some protection against the 'nibbling' of the rear aircraft in the formation, but this rendered them vulnerable to mass attacks. These attacks could be 'easily upset' by a rapid closing of the vic. If this closing movement could be carried on into a 'scissors' formation, a mass attack might be prevented altogether. The 'scissors', however, exposed the rear aircraft to 'nibbling', so it was thought that these rear aircraft should be heavily armed and armoured 'escorts'. As an alternative, two boxes of six aircraft might provide some protection against both mass and 'nibbling' attacks until the heavily armed escorts became available. However, boxes were 'bad for surprise from AA fire, *rather tiring to fly without a great deal of practice* [italics added], and possibly more open to surprise than some wider formations'.

From these trials, the 'main lesson learned' was that quite small alterations of course could be effective. The report went on:

> To make an extreme case, a formation might enter a long fighter zone in two boxes, change to independent sections through an AA zone and when again in boxes might throw the section of the second box onto the top section of the first to form a vic ready for scissors, so as to reach a cloud cover before a full fighter attack could develop.

In what must have been the understatement of the year, the report concluded that 'such action calls for very effective fighting control'. It might be considered that, in the heat of battle, the poorly armed bombers, assailed by highly manoeuvrable eight gun or cannon armed fighters with 100 mph speed advantage, might need all the skills of a top display team to achieve these formation changes. But the huge expansion of Bomber Command and the vast pilot training programme meant that pilot training was mostly carried out in the much expanded and diluted squadrons themselves, by the small nucleus of highly trained pilots. 'The problems of handling large mass formations of aircraft were only just beginning to receive attention even at the Air Ministry.'[14]

Another hope lay in the Short Aerial Mine. This device was intended to provide protection to the bomber from attacks from astern, and consisted of a small mine released from the rear turret, which dangled from an 800 foot cable, supported by a parachute, into the path of attacking fighters. If the fighter did not attack from dead astern of the bomber, the bomber pilot would 'wiggle' his aircraft from side to side, or up and down, until the fighter entangled itself in the cable. That hopes were raised by this device is a sure indication of the desperate pessimism with which the possibility of the defence of the Blenheim and Battle, the Wellington, Hampden and Whitley against the modern fighter was viewed; and even the new heavies, when they came, although they would possess power operated turrets and eight machine guns, would still be armed with the .303" gun. How would they cope with cannon armed, and armoured, single-engined fighters?

Notes

1 P Colin Sinnott, *The RAF and Aircraft Design 1923–1939*, Frank Cass, London, 2001, 172–3.

2 PRO Air14/251.

3 PRO Air5/1137.

4 PRO Air5/1137.

5 CA F29/23-9.

6 PRO Air9/82.

7 PRO Air14/385.

8 In July 1940 the Brooke-Popham Report concluded of the Blenheim that 'as a fighter it wants more speed and as a bomber it wants more defence behind', see PRO Air16/504.

9 PRO Air14/243.

10 PRO Air14/243

11 If, say, a ball were to be thrown at 50 mph from the back of a lorry travelling at 30 mph, its speed relative to a fixed point would be 50 – 30 = 20 mph to the rear. If it were to strike a following lorry, it would add the following lorry's speed, and impact at 20 + 30 = 50 mph. But a ball thrown from the following lorry towards the first would have a speed relative to a fixed point of 50 + 30 = 80 mph, yet the speed of the lorry away from it would mean that it had an impact speed on the lorry of 80 – 30 = 50 mph. Both balls would be in the air for the same time, and both would therefore slow down at the same rate, and wind resistance would only be marginally greater for the fighter's *bullets*.

12 JBS Haldane, who had witnessed the bombing in Spain at first hand, had seen the value of fighter escort. Speculating that such escorts would not have the range to accompany the bombers in a knock out blow on London, he berated the 'tragic' fact that the RAF had concentrated on bombers. See JBS Haldane, *ARP* [Air Raid Precautions], Victor Gallancz Ltd, London, 1938, 69–70.

13 PRO Air41/39.

14 PRO Air41/39.

CHAPTER FIVE

Defensive Armament, Guns and Turrets – The Bills are Cashed

The decisions by arms is, for all operations in War,
great and small, what cash payment is in bill transactions.
Karl von Clausewitz[1]

For all the inter war fears of a knock out blow in the first days of war, the Second World War in the air began quietly. There were no German attacks on London at all, although the alarm was sounded. Bomber Command conducted night leaflet raids on Germany, using the Armstrong Whitworth Whitley, a bomber dedicated to the night, which had 'little inherent stability', was 'heavy and unpleasant on the controls', and was 'fatiguing to fly'. The Whitley was very difficult to navigate, needing course and airspeed to be maintained exactly, otherwise dead reckoning became difficult. 'If it did not look like sarcasm', wrote a pilot in 4 Group, 'I would like to add, "as a flying machine, the Whitley has a very good undercarriage."' The author added that, given more co-operation between designers, 'we may never again be infected with any bomber having the characteristics of a Whitley'.[2]

Leaflet dropping had the support of the Archbishop of Canterbury, who no doubt regarded it as a more persuasive and bloodlessly mild form of warfare, although the Germans, who had inflicted no punishments on captured bomber pilots in the Great War, had threatened to execute leaflet droppers in that conflict. Much was hoped for from this form of propaganda. Given the known difficulties with navigation at night, particularly in a Whitley, and the fact that a leaflet took from twenty to forty minutes to reach the ground after release, the German countrymen might have been puzzled, and the townsfolk relieved, by the placing of the leaflets.

These deep penetration night operations resulted in the loss of only four aircraft in 113 sorties from the outbreak of war until 24 December 1939. However, the Wellingtons and Hampdens, which carried out day raids on German naval installations, met a very different fate. On 29 September a flight of five Hampdens made a reconnaissance of the Heligoland area – none returned. On 14 December forty-four aircraft set out on a shipping search, and twelve Wellingtons found a convoy in the Schillig roads, north of Wilhelmshaven. Only seven returned. Four days later, of twenty-two Wellingtons attacking shipping, only ten returned. The Germans had lost, it was believed, three fighters in all during both these operations. Clearly, 50% casualties could not be sustained. On 1 October, before these disasters, Ludlow-Hewitt had written that 'there is no more valuable ally in air operations than surprise…and the next most valuable is clouds'.[3] Surprise had been lacking on 18 December, the Germans having detected the Wellingtons by radar – and cloud was fickle. The only ally for the slow and ill-armed bombers seemed to be the night. But night bombing was inaccurate and accidents, never a small factor in losses, were more common – and German fighters would soon be hunting in the night skies.

The British bombers, with either no rear turrets at all or a turret with two .303" machine guns, and with a fighter escort ruled out by doctrine, were sitting ducks for German fighters without the need for the latter to be so heavily armed as to become vulnerable in themselves. Indeed, in December 1939 Sir B Melville Jones, FRS, armament expert and professor of Aeronautics at Cambridge University, noted that:

> …if the fighter approaches to close range he is almost certain to bring the bomber down, provided he is not himself hit and that the guns are correctly harmonised for close range attacks…the advantage of close range is particularly marked when the target takes avoiding action.

Clearly, the .303" rifle calibre machine gun might be hard put to keep an enemy fighter from closing.

Yet many hopes lay in the new four-engined heavy bombers, which would be armed with eight machine guns, four in the rear turret. These, as discussed, would be .303" calibre, with all the limitations of range and hitting power that this implied. Operational Requirements Section, however, under a new Director, Air Commodore R Saundby, were now belatedly arguing for 20 mm cannon armament in the new bombers. This was set out in a paper which began: 'The number of guns which a bomber can carry for its defence must, if the aircraft is to carry bombs in addition, be limited.' This, although obviously true, was a significant comment with which to open a paper which might more agreeably have begun with Ludlow-Hewitt's comment that 'It is much more important to halve the risk of losing an aircraft and its crew than to double or even treble the bombload – it is the size of the casualty rate in our fighting forces which will lose the war', or Sir Henry Tizard's thought that Bomber Command should look at the problem 'more in the light of the number of bombs one can get on to a target per bomber casualty'.

Saundby's paper set out two possible layouts for defensive guns in the bomber. 'The first plan', it was suggested:

> …aims at so disposing the guns as to eliminate all blind spots. To do this requires a large number of gun positions, with the result that the number of guns in each position must be small. [It was scarcely necessary to add the implied rider 'if bombload is not to be affected'.] This method [would ensure] that attacks coming from any direction will be covered by at least one gun, but it suffers from the drawback that fire cannot easily be concentrated in any one direction and that a large number of gunners is required. A good example of this is the Boeing 17, the well known 'Flying Fortress', *the weak defensive armament of which is perhaps its most characteristic feature* [italics added].

Here a small diversion into the history of the United States Army Air Force's Flying Fortress might provide a useful commentary on the armament discussion. The original aircraft had been dubbed 'Flying Fortress' by the press not because of its defensive armament (five .30" calibre machine guns) but because its purpose was to defend the sea approaches to the United States, and the provision and manning of coastal *fortresses* was the responsibility of the United States Army. But the significance to the Operational Requirements paper is that, as stated above, the B17 had progressed from five .30" machine guns to thirteen .5" in the light of British experience. Its armament and performance were much superior to the new British bombers, which had not yet even flown, although its bombload was considerably less.

The paper continued, going on to the second method of bomber defence, which:

> …aims at concentrating fire in the direction from which attack is most likely to come, and relies upon tactical manoeuvre to avoid or render ineffective attacks coming from other directions. The advantage of this system is that it enables the guns to be concentrated into a smaller number of points, the number of gunners to be reduced and fire to be concentrated where it is most likely to be

needed. The system also facilitates the provision of armour protection for the crew…

It was noted that the heavy bomber then in production, the Wellington III (with a four-gun tail turret), and the planned Manchester, the Halifax and the Stirling conformed to the second plan, and would have a four-gun tail turret and a two-gun nose and under (ventral) turret. These would deal with attacks from front and rear and below, but not from the beam or quarter (unless from the lower hemisphere). To defend against this, it was noted that an upper amidships turret had been suggested, which would increase the weight by approximately 700 lbs.

> …an undesirable addition to the weight of these aircraft, which have already been very considerably increased since they were first designed, by the addition of balloon barrage cutters, de-icing equipment, armour protection and self-sealing fuel tanks, *with a corresponding reduction in the bombload* [italics added]. If, however, it should prove possible for the enemy to carry out effective attacks from the beam or quarter in the upper hemisphere, then heavy bombers may prove to be so vulnerable that the addition of another turret would be essential, and it is therefore recommended that provision should be made forthwith for the fixed fittings to carry a mid upper [dorsal] turret.

It was noted that a suggestion that some bombers should carry upper, and others lower, turrets had been made, on the supposition that they could protect each other from beam and quarter attacks in both hemispheres; it had been suggested that all Wellington III bombers made at Weybridge should have a lower turret, and all made at Chester should have an upper. This would not work, of course, if the aircraft were flying alone – but at night, when this was most likely, the enemy fighter 'would not readily be able to discover before carrying out his attack in which hemisphere the bomber was most strongly armed'.

Next, however, it was noted that the RAF already gave its fighters a reasonable degree of protection from .303" fire ahead:

> …and it would be unwise to assume that the enemy will not also give similar armour protection to his fighters. When this occurs we may discover that the .303" gun has insufficient stopping power to deal with the attacks of these fighters, and it will be necessary to equip the bombers with guns of larger calibre…this raises new problems...

Professor Melville Jones' ideas were then discussed,[4] in which it was suggested that the primary armament of large bombers should be carried in turrets in the nose and tail of the aeroplane, and that both upper and lower midships turrets were unsatisfactory. Professor Melville Jones thought it a matter of 'great urgency' that the .5" machine gun turrets should be developed, since the 20 mm gun might be too heavy to be carried in the tail. With upper and lower midships turrets, Professor Melville Jones thought that a fighter might pass quickly from the field of fire of one turret to another.

The Operational Requirements paper then summarised the views of the Commander in Chief, Ludlow-Hewitt, who, it suggested, had originally thought that a gunner in the rear turret would be 'unduly vulnerable to enemy fire', while a gunner amidships would have more protection from the body of the aircraft. Later, however, he had become convinced of the need for some sort of tail turret.

But despite this, the paper still suggested that 'the balance of opinion both in the Air Ministry and in the industry' was 'against the tail turret'. From the aircraft designer's point of view it represented a 'heavy weight in the extreme after end of the fuselage which conflicts with the ideal distribution of weight which should be concentrated as near to the centre of gravity as possible'. The tail turret 'also added considerably to the structure weight of the aircraft as the after end of the fuselage must be considerably stronger to bear the extra stresses involved'. It also prevented streamlining of the tail, which would add to the speed of the bomber.

'The disadvantages described above', continued Operational Requirements, 'though serious, can just about be tolerated so long as the guns in the tail turret are no larger then .303" calibre', adding that .303" would be ineffective! But increases in gun sizes, according to the paper, meant fewer guns with less chance of hitting.

The paper then argued that because the fighter can choose the range at which it wishes to fight:

> …the effect…of a substantial reduction in the volume of fire on the defensive power of the bomber is very serious, since it may mean that the fighters are able to attack in from ranges at which it can make no effective reply.

This seemed to stand the usual view of the range of armaments on its head. The absolute range of a .303" bullet was 1,000 yards, and that of a .5" bullet was 7,000 yards, with a 20 mm gun firing much further still. Obviously, the gravity drop for a .303" round was greater than that of the .5", as the bullet was losing velocity far more quickly – at 400 yards a .303" bullet dropped 8 feet, and at 1,000 yards 61 feet. But four .303" guns could spew out bullets much faster that two .5" or two 20 mm guns, even if the weight of fire is less – although any hits made would, of course, be less effective. Yet on 9 November 1937 the Director of Armament Development and the Chief Superintendent of the Royal Aircraft Establishment at Farnborough had received a mathematical paper by Dr LBC Cunningham, which showed that it was better to fire explosive bullets (which only the 20 mm cannon could effectively do) because the reduced rate of fire was compensated by an increase in the *effective area* of the target.[5] This seemed to have fallen on deaf ears. Later on, Bomber Command's own Operational Research Department would confirm and quantify the vulnerable areas of German night fighters to various calibre weapons.

To return to the Operational Requirements paper, the suggestion was now made that the tail turret was too limited in size for the 20 mm gun to have as full an arc of fire as the .303".

> *One* 20 mm [italics added] might still be unable to ensure a sufficient number of hits to make the defence effective; and two would mean a considerable addition to the weight of the installation and also of the aircraft structure designed to carry it, and it is certain that further increases are out of the question. The possibility of an adequate supply of ammunition for these guns in the tail would also present a difficult problem.

It was noted that:

> ...the possibility of installing .5" guns in tail turrets is still largely unknown, but as the gun is twice as heavy as the .303" Browning, and the ammunition approximately three times as heavy, and as the weight of the turret itself would also be greater, it is clear that the number of guns and amount of ammunition that could be carried would be substantially less than in the case of the .303". To sum it up, it is clear that, as the amount of weight that can be carried in the tail of a bomber is limited, any increase in the calibre of the guns mounted in such a turret must be accompanied by a corresponding reduction in the number of guns and amount of ammunition that can be carried. This in turn will involve a reduction in volume of fire and chance of hitting.

The inevitable trend of this argument was to say that the bomber was indefensible. A classical dilemma presented itself – only nose and tail turrets could be effective, thought Melville Jones, and tail turrets could only be armed with .303" guns, thought Air Vice Marshal Saundby and his Operational Requirements Department, and .303" guns would soon be ineffective, if they were not so already. The new heavy bombers seemed to be damned before they could even take the air. The whole thing obviously needed sorting out, or bombing hopes would all rest on an unarmed speed bomber, which had not yet even been built, for fighter escort – the only other option – seemed to be ruled out on doctrinal grounds. Yet, fenced in to this conclusion by logic, the paper simply overrode the dilemma by arguing that, 'when it became evident that larger calibre weapons must be carried in bombers, it was decided to mount these guns in midships turrets close to the centre of gravity'. It was suggested that *both* midships turrets should be carried – upper (dorsal) and lower (ventral) – and that *both* should be armed with 20 mm guns. Yet because placing sole reliance on these turrets might be misguided, .5" guns should also be carried in the tail turret, although in the interim while these were developed, one 20 mm cannon should be placed in the tail. Both Professor Melville Jones' ideas and those of Operational Requirements required, therefore, the 'very urgent' development of a tail gun turret with .5" guns for the new heavy bombers, although it had been accepted that the first marks, because of the comments of Operational Requirements in 1938, would be armed with .303" guns.

These proposals, from both Professor Melville Jones and from Saundby's Operational Requirements, were put to the twenty-first Meeting of the Air Fighting Committee held at the Air Ministry on 5 April 1940, under the chairmanship of Air Vice Marshal W Sholto Douglas, the Assistant Chief of the Air Staff (Training) [ACAS(T)]. The Commanders in Chief of both Fighter and Bomber Commands were present, as well as the Director of Armament Development and the Director of Operational Requirements. The Chairman opened by stressing the great importance of the meeting, since the Committee was being asked to decide on a policy which would in all possibility have to stand until the end of the war, and it was therefore of great importance that the right decisions should be reached. Yet, for all the importance of the discussion, there was one notable absentee. A new Commander in Chief of Bomber Command had been appointed *just the day before* – Air Marshal Charles Portal, Ludlow-Hewitt having become Inspector General of the RAF. Although Portal had with him the redoubtable and very knowledgeable Air Vice Marshal Harris of 5 Group, and was himself a man of high intellect, the absence of the brilliant Sir Edgar Ludlow-Hewitt, who had had so much to say on bomber defence during his tenancy of the command, and whose experience in a purely advisory capacity would surely have been invaluable, must have been missed. It does seem that, on occasion, the rulers of the Air Ministry seemed more concerned with personnel 'development' and etiquette than the prosecution of the war by the best men available.[6]

The first question for discussion was that of attack on the bomber from the beam or quarter. Here Sir Hugh Dowding of Fighter Command was able to reassure the meeting that beam attacks by fixed gun fighters, possible when the bomber was flying at 140 mph (at which speed even the Wellington had sometimes been flown), was rendered very difficult by even a small increase in speed. The guns would have to be aimed at a point well ahead of the bomber – a deflection shot – and this was very difficult to estimate, for the bomber at, say, just 200 mph, was flying at nearly 20% of the initial speed of the bullet, and the bullet would, of course, be slowing down while the aeroplane would not. However, Saundby, although he agreed that beam attacks from fixed gun fighters could be discounted, thought that a problem might arise with the turret fighter (which could fly alongside the bomber firing sideways from the turret). Indeed, the RAF placed some hopes in their own turret fighter, the Boulton Paul Defiant.[7] Although it was agreed that this form of attack was unlikely, no German turret fighter having been detected, it was also agreed that provision should be made in the new bombers by leaving a (covered) hole for the fitting of a mid upper (dorsal) turret so that the bomber could reply to fire from the beam if the Germans did eventually produce a turret fighter.

The Director of Armament Development (D.Arm.D.), Air Commodore J O Andrews, anticipated much difficulty in obtaining turrets, estimating a fourteen-month waiting time. Portal, however, 'did not recede' from his view that they should be provided, and Saundby, more optimistic, thought that they might be obtainable from other sources.

Next, the meeting considered the arming of some bombers with dorsal, and some with ventral (dustbin) turrets. Portal thought that they should all be of one type, since aircraft might have to operate singly – and inevitably, one type would prove more popular among crews, leading crews in the less popular version to be 'unhappy and less confident'. Air Commodore Andrews added that by trying to 'cram on' turrets (and thereby reducing speed) they might bring about the very circumstances they were anxious to avoid – the beam attack! This seemed a curiously negative comment, since the question had been one of a mixture of turrets – some upper, some lower – on different aircraft, not both turrets on all, and the under turret, at that time, was standard.

Air Vice Marshal Harris, an expert in night flying, commented that the under turret was more useful by night, and the dorsal by day. This was a crucial point. In April 1940 there had been no clear decision to abandon daylight bombing; in effect, almost all bombing had been abandoned, for the main effort had been directed against seaplane bases and German warships, and heavy losses had forced Bomber Command to curtail the reconnaissance of North West Germany. However, as Saundby pointed out, it had only been possible to fit into the new Manchester and Halifax designs a dustbin turret, which could not fire above 30 degrees below the horizontal, and 'could not therefore support the tail turret unless the attack came from below'. No other type could be fitted owing to centre of gravity problems; this turret might not be popular, and it was for this reason that he had advocated both dorsal and ventral turrets.

On the subject of larger calibre weapons, the Chairman summed up the position succinctly; if tail turrets were essential, larger calibres than .303" could not be used because of the effect on the centre of gravity of the aircraft. If larger calibre guns were to be put into ventral and dorsal turrets, a fighter could conceivably dodge between the fields of fire of both and avoid being engaged by either. In reply to a question from Portal, the Chairman stated that both 20 mm and .5" guns could be considered, as the 20 mm was in production, the Browning .5" was being bought in America to fit into aircraft supplied by that country, and the Air Member for Development and Production (Air Marshal Sir Wilfrid Freeman) was also determined to produce some at the earliest possible date.

Now Andrews, the Director of Armament Development, made another surprising intervention. Referring to the Operational Requirement's paper, he pointed out that it stated that 'There is no doubt that the fixed gun fighter can provide itself with sufficient armour to give itself reasonable protection from .303" fire coming from ahead'. He felt, however, that it would be very difficult to armour fighters adequately against .303" bomber armament. Saundby pointed out that it was necessary to look ahead, and that it was dangerous to presume that they could count on the .303" indefinitely. 'It must be borne in mind', he said, 'that it was necessary to kill the fighter quickly or the fighter would be able to deliver his attack.' What impact might Ludlow-Hewitt have had, Commander in Chief of Bomber Command only two days before, and long a critic of the ineffectiveness of .303" fire!

Dowding, the Commander in Chief of Fighter Command, now made the very significant remark that 'by the time they had armoured the fighter all round it would probably not be very much of a fighter'. Nobody, unfortunately, took up the point that this might reduce its performance sufficiently to make it vulnerable to a long-range escort fighter. Dowding added that an armour piercing .5" bullet could probably penetrate any armour that the fighter could afford to carry, and certainly no fighter windscreen could withstand it. A bomber, however, if it gave up the necessary amount of weight, could armour itself to withstand .5" ammunition; therefore, the fighter needed heavier armour than the bomber. Here, however, the Chairman thought [a] 20 mm [gun] would stop a fighter, but .5" would not.

But now Portal pointed out (and Harris concurred) that the tail turret was essential, for beside the disadvantages already listed of relying on the dorsal and ventral turrets alone, at night the gunner must be able to 'look out straight into the void with no obstructions [such as the tailplane] obscuring his view'. The tail turret must therefore be retained, with either two .5" guns, or four .303". Harris added that the main disadvantage of the midships turrets was *not* bringing both guns to bear simultaneously, but seeing the attacking fighter before it was too late; the problem was laying the guns, not bringing them to bear.

However, both the Director of Technical Development (Air Vice Marshal Roderick Hill, who would later command the Air Defence of Great Britain, as Fighter Command became) and Saundby were in favour of deleting the nose turret (particularly in the Halifax) on aircraft performance grounds, and Hill was in favour of deleting both nose and tail turrets on the same grounds. It was the majority opinion (Bomber Command being opposed) that when the 20 mm upper and lower midships turrets were installed, the nose and tail turrets should go. However, in a discussion on remote control of guns, the Chairman thought that a man positioned in the tail turret might operate the upper and lower midships guns to ensure their being brought to bear together. Additionally, some hope was still placed in the Short Aerial Mine for rearward defence.

Yet at this meeting no final decision on the position and calibre of guns was agreed. The .5" was to be tested against armour and compared with the .303" for penetration, to arrive at a decision as to whether four .303" guns were better than two .5" guns; development work on the 20 mm turrets was to proceed on top priority, and when it was perfected, both nose and tail turrets in the Stirling and Halifax would be deleted; remote control guns were to be pursued as a long-term development; and the development of the Short Aerial Mine was to be expedited.

These were remarkable examples of a compromise that seemed to cover all eventualities, yet which solved nothing. Nobody disputed Professor Melville Jones' contention that guns should be placed in the tail and front turrets. Few disputed that the .303" was on the verge of ineffectiveness, yet only this could be carried where guns were most effective, although the effectiveness of two .5" guns in the tail would be tried by an officer (the Director of Technical Development) who thought the .303" effective and therefore both .5" and 20 mm turrets unnecessary (and difficult). Harris had noted that the ventral turret was more useful by night, and the dorsal by day, yet when, soon afterwards, bombers were virtually confined to night attacks, the dorsal turret was adopted and the under turret deleted. These false compromises were to be made on the new bombers, the ones which would eventually carry out the relentless offensive. During the meeting, Roderick Hill had mentioned, when Andrews had stated that an additional .303" turret would weigh some 700 to 800 pounds, that with 'armour, de-icing, self sealing petrol and oil tanks, self sealing petrol piping etc …all this was reducing the available bombload. They were getting to the stage where a 30 ton aeroplane would only carry 3 to 3$\frac{1}{2}$ tons of bombs'. The B17 Flying Fortress carried 2$\frac{1}{2}$ tons, but carried it faster and higher, and was armed with thirteen .5" machine guns.

A month after this meeting, the 'ideal bomber', the B19/38 (later redesignated B1/39), the intended replacement for the Halifax, Stirling and Manchester, was finally laid to rest. Consideration had been given to a range of sizes, with bombloads varying from a minimum of 8,000 lbs to a maximum of 44,000 lbs and tare weights of from 9,000 lbs to 91,500 lbs. The design of the bomber 'was to be arranged to conform with the size of the two [midships] turrets',[8] each of which would carry four 20 mm cannon. Weapons of .303" calibre were considered ineffective, for a trial at Orfordness in summer 1938 had shown that 500 .303" bullets fired from astern into a Blenheim had 'failed to destroy the structure, the controls or the hydraulics'.[9] Yet the Director of Armament Development had maintained in April 1940 that .303" fire was still effective.

Unfortunately, time now ran out for the bombers. Four days after the meeting, the Germans, rightly fearful that their iron ore supplies from Sweden might be interrupted, invaded Denmark and Norway. The Danes, taken by surprise, offered minimal resistance. The Norwegians fought back hard, although their efforts were soon overwhelmed by the well planned and well executed German attacks. Allied forces were despatched quickly, but air support was difficult to provide so far across the North Sea, southern Norway (all that could be reached) being a round trip of some 1,000 miles, and strongly held by the German Air Force. On 12 April 1940 eighty-three aircraft attacked Stavanger and nine were lost in what has been described by Martin Middlebrook and Chris Everitt[10] as 'undoubtedly the most important turning point of Bomber Command's war'. With some exceptions, night bombing now became the standard form of attack. Blenheims of No. 2 Group sortied by day – but only if there was cloud cover into which they might escape if attacked by fighters. This selection of night and cloudy days obviously did nothing for bombing accuracy, as will be seen later.

But far, far worse was to come. On 10 May 1940 German forces attacked in the West. Their plans, originally for a sweep through Holland and Belgium, were compromised by their falling into Belgian hands after a plane landed in that country by mistake. New plans were laid by Von Manstein, which agreed with ideas which Hitler had formed. The attack on Holland, Belgium, Luxembourg and France would continue, but seven *panzer* divisions – mobile forces of tanks and motorised infantry – were to strike from the difficult, wooded country of the Ardennes, cross the Meuse at Sedan, and cut off the Allied forces which it was correctly presumed would advance into Belgium to meet the attack on that country. Much is made of the 'Maginot' mentality, the reliance of the French Army upon a very heavily fortified defence line, which unfortunately ended at the Belgian frontier (which, had it been fortified, would not have encouraged the Belgian Army in the belief that France would advance to her relief if attacked!). The French, it is argued, were fighting the last war again, for instead of concentrating her mobile forces for a counterstroke, they were spread along the French line.

Yet the RAF might be equally accused of *not* fighting the last war again. Trenchard's relentless offensive over the lines by bombers and fighters, which in 1918 had done so much to break the German advance, and to harass the German retreat, was simply not there. Over fields and towns where twenty-two years before the RFC and the RAF had, despite very heavy losses, made all enemy movement difficult, it was very largely German planes which were heard. The Junkers 87 *Stuka* dive bomber with its unnerving siren, and the Heinkel 111 bomber acted as gigantic guns – the explosive power of a 250 kg bomb being roughly equivalent to fourteen 15" shells – a broadside from a battleship[11] – and far more powerful than the aircraft bombs of 1918. The skies above were protected by Me109 and Me110 fighter planes. The only thing which remained in the skies to evoke the ghost of the RAF of 1918 was courage.

The RAF in France was divided between three branches of the service. Firstly, the RAF component of the British Expeditionary Force, commanded by Air Marshal AS Barratt, consisted of five squadrons of Lysander tactical reconnaissance and photographic reconnaissance aircraft, four squadrons of Blenheim Strategic Reconnaissance aircraft, and six Hurricane squadrons. Secondly, an Advanced Air Striking Force possessed ten squadrons of Battle and Blenheim bombers, which also supplemented a force of 100 French bombers, a mere twenty-five of which were modern. The third component consisted of seven Blenheim and two Whitley squadrons of Bomber Command. Portal objected to the latter deployment on the grounds that the enemy fighter support provided for their offensive would inflict crippling losses. It was also doubted that bomber support against an *advancing* army, well equipped with anti-aircraft guns and fighters, would be effective.[12]

The strength of the RAF – some thirty-four squadrons including the Bomber Command squadrons allocated to strategic duties – was a third of the strength of the RAF in France in 1918. The Battle and Blenheim squadrons were horribly vulnerable. On 17 May 1940 twelve Blenheims attacked German troops who were well protected by flak. Loosening their formation to minimise the danger from this, they were attacked by fighters. *All* were lost – the one temporary survivor from the attack crashing in England.[13] The Battles were even more defenceless. In a report dated 16 July 1940,[14] Air Chief Marshal Sir R Brooke-Popham wrote of the Blenheim that:

> As a fighter it wants more speed and as a bomber it wants more defence behind. I realise that these points are fully appreciated but I would urge that every effort be made to embody more guns in the Blenheim at the earliest possible moment…There is a pressing need for a long distance fighter which would enable us to reinforce the offensive action of our heavy bombers by fighter action over the enemy's aerodromes…In view of the very heavy losses by day it is remarkable how the Battle squadrons kept their morale.

Brooke-Popham added that 'The Battle will still be able to do good work against invasion and will certainly be very valuable for training so soon as it can be replaced by some more efficient operational aeroplane'. He might have been surprised, however, to find that production of the Battle carried on until December 1940, and the production of Blenheims until June 1943. In the draft of Postan and Hay's official history of the *Design and Development of Weapons*[15] occurs the comment that 'There is little doubt that even the most public spirited of the firms did not exert themselves in changing over to new types when orders for the old ones were to be had'.

Bomber Command now seemed to have arrived at the point feared by Ludlow-Hewitt in his letter to the Chief of the Air Staff of 3 December 1938. The bombers' .303" calibre weapons were 'practically ineffective against single seat fighters', and the 'difficulties of fitting large calibre guns to the 36 and 37 class of bombers seemed insuperable'. Bomber Command, with 'no other strings to its bow', found that its striking force was 'disappointingly weak in striking power over enemy territory.' Bomber command was at its nadir.

We have seen that, paradoxically, the unarmed speed bomber would provide a solution to the problem of bomber defence, but only a partial one. Apart from the speed bomber, however, whose promise still lay in the future, by June 1940 the attempts to provide sufficient defence for the bomber had been a complete failure. Only evasion, by cloud or by night, seemed to have worked at all. This failure had been foreseen by both Ludlow-Hewitt and Tizard. The bomber and the offensive had been the *raison d'être* for the RAF as a separate service, and by day it had proved indefensible.

The Great War had been won by the Allied armies' defeat of the German Army in the field, aided directly by air power, and indirectly, but importantly, by the naval blockade. Now, by June 1940, the Second World War had been virtually lost because the Allied armies had been defeated in France, and the great French Army had fallen. In 1914–18, Germany had faced France, Britain, Russia, Italy and, when Russia was defeated, the United States. She had the weak and disunited Austria–Hungary for her main ally, while backward Turkey, and Bulgaria, were allies. In that war Britain had provided some fifty-five divisions on the Western front, and ninety-nine squadrons of fighting aircraft. Now, with ten divisions and some thirty-five squadrons to aid France, she had presumed that Germany and Italy could be held until the economic strength of Britain and France prevailed.[16] Neville Chamberlain had not wanted another terrible land war like the Great War had been, with the sacrifice of another generation of young men. He had also felt the general, almost universal, fear of air attack, and had strengthened Bomber Command in accordance with the Trenchard doctrine, in order to provide a striking force. Fortunately, he had also strengthened Fighter Command, although not in accordance with RAF doctrine. But Army air co-operation was sacrificed to the strategic striking force. Germany had ruled the air over France during the land campaign, and this had been a considerable factor in her success. Now Germany sat in triumph on the Channel coast. Field Marshal Sir Douglas Haig, so long unfairly thought of as the general who had hurled troops in stupid and needless sacrifice against machine guns and barbed wire, had been right – the fear of the bomber had perverted military doctrine and resulted in a catastrophe, while the Germans had combined tanks, aircraft, artillery and infantry in a manner foreshadowed by the British '100 days' offensive in 1918, but with modern, much faster[17] tanks organised with motorised infantry and artillery into mobile, *panzer* divisions. Paradoxically, the futuristic belief in the destruction of cities and the relentless offensive by bomber aircraft which had dominated and perverted British strategy between the wars was now the only hope of victory left.

Yet since fighter escort was ruled out by doctrine and defensive armament was ineffective, the only way the bombers could operate was by evasion. To seek refuge in clouds by day was an unreliable form of defence and losses had sometimes been very heavy when Blenheims had attempted to attack in this way. The offensive could therefore only be carried out by night.

Bomber Command was now forced by the failure of the bomber's defence into a great paradox. The provision of 20 mm cannon had been thought to be impossible in the only place where it had been considered by Melville Jones to be effective – in the tail. The reason for this was the effect of the extra weight on the centre of gravity – not only the weight of the cannon and ammunition, but the extra weight engendered by strengthening the fuselage itself. The drawback of all this extra weight was that it had a direct, arithmetic relationship to the bombload. Every ton extra carried in the turret meant a ton less of bombs carried. But it will soon be seen that the progression in the number of bombs required to achieve various probabilities of hitting a target at increasing distances of bombing errors is geometrical. Bombing by night meant that each bomb was far more likely to be wasted, ie, that it would not hit the target. So, if increasing the bomber's defence at the expense of bombload could have ensured day bombing, and it is, of course, by no means *certain* that it could, then the question of the armament of the bomber can be seen to be of absolutely vital importance to the whole of the British war effort in the Second World War, since the night bombing campaign meant that far fewer bombs would be on target. Indeed, it was only by expanding the perceived vulnerable areas of Germany to include whole cities that targets could at first be hit, and even these were often missed. It demonstrates that the argument that heavier defensive armament would be at an unacceptable expense of bombload was quite fallacious, even ludicrous, unless daylight bombing was simply given up on as too expensive.

There were, of course, the new heavies – the Stirling, Manchester/Lancaster and the Halifax, with eight machine guns each – coming along. Much hope was placed in them, and in the supposition that the range of the gun was more a function of the firing rate – that is, the number of hits to be expected at a given distance – than the actual force of the impact and the increase in the vulnerable area of the target with heavier weapons. The former argument, of course, always favoured the .303", which not only had a higher firing rate per gun, but which was so much lighter that more could be carried. Nothing therefore needed to be done. Inertia ruled.

Gun Turrets

The problem of bomber guns was, of course, intimately connected with gun turrets and gunsights, both of which determined the accuracy of the gun. The results of the decisions on guns, turrets and sights were major determinants in bombing policy, and in Great Britain's war strategy at the highest level. That the bomber could not be defended by day was the proximate cause of the area bombing offensive, the indiscriminate bombing of whole towns, for it was soon found, once again, that Ludlow-Hewitt had been correct in his forecast of the need for night bombing aids in order to achieve any standard of accuracy. But then, after mounting losses in the night offensive, the whole campaign almost foundered on the indefensibility of the bomber, and the secret war of high technology radio aids was begun in order to hide the bomber from the night fighter's increasingly clear gaze.

The power operated gun turret, although it seems to have originated in France, was developed to such an extent in Great Britain that by 1939 they were world leaders. Boulton & Paul had developed a pneumatic turret with de Boysson, which the Aircraft and Armament Experimental establishment at Martlesham Heath considered 'so promising that it should be developed' in 1933; and Captain Fraser Nash developed another hydraulically operated turret at about the same time which had also won approval. The hydraulic turret proved to be superior, and Boulton Paul subsequently converted their turrets to electro-hydraulic operation, taking over the de Boysson turret.

By 1940 the turret manufacturers were engaged on the design of .5" and 20 mm gun turrets, the 20 mm upper and lower turrets for the Stirling and Halifax being confirmed as top priority at the twenty-first meeting of the Air Fighting Committee of 5 April 1940 which was discussed above. But on 15 May a change in the organisation of the Air Ministry was made, which would have very far reaching consequences for all matters of aircraft production and development. On that day, the Air Member for Development and Production (Sir Wilfrid Freeman) and the whole of the Directorate of Scientific Research at the Air Ministry, including the Directorate of Armament Development, were placed under a new department, the Ministry of Aircraft Production (MAP). The first Minister of Aircraft Production was Lord Beaverbrook, the newspaper magnate and friend of the new Prime Minister, Winston Churchill. In the crisis after the fall of France, harsh production measures were taken.

Beaverbrook certainly galvanised the whole country into thinking in terms of aircraft production, even if some of his measures were unfortunate. One of the unfortunate results for Bomber Command was that turret development was suspended in favour of other priorities – which included the Blenheim and the Whitley bombers – although experimental and development work was still carried out privately by the companies themselves.[18] Perhaps fortunately for Britain, Hermann Goering, the *Reichsmarshall*, head of the *Luftwaffe* and in charge of German industry, suspended projects at the same time, but for the opposite reason – he felt them to be unnecessary in the war which now seemed won. One of these projects was the jet engine.

As if it were not enough that the new gun turrets should be delayed, the Armament Department itself had no high reputation. On 7 August 1940 Professor Tizard wrote a critical note to Brooke-Popham:

> …The armament department of the Air Force has always had a bad name, and although a good deal of ill-informed gossip flies about, and that it is one of the chief characteristics of Englishmen that they can see other people's faults so clearly, I still feel that the Air Force cannot be proud of its armament department. Things do not get done quickly enough and efficiently enough. The same criticism can fairly be made of other technical branches. I think the faults are all based on the fact that there is no proper professional training in the Air Force. The scientific branches are good, in this sense, that we are generally well in front of new scientific ideas, but when it comes to putting them into practice for use by the Air Force, I am always appalled by the shortage of engineers and professional Air Force officers. The contrast between the Air Force and the Navy and War Office in this respect is distressing. What can be done now to improve matters rapidly I find it hard to say, because there is a general shortage of engineers, but I feel that the Air Staff should realise that, broadly speaking, they have too many scientists and too few engineers, and that they ought to consider very seriously the possibility of importing officers, if they are available, from the Army and Navy…[19]

Tizard had written as early as 20 July 1939 with strong criticisms of armament developments, for he had noted that:

> …We have no research stations of sufficient size and sufficiently equipped in this country for armament work. Much important armament work is sent to Farnborough where the facilities are inadequate and the staff is too small.
>
> During the last two years, since the date that I have already mentioned [January 1937] I have had frequent talks with senior members of the staff at the Air Ministry on the desirability of taking away most of the armament research from Farnborough, decentralising it, and developing properly equipped stations elsewhere. There are many difficulties in the way, more perhaps than

I know of…we must get into the way of envisaging a scale of armament research and experiment for the Air Force comparable to that of the Navy…The new policy of developing a special corps within the Air Force will, I am sure, help to the desired end. The bulk of experimental work done on armaments is better done by serving officers if the right type of officers can be recruited and trained, and I see no serious difficulties here.[20]

On 22 July the Director General of Research and Development, Air Vice Marshal Tedder, noting Tizard's comments, added:

…In my opinion the lack of armament research and development is, and has been ever since the [Great] war, one of our most serious weaknesses. Armament development has throughout lagged behind aircraft development. That was always deplorable, now it may well be disastrous since, with the use of heavy guns, *the aircraft must to a certain extent be designed round the weapons they are to carry*…[italics added]

In my opinion armament development has in the past been hampered by:

1. Apathy and ignorance on the part of most G.D. officers who have regarded armament as being a job for 'specialists' (and grand ones at that) – instead of being as it is *our only excuse for existence as a service* [italics added].

2. Lack of suitable range facilities ie sea and land ranges where all types of live bombs can be used and where typical targets can be erected, also air ranges where all calibres of guns can be fired at air targets.

3. Lack of suitable men (partly the result of (1)) and organisation. The armament group was intended to be a beginning towards this but, like most of the rest of training, it has largely become a mere cog in the training factory for the mass production of pilots etc.

4. Lack of aircraft, We are feeling the result of this very severely now and urgent work at Martlesham is hung up as a result…

On 22 August 1940 Cherwell would write to the Air Ministry[21] that:

I hope I am right in thinking that the departure of D.Arm.D. (Andrews) implies that you are considering what you want to do with the Directorate in future, or indeed whether you want it to have a future at all in its present form. As it seems to me, the Directorate has hitherto been standing between the designers of Armament Equipment and the Service users. The result has been that apparatus has been developed which has often been either too complicated to use under the stress of operational conditions, or too complicated to manufacture under war-time conditions.

...If the Directorate were abolished in its present form... [it would avoid] many of the troubles from which we have suffered in the past. I am of opinion, from what I have heard, that a new broom is needed...I have heard a good deal about the delays and difficulties which have beset the introduction of important gadgets into the service.

This was not a good background for the development of Bomber Command, which was reliant for the defence of the bomber on guns, and for offence (the reason for its existence) upon bombs, for the development of neither of these essentials gave grounds for much optimism. We shall encounter far more fierce and intemperate criticism of the Armament Department from Arthur Travers Harris when he assumes the mantle of Commander in Chief of Bomber Command in February 1942; but it is well to be aware that his fury was not altogether misplaced or unreasonable, since there were grave weaknesses in the development of both guns and bombs. However, Bomber Command did not always help itself in these matters.

Air Marshal Sir FJ Linnell had been appointed Controller-General of Research and Development at the MAP in June 1941. On 25 August 1941 he wrote to Peirse, then Commander in Chief of Bomber Command, on the subject of a certain Wing Commander GA Walker.[22] Linnell wrote:

You are quite right, I am interested in getting hold of him. I have recently started a special body to sponsor, sort out and develop, all the various possible ways of improving the defences of heavy bombers so as to bring us nearer the time when day bombing can be resumed as a routine, without crippling losses. It is in connection with this particular work that I wanted to get hold of Walker. Owing to his intimate knowledge of turret work and his close connection with Bomber Command [he had commanded a squadron] he seemed the ideal fellow for the job I had in mind.

You will see, therefore, that his removal would be a job directly to the benefit of Bomber Command. But if, with knowledge before you, you feel that he will be of more value to you as a potential Station Commander, then I will not press the matter...I do earnestly ask you to let me have Walker in the job where he will directly benefit your Command, instead of letting him go into the normal round of postings...

It might be thought that Air Chief Marshal Peirse, who had been such a critic of indiscriminate bombing, might have been pleased to expedite any appointment which promised, however remotely, to end the reliance on night bombing and bring the far more accurate day bombardment closer. However, Peirse replied to Linnell on 3 September, thanking him for 'co-operating in this', and to say that he would do:

> …what I can with the Air Ministry to retain Walker in command of his squadron and, I hope, later, in command of a Station. If, on the other hand, I fail, I will certainly do what I can to see you get him.

Linnell did not get Walker, for he wrote to Air Commodore JJ Brown at the Directorate of Personnel, Air Ministry, on 24 October:

> …The question of Wing Commander GA Walker is an awkward one and so that there shall be no further misunderstanding I am putting my views on paper.
>
> In August, as you know, I badly wanted Walker for work on the Bomber Command Defence Committee. In deference to the Commander in Chief's wishes I undertook not to press the point at the time. My letter of 25th August to the Commander in Chief gave the undertaking which I have observed. That Walker's case was again under consideration came to my knowledge through a long personal letter from the Air Officer Commanding 5 Group dated 21st October and commencing 'I am told that you are after Gus Walker for an armament development job'. The question of Walker had not been re-opened by me, but on going in to the matter I find that a query had been raised from your Department to D.Arm.D. [Director of Armament Development] asking whether the latter wanted Walker as he was due for relief from the command of his squadron. Naturally, D.Arm.D., knowing Walker's qualifications, jumped at the opportunity of employing him when he urgently needed him.
>
> So much for the history of the thing.
>
> Walker is one of the few really skilled armament officers we have in the service (*I know we have hundreds on paper, but the percentage of dead-heads is a high one*) [italics added]. He has a great deal of experience in this Directorate on the design of turrets and the problems connected therewith. This is a branch of D.Arm.D.'s Department where we need strengthening and Walker is one of the few people with the requisite knowledge and experience. His recent operational experience would be invaluable to us and it is perhaps pertinent to remark that Bomber Command's general impression of

the MAP appears to be that it is out of touch with realities. I am sure that the posting of Walker to this job would be for the ultimate good of the service.

I am, of course, biased and I do not know the urgency of the need for Station Commanders in Bomber Command. The Air Ministry are the only people who know all sides of the question and it is up to them to decide.

This is the case as I see it and I want to reiterate that I have not gone back on my undertaking to the Commander in Chief in that the case was re-opened for the Air Ministry and not for me.

Linnell sent a copy of this letter to Peirse, who replied on 27 October.

I was very grateful to you for ringing up and also for your letter. I felt quite certain that your finger was not in the pie, but the manoeuvres of Director of Personnel's Department certainly seemed strange and I told Director of Personnel so. …I am wondering whether WC Warfield, who has either just left, or is about to leave Malta, would be of any use to you. HC Lloyd telegraphed to me personally to say that he regarded him as a first class armament officer should I want to get hold of him.

In view of the subsequent history of turret development, which is one of failures and mutual accusations, and of the very considerable disadvantages of being forced by the defencelessness of the bomber into night bombing, this obstinacy by Peirse must be considered as confirmation of both Tizard's and Tedder's remarks on the RAF's seeming blindness to the paramount importance of armament; and these views will be doubly confirmed when the serious failures of the bombs themselves are considered.

The question of the defence of the bomber, and how science might aid it, was discussed by the Committee for the Scientific Survey of Air Warfare (CSSAW) at Exeter on 22 June, 1940. Professor Tizard, the Chairman, stated that he had called the conference 'To review the present position of aerial gunnery with a particular reference to the use of tracer and to deflection firing, and to consider the lines of future development, especially any which would produce results during the next few months'.

It was noted in the minutes that the use of tracer was 'always advantageous', owing to 'the impossibility of establishing the direction of the necessary allowances with sufficient accuracy'.

On gunsights, it was agreed that 'every effort should be made to develop means of shooting accurately at longer ranges and with larger deflections'. The idea of the gun firing very high velocity bullets appears not to have been mentioned. It was noted that the Royal Aircraft Establishment were developing a gyro gunsight, the design of which was well advanced. However, it was noted that 'it is not practicable for an air gunner to keep his sights on the target and at the same time read a range finder', and therefore it was thought that a 'simple modification' to the Airborne Interception (AI) radar set would give the range to the nearest target in a given hemisphere, 'which would give serious drawbacks for bombers in widely spaced formations', since it was non directional. A directional radar would need a much shorter wavelength, but the development would be a long term project. It was agreed, however, that as a first step, the non directional range finder 'could proceed in parallel with the gyro gunsight'.

There were twenty-six persons present at the meeting, including five fellows of the Royal Society, and numerous other learned doctors and professors. The minutes give an impressive idea of the efficiency with which these scientific minds processed the agenda and arrived at its measured conclusions. However, as most people who have attended large meetings, especially those in which scientists and engineers gather, are aware – especially those who have the difficult duty of summarising the conclusions and the views which have been expressed – the minutes often reflect a more orderly summary of what it was thought *ought* to have been said, rather than the facts. A Group Captain Davis attended the meeting on behalf of the armament section of Bomber Command, and he duly reported on the meeting to his Commander in Chief, Sir Charles Portal.

He began by commenting that there had been no agenda or any information given before the meeting, that three members arrived late, that most members were therefore ill prepared and the discussion 'definitely woolly'.

Group Captain Davis went on to say that:

The most important item on the whole programme was the design of gunsights. When this subject had reached a somewhat critical stage, one member of the conference had to leave in order to catch a train, consequently the discussion [was] switched to his particular subject of ballistics and ground defence. Before the original subject could be re-opened, the majority of members hastily dispersed therefore nothing conclusive was decided.

...The RAE are developing a gunsight for the determination of angular velocity. The necessary offset for bullet trail [the movement given to the bullet by the speed and direction of the aircraft] which is dependent on height and air speed, is effected by electromagnets which influence the orientation of the gyro which in turn gives a lead to the sight. It is designed for a fixed range. It was agreed that the inclusion of some form of range finder is highly desirable and it was proposed to investigate some form of RDF [Radio Direction Finding, ie radar] for this purpose...

Group Captain Davis noted that the radar was non directional, and added:

I mentioned that I required a higher degree of selectivity and, if possible, some form of directional control...

Mr Bowen (ADR Arm – Assistant Director of Research, Armaments) mentioned that Nash and Thompson had been developing [a turret] along these lines for many months but little interest was taken in the statement, favour being mainly bestowed on RAE and DCD.

Although DSR supported my contention that we must ultimately come to directional control and therefore, it was preferable to concentrate on this subject, ACAS (T) (Air Vice Marshal Saundby) thought that it was better to improvise with the AI set and get something now rather than a promise of a better instrument later. I did not support this argument as my last 6 years experience has shown it to be fallacious. The Chairman agreed with the ACAS and before I could register a strong minority opinion, the meeting broke up in confusion [the last two words were subsequently deleted from Davis' comments] in order that members might catch trains...

I feel so strongly on this subject, I would like to write to Sir H Tizard to amplify my comments at the meeting but I will refrain from doing so, unless you support my views, I would therefore appreciate your opinion.

I regret I cannot go into great detail about RDF as it is black magic to me. Furthermore, I could not gather the full scope of the discussions, as with interruption of late arrivals, distribution of teacups and several 'opposition' meetings being held simultaneously by various members of the conference, it was extremely difficult to hear what was being said, or to glean much enlightenment therefrom.

Portal commented on the file that: 'We discussed this, and I agree with you that an automatic range finder which is not directional would be a greater menace to our aircraft than to the enemy's.'

Later, as we shall see, the gyro gunsight was developed with its own integral range finder, which consisted of a set of diamonds which had to be lined up onto the extremities of the target, the type of enemy aircraft (and therefore its wingspan) having been determined and entered onto the instrument. The radar range finder would become the AGL(T), the

Airborne Gun Laying Turret which would eventually equip two Lancaster squadrons. However, although the directional issue was solved, the question of target identification remained a problem to the end, despite advances with infrared recognition systems.

Sir Henry Tizard resigned in June 1940 over having been in error about the probability of German navigational radio beams, the existence of which had been predicted by Lord Cherwell's protégé, the brilliant RV Jones. In September, Tizard headed the mission to the United States which bears his name, an exchange of secret scientific information which was of the first importance to the war effort. Much equipment was sent to the United States for their information, including the latest Boulton Paul, Frazer Nash and Bristol powered turrets and ASV (Anti Surface Vessel) radar. The Americans in turn handed over a comprehensive manual of the Browning .5" gun, including details of the impact of the .5" cal bullets against running engines, parts of engines, equipment, fuel tanks, bombs, personnel stations and airframes. This *ought* to have speeded up the process of evaluating the .5" gun, which as we have seen was thought by Professor Melville Jones to be essential for bomber defence.

A top secret American invention of special interest to Bomber Command was the Norden bombsight, developed by the US Navy, which they proposed to give to Great Britain. Tizard considered that there would have been no doubt about disclosure of this important instrument had the ASV equipment arrived in accordance with the arrangements made prior to the mission. The non arrival of the apparatus, in which the Americans were exceedingly interested, had had a very bad effect on the Navy, ever suspicious of the British (and indeed, of the US Army). Tizard registered a formal complaint. Needless to say, when the equipment did not arrive, the US Navy declined to hand over the Norden bombsight, and the British delegation had to be content with the Sperry (which was itself considered to be 'better than anything we have for high level bombing' anyway). The effect of this will be seen in the next chapter. However, the incompetence was not limited to the ASV apparatus, for it was reported to Tizard by one American source that he had been asked for practically the same information from six British sources. 'This naturally gives the impression of inefficiency on our part', wrote Tizard to MAP, adding 'Are they far wrong?'

The bomber was defenceless by day, and little had been done to alter this fact by the end of 1941. We have seen the opinions of the Armament Department expressed by Tizard and Tedder and others, yet we have also seen the Bomber Command themselves were reluctant to support them by releasing personnel, betraying in the process that attitude to armament which Tedder had criticised. Added to this, the MAP had halted design work on 20 mm and .5" turrets at a critical time. Yet Bomber Command were able to more or less slumber on the question of bomber defence; because losses at night were at first not at all heavy, they had an unduly optimistic view of the accuracy of night bombing – and the new four-engined heavy bombers with their four .303" tail turrets and two .303" mid turrets were on the way. The Air Ministry had refused to sacrifice bombload for armament, yet had wasted bombs by the gross inaccuracy of night bombing, an inaccuracy foreseen by Ludlow-Hewitt, and soon to be revealed by Lord Cherwell's staff.

Yet the apparent safety of bombing by night would be a mere interlude, for it relied solely on evasion, and the technically gifted Germans were hardly likely to fail to develop effective defences eventually. And once the fighter was brought into contact with the bomber, the bomber's chances were less by night than by day, for the odds of battle were even more heavily weighted against them.

By day the bomber could at least see the fighter, although it had been noted during trials that a Hurricane fighter had been very hard to spot against the background of the earth. The bomber, however, presented a bigger target. The fighter could choose the time and direction of attack, could be more heavily armed and was anyway a more stable firing platform. These were grave disadvantages, mitigated only by the possibility of the massed firepower from a formation of day bombers, and the possibility of being protected with a fighter escort.

By night, however, there could be no formation and no escort. And the bomber could be seen at night more easily than the fighter, which could choose the darkest part of the sky to creep on to the bomber. Norman Bottomley, when a squadron leader in the Great War, defending Hull from Zeppelin attack, was 'struck forcibly' by the fact that:

> It would be almost impossible to sight a Zeppelin from above, but …looking upwards there appeared to be a surprising amount of light in the sky which was unclouded, and objects showed up against this much more than when on the ground…

He also noted that:

> …By July 1916 the BE2c was replaced by the BE12, a machine with a much faster climb and higher speed. A machine gun, firing over the top at 45 degrees, was mounted…[23]

It was well known in the RAF, therefore, that an aircraft was difficult to detect, even by day, against the ground – but especially so by night. Indeed, on 12 January 1940 a paper was produced by the A&AEE at Boscombe

Down, showing the advantages of an upward firing gun, which were that, in an attack from below, the maximum vulnerable area of the bomber was exposed, while even in daylight, the bomber may be surprised through failing to discover until it is too late a well camouflaged aircraft which attacks from below. If the fighter could not be seen, then he could approach to very close range, where, as Melville Jones had warned, the bomber stood little chance of survival. It could therefore be expected that the Germans would not be unaware of this; yet later, as we shall see, much doubt was expressed at the likelihood of this deadly form of attack.

The problem of visibility, especially from below, where the fighter was much more difficult to see, meant that, potentially, the bomber was far more vulnerable by night than by day. The main problem of bomber defence at night was therefore one of evasion, whether by devious routeing to the target, feint attacks, or confusing the enemy radar. But if this could not be achieved, and the fighter saw the bomber, then an important secondary defence was that of the bomber crew, usually the rear gunner, seeing the fighter quickly, and conducting violent evasive manoeuvres.

This latter was, of course, very difficult; the fighter could pick his approach – perhaps from above if the bomber was silhouetted against white cloud or a choppy sea, or below with a moonlit night, or a dark one. The fighter was much smaller. At first – and as we shall see it took some time to be corrected – the bomber could be revealed because of its unshrouded exhaust, a British night fighter reporting that the Halifax could be seen at a distance of $1\frac{1}{2}$ miles due to its exhaust flames.

By night, the gunner in the rear turret had one small, compensating advantage. Not being placed directly in the slipstream of the aircraft, he could have a clear vision panel in the turret, through which he could look out into the night with unimpeded vision. In contrast, the fighter, its cockpit being directly exposed to a 250 or 300 mph slipstream, had to have an armoured glass windscreen. This armour was $2\frac{3}{8}$" thick in the Me110, the most common German night fighter. It was estimated that flint glass absorbed 10% of incoming light, so the theoretical ability to look out without any loss of incoming light was perhaps the bomber's sole advantage. The Perspex material absorbed 6–7% of incoming light, so having to look through this lost the gunner most of his advantage. In addition to this, both Perspex and glass could become scratched and get dirty, both of which would seriously impede vision. Given that in nine out of ten combats the bomber did not see the fighter,[24] this advantage of vision could be crucial. Obviously the turret heating system would need to be efficient, or the rear gunner would need a heated suit. These, given the advantages accruing from the clear vision panel, might be expected to have been the subject of much research and vigorous development. Yet it does not seem to have been pursued with any great vigour, as we shall see when we reach the time when Harris was in command of the bombers, despite the fact that losses were to become so heavy as to threaten the night offensive with defeat.

In October 1940 Peirse had written to the Under Secretary of State at the Air Ministry, strongly recommending that a tail turret should be produced with an open view, as Perspex would, when wet or dirty, restrict the rear gunner's view, and Bottomley, in a reply to Peirse and to Saundby as well, said that he thought a clear vision panel might be opened and shut at will by the air gunner. Yet on 6 April 1941 Group Captain Rice of 5 Group (who would later co-design a turret himself) wrote to Saundby to express

> ...considerable misgivings as to the effectiveness of the tail turrets for defence in night fighting, owing to clear vision having been sacrificed to provide atmospheric protection for the gunner.
>
> It is reasonable to suppose that the enemy's efforts to solve the night fighting problem will eventually meet with some success...
>
> At present final engagement in the dark is a matter of visibility...It is my opinion that unless this defect in the night fighting equipment of our bombers is eradicated in the very near future, a period must arrive when improvements in the enemy's equipment will enable him to inflict heavy casualties on our Bomber force, which could largely be avoided if the necessary action is taken beforehand to ensure that air gunners have the advantage of a completely unrestricted view astern...

Saundby agreed.

However, one of the great difficulties in the whole question of turrets and armament for the new heavy bombers was whether they should be considered as night bombers, or whether they would be expected, with their superior armament, to be able to operate by day as well. The latter gave considerable advantages in flexibility. As we have seen, the most considerable disadvantage of the night bomber was that it could be seen and attacked without being able to see its attackers, and this called for priority for the clear vision panel at the very least. But at night the front turret was scarcely ever needed, for head on attacks were almost impossible – given the very high closing speeds and the very short range at which the bomber must be visible to the fighter, there was very little time to take aim. The mid upper turret was also of debatable value at night, although essential by day. The under turret, thought originally to be useful at night to back up the rear gunner, was a major cause of drag on the aircraft, and was soon abandoned for both night and day work. This seems surprising, given the British trials with Blenheims fitted with upward firing guns, and the well known (to Fighter Command) advantages of this form of attack. Indeed, the German use of upward-firing guns was not suspected by Bomber Command for a long time after these attacks had begun, even when bombers began to return with damage consistent with this form of attack. So deadly did this tactic prove to the British night bombers that very few aircraft lived to bear the tell-tale scars. But when all began to be revealed, hand-held guns rather than turret-fitted guns were placed in the under position, so great was the drag from under turrets.

Thus, by the beginning of 1942, the heavy bomber was a machine on which Britain had initially placed great hopes as a deterrent to preserve her cities from attack, and a means to prevent another Somme or Passchendaele. It now bore the burden of being Britain's only hope of carrying the war to Germany, and since the German invasion of Russia in June 1941 it was the only real hope of diverting German air forces from the east – but it was still unescorted, still defenceless and reliant on evasion by night, which ensured that the carefully preserved bombload would be largely wasted. The spurious argument of the advantage accruing to the bomber from relative differences in distance between bomber and fighter meant that the bombers were still armed with .303" guns, despite the well known limitation of the power and penetration of these weapons, a knowledge repeated in RAF lectures in 1925. Having designed bombers with eight .303" guns, it was then decided to uprate them to 20 mm, jumping over the next highest calibre, the .5", because it was thought that even this size would soon be ineffective. These great 20 mm cannon were, however, to be installed in the next heavy bomber design, the B1/39. Attempts to install them in the 1936 classes had come up against problems of the centre of gravity when installed in the tail, the most useful position. So it had then been decided to put two 20 mm cannon each in upper and lower turrets, and .5" guns in the tail. Then the newspaperman and friend of Churchill, Lord Beaverbrook, appointed Minister of Aircraft Production, stopped development work on the turrets.

However, in late 1941 No. 5 Group decided to 'go it alone' on turrets, for on 27 October Group Captain Lewis Roberts, the MAP overseer Lancaster production, No. 5 Group, wrote:

My assistant tells me that he received a telephonic enquiry this morning from Flight Lieutenant Masters, the Gunnery Officer of 5 Group, as to the maximum diameter of the turret ring of the

'Lancaster' mid upper turret, the enquiry being prompted by consideration of the installation of cannon…

The Officer Commanding No. 5 Group, Air Vice Marshal Coryton, wrote on the next day that the information required was not the diameter of the ring, but the maximum permissible diameter of a mid upper turret ring, as the cannon were under consideration, and the turret would need to be moved nearer the mainframe.

On 1 November, Group Captain Lewis Roberts commented that the fitting of a larger turret ring would cause disturbance to the airflow over a much bigger surface area of the Avro Lancaster, with a consequent reduction in speed and range, and that the nearer the turret approached the wing, the more the wing would interfere with the field of fire of the turret. A further consideration was the blocking of the walkways inside the aircraft. Avro were 'very anxious' to provide some form of cannon turret, and Lewis Roberts therefore suggested that it would be worth visiting the firm.[25]

The cannon were not installed.

The arguments for heavier calibre weapons were different for the day and the night bomber. Long-range firing was not possible at night, though it was perhaps sometimes possible for the fighter, since the bomber simply could not see the fighter at long ranges. It was the contention of the Director of Operational Requirements and of the Armament Department that the larger calibre guns simply did not increase the range anyway. This argument was put succinctly in a paper by the Director of Operational Requirements in October 1942:

> …It may be argued that the two .5" guns would be more effective at long range and would have greater stopping power, but against this is the disadvantage of a smaller and less dense bullet group and the weight of ammunition necessary to cater for long range fire. Even then, on the score of ballistical accuracy, .5" armament would only be advantageous at ranges in excess of 700 to 800 yards. This latter argument applies equally to the 20 mm armament. Heavier calibre guns do not facilitate longer range shooting in air combat as is the popular conception, but rather tends to reduce it because of the greater difficulty of hitting with the smaller bullet group and very much less volume of fire.
>
> It is axiomatic that the effect of aiming errors increases in proportion to range whatever weapon is used and therefore the probability of hitting at the longer range for which the bigger calibre guns would be otherwise effective is likely to be very small. The

bomber cannot afford to expend such heavy ammunition unless there is a reasonable chance of hitting. It may be however, that when the Mark II gyro sight becomes available the increase in accuracy of gunnery will improve so much that that the longer range shooting will be practicable but this will apply also to .303 gun turrets for the present effective range in air combat is governed by the ability to hit rather than any falling off in striking power of the bullets.

The purpose of the heavier calibre is to penetrate and damage aircraft structure, to defeat self-sealing tanks and armour protection for the crew and the vital parts of the aircraft. Single .5 or even 20 mm guns could be fitted to aircraft without much difficulty, if restricted arcs of fire are accepted, as is the case with German aircraft, but the small cone of fire and bullet density would render the chance of hitting immeasurably smaller than that with the present battery of machine guns. It is for this reason that consideration has not been given to the mounting of less than two of these guns.

It has been our practice to protect the bomber over as wide an area as possible by providing each turret with the widest practicable field of fire. The prudence of this policy was confirmed in the early stages of the war when the enemy fighters, discovering the sting in the tail of our WELLINGTONS, exploited beam and quarter attacks. It was because of these attacks that it was decided to install fully-rotating dorsal turrets in heavy bombers.

A further factor which must still be borne in mind is gun flash. This has been reduced to an undisturbing amount in the .303 calibre, but is still a serious drawback in the use of the .5 and 20 mm guns in turrets at night because the flash from these guns is so blinding to the gunner. Much promising development work has recently been done on flash eliminators for .5 guns but until this defect has been overcome, it is doubtful if, on this score alone, heavier calibre guns would be acceptable for the defence of bombers or GR aircraft employed in a night role.

The Director of Operational Requirements had then gone on to comment that plans for the Lancaster, Stirling and Halifax were all for .303" armament, and that a projected bomber, the Shetland, which was originally specified to carry four 20 mm turrets, had now been scaled down to three .5" turrets 'to save structure weight'.[26]

This paper was forwarded to Harris by Sorley, the ACAS(TR), on 30 October with a letter which proposed that a four .303" dorsal turret should be put in the Halifax, and four .303" guns in a new Bristol dorsal turret for the Lancaster and Stirling – which *could* be adapted to take two .5" guns. Sorley also proposed to fit twelve Lancasters with 20 mm dorsal turrets, which if successful could be extended to replaced the projected four .303" guns. It was also proposed 'for the more distant future' to install two 20 mm dorsal turret guns in any redesigned Halifaxes and Lancasters, and to provide two .5" guns in the tail turret 'provided the weight distribution will allow'. Sorley added that 'it must be recognised that bomb load and range will have to be sacrificed to some extent'.

But Harris was not to be deterred from his quest for larger calibre guns, replying on 18 November that the new Bristol dorsal turrets for the Lancaster and Stirling should be designed 'from the beginning' to take two .5" guns rather than four .303"s, and adding that although the gyro gunsight was most desirable, the changeover should not be delayed while it was introduced.

Harris approved of the proposal to equip twelve Lancasters with 20 mm guns as a trial, but insisted on the introduction of two .5" guns in the tail of every heavy bomber as soon as possible, adding that 'every effort' should be made to find a solution to the problem of gun flash in both .5" and 20 mm guns. Significantly, Harris mentioned nothing about the heavier guns making it possible to return to daylight bombing.

There was no doubt, of course, that volume of fire was an important factor in range. Hitler had ordered the use of 50 mm cannon for bomber destroyers, with a rate of fire of one per second, but Adolf Galland, a German fighter ace, had observed that, although it had been installed to improve the range, it could not hit anything above 400 yards away.[27]

However, the argument about range contained in the paper had ignored the important factor of the area of the target vulnerable to each weapon, which was, of course, considerably greater for the heavier calibre weapons, and effectively increased the size of the target. It also ignored the effective weight of the bombs carried, which, due to problems of navigation, target identification and bomb aiming was considerably less at night, as we have seen.

These arguments about group size and range ignored the comments of perhaps the greatest expert on the matter, Professor Melville Jones, who had thought that two .5" guns in the tail were *essential* to the bomber. It dragged out the old story of the beam attacks made on Wellingtons in 1939, while ignoring Dowding's comment that beam attacks were avoidable by simply flying faster, thus making a difficult deflection shot almost impossible. Indeed, the argument on range and group size became almost a question of political correctness; a report on tactical trials of the Lancaster which commenced on 24 April 1942 originally stated that:

> It has been found in the majority of recent daylight operations that the German fighters are shy of the power operated turrets and stand off at 400–600 yards using their cannon. The result is that if any close formation is adopted by the bombers they present a mass target while adding nothing to their mutual fire support *owing to the limited offensive range of their .303 ammunition* [italics added].

This last comment was, however, changed on at least one copy to *'owing to the extreme difficulty of achieving a correct aim at long range with our present sights'*.[28] This seemed to ignore the fact that the German fighters, armed with slower firing cannon, had experienced no such 'difficulty of aim'!

After the famous daylight Augsburg raid of April 1942 it was reported that Captain Frazer Nash (the turret manufacturer) was on the airfield as the survivors came in from the raid and got first hand information from the pilots:

> Everyone said that if only they had had 20 mm armament they would have been all right. The Germans just picked them off with their cannons from a distance and the machine guns could not reply as they were out of range. Nash dashed back to his factory and got all his people working. Within a week he told D.Arm.D. [Director of Armament Development] that he had a 20 mm turret which was what the service was looking for. This was the FN79 twin 20 mm.[29]

This turret was later rejected by Harris.

The whole question of turrets and guns, and the priorities in design, seemed therefore to be in some disarray; were they intended for day or night fighting? Was the dorsal turret, which had seemed so necessary to ward off beam attacks by day, a hindrance at night, when beam attacks were out of the question? Should the priority in turret design be given to vision, as was demanded by the night bomber, or to firepower and sighting, which was essential by day? Should bombers be capable of both day and night operation in order to avoid the inflexibility which would arise if two separate bombing forces were necessary? If a flexible force was desired, the actual installation of the gyro gunsight and larger diameter guns would need to be delayed until the brightness of the sight could be reduced for night work, and a solution found to the flash of the .5" and 20 mm guns.

There were further possibilities being investigated for the defence of the bomber which perhaps added complications to the decisions which needed to be made on the gun question. On 31 December 1941 Squadron Leader Fielding Johnson reported on the trials of a backward looking radar device code-named 'Monica', and recommended that the highest priority be given to its installation in night bombers. And the Airborne Gun Laying Turret (AGL(T)) was, as we have seen, already under development, promising to lay the guns automatically onto an attacking fighter – although there had been little progress in the identification of the tracked aircraft as friend or foe, making it too dangerous to use until this problem was solved. Vast scientific and technical resources were poured into both making the bomber safe at night, whether by evasion or gunfire, and, as will be seen, enabling it to navigate to the vicinity of the target. Yet the simpler engineering problems, that of putting sufficient firepower into the bomber and developing an efficient gunsight, or just of putting two .5" machine guns into the rear turret and arranging the turret so that the gunner had a clear view into the night, were not solved until Bomber Command took things into their own hands and solved it themselves.

In February 1942 came two significant changes. First, on 14 February, a new direction for the Command, that the morale of the civilian population, especially the industrial workers, should be the primary aim; the second, on 22 February, was the appointment of Harris as Commander in Chief. Almost immediately Slessor, now commanding No. 5 Group, suggested getting rid of the front turret for the new Lancaster, saying that 'I have yet to hear of a front gunner firing his guns in anger against an enemy at night' – but Harris' reply was that both the front and mid under turret were required for daylight attacks. The front turret, thought Harris, was also good for morale – and for the centre of gravity of the aircraft!

By 8 April Harris wrote to Freeman,[30] giving his priorities for bomber defence, which were, in order of importance:

1. Provision of a clear view panel in the rear gun turret.
2. A flash device, to dazzle the night fighter pilot.
3. Monica.

On 17 April Freeman replied, saying that the clear view panel was being given all the 'shove' they could, but adding 'it is going to be a difficult problem to solve'. He also hoped that 2,000 'Monica' sets on order would be delivered by November 1942.

On 21 April Harris wrote to Air Vice Marshal Sorley, the Assistant Chief of the Air Staff (Tactics and Requirements), ACAS(T) in true Harris style:

For years I have been a voice crying in the wilderness over the necessity to provide adequate escape hatches in our heavy bomber aircraft. While I realise that the Liberator is inflicted on us by the American designers, and therefore its shortcomings are not of our choosing, yet we have as many beams in our eyes as they have in theirs.

I appreciate the length of time it takes to make alterations and that where existing aircraft are concerned we must necessarily wait until essentials can be worked into the production line without too much interference. But the sickening regularity with which these shortcomings repeat themselves in new types certainly indicates that we should tighten up the whole of our methods of controlling manufacturers and designers in such a manner that no future types can ever get as far in the production line without the incorporation of minimum requirements as specified by us in such directions.

You will recall the regularity with which every heavy bomber is produced with yards of flame streaming from undamped exhaust pipes, and also the fearful casualties we have suffered from frostbite after spending years waiting for the provision of adequate heating. The Hudson, for example, is an aircraft in which the heat provision has always been adequate and achieved by the simplest means. The opposition to universal adoption of the Hudson system has, I believe, arisen mainly from Farnborough and I seriously suggest that the time has arrived when disciplinary action should be taken against the individuals at Farnborough who have been responsible in the past for the lack of adequate heating in our time. There are plenty of countries where such failures would be expunged by the firing squad on the charge of sabotage. While I do not make accusations to that extent, I consider that the gross incapacity exhibited by responsible persons in such matters as the provision of heating and adequate safety hatches should be the subject of an enquiry with a view to appropriate disciplinary action.

On 22 May 1942 Harris wrote to the Air Officers Commanding 1, 3, 4 and 5 Groups that a Taylor flying suit was being issued, and ordered that:

…Tail gunners are to have priority on the issue of these suits, and when they are worn, the direct vision panel in rear turrets is always to be kept open in the hours of darkness when attack by fighters is possible. The modifications for providing direct vision panels…are to be incorporated as quickly as possible.

However, on 27 May the Secretary of State for Air, Sir Archibald Sinclair, wrote to Harris with the following information:

…I understand that it has proved difficult to design a clear view panel which will avoid excessive draughts. One is available with a metal edging which I believe has not found favour with you because of the obstructions to vision caused by the metal edges. It will be difficult to produce a panel with Perspex without any edging, but ACAS(T) anticipates that it can be done in about three months' time and has asked for it to be introduced into the production line. In the meantime, however, the metal edge panel is the quickest way of doing the job and I should be grateful if you would consider whether you cannot accept this type of panel as an interim measure.

Harris' reply to Sinclair of 29 May showed a serious weakness in the whole system of communicating Bomber Command requirements; he thanked Sinclair for his efforts, and replied that he did not know why Bomber Command did not want the metal edge, since the Perspex would have become scratched and opaque without it anyway. Here, Harris showed that his vigorous approach could reward Bomber Command by enlisting aid at the highest level – yet the communications from the top of Bomber Command to those officers who liaised directly and almost daily with both MAP and suppliers were not as strong. We shall see that later, when Harris' indignant accusations of incompetence were answered by detailed data concerning Bomber Command acceptance of designs at ground level.

Sinclair wrote to Harris again on 31 August 1942,[31] stating that he was assured that 'all tail turrets for Stirlings, Lancasters and Wellington IIIs leaving the production line after 1 August will have Perspex clear view panels fitted'. He went on:

> I am further told that a substantial number of these panels with metal frames for application to aircraft in Squadrons are now available for Lancaster, Stirling, Wellington III, Wellington 1c, Manchester, Whitley and Sunderland, and that supply will be regulated according to the detailed priority list which you have sent in.

However, Sinclair noted, in the case of the Halifax, that the problem was one of draught elimination, which applied to all mid upper turrets as well, but adding that 'RAE is on to it'.

As well as increases in firepower, bomber defences could also, it was thought, be improved by the provision of additional armour plating over vulnerable areas. Sir Wilfrid Freeman, the Air Member for Development and Production, who became Chief Executive at the MAP from October 1942, and who we have seen as the very far sighted 'father of the Mosquito' (it was known at first as 'Freeman's Folly') proposed that twelve Lancasters should be specially armoured and tested in action to see whether they might enable Bomber Command to resume daylight bombing.[32]

Harris did not approve, and wrote to Freeman that although the trial would have the advantage of a statistical comparison of vulnerability, the disadvantages would be that '2nd or 3rd rate targets' would be bombed, that since the bombload would reduce by 2,000 lbs three aircraft would be needed for every two before, and it would result in the loss of valuable aircrew and lives. However, he recommended trials with German ammunition, and suggested that the armour should be detachable so as to allow for flexibility of use.

Freeman replied on 3 June 1942:

> I thought that over a period of one and a half years I had got used to your truculent style, loose expression and flamboyant hyperbole, but I am not used to being told…that I am deliberately risking human lives in order to try out an idea of my own, which in your opinion is wrong.
>
> When it was first decided to add additional armour to the Lancaster, it was considered that a return to daylight raiding would be necessary and that every effort should be made to reduce casualties to the minimum. It was recognised that a reduction in bomb load would be necessary; *but why not, if the weight of bombs reaching the target is greater than it would otherwise have been?* [italics added] It is possible, for example, that our casualties on the Augsburg raid might have been 50% less if the additional armour had been carried by our aircraft…

This very valid point had been made before, by Sir Henry Tizard, by Air Marshal Sir Edgar Ludlow-Hewitt and by Air Vice Marshal Tedder, that it was bombs on target per aircraft casualty which was the critical measure of success. However, the Air Ministry Directive of 14 February had simply expanded the definition of the target to include whole cities, which by a stroke of the pen increased the 'accuracy' many times, and changed the argument from Freeman's and Tizard's to Harris'.

A 'Virtual Failure of the Type' – The Stirling and the Halifax
Since the introduction of the new heavy bombers, it was becoming obvious that the Lancaster was definitely superior in terms of bomblift, operational height and cruising speed. The Stirling began to be discounted as a heavy bomber type, and it was soon recognised that the defence of the Halifax was more difficult than the Lancaster, and required a different approach as far as turrets were concerned.

Harris wrote as early as 12 August 1942 to the Assistant Chief of the Air Staff (Operations),[33] saying that:

> …they [Halifaxes] were first called upon in the exigencies of the war situation to train for and to stage the attack on the Tirpitz, in the course of which they suffered heavy casualties. Since then casualties

on normal operations have been very excessive, amounting to no less than 140 crews in two and a half months. Every effort has been made to discover the causes of those casualties, so far without success. It is, however, suspected that a combination of poor performance in the aircraft, lack of effective flame dampers and possible fuel systems and installation troubles may be found, in the detailed investigation now taking place, to be behind these losses.

The next day Harris wrote to Sorley, ACAS(T), stressing the importance of producing satisfactory flame dampers 'which do not cause appreciable drag' before using turbo blowers on any bomber. And on the following day he wrote to Portal,[34] saying that further detailed investigations into the Halifax were being made with the engineering staff, Operational Research, Rolls-Royce and Handley Page, 'to see if we can get to the bottom of the Halifax's vulnerability', adding that 'we are reaching the conclusion that it is mainly due to the poor performance of our overloaded aircraft'.

By 25 August Harris was referring, in a letter to Freeman, to the 'virtual failure' of the Halifax.[35]

On 6 September Harris wrote to the ACAS(T) that the Halifax[36] should be produced as a transport aircraft, adding '…In my view the Halifax is unlikely to remain fit for use as a bomber under tactical conditions likely to prevail in a year or 18 months' time'.

By 12 November 1942 Harris suggested to Portal[37] that all Lancasters should have Merlin engines, and that the Hercules engine should be reserved for the Halifax, as it was 'useless anyway'. Turning to Short Bros, he suggested to Portal on 6 December that '…we shall get nothing worth having out of Shorts until Oswald Short and a good many others in the firm are thrown out on their ears'.

On 23 December Harris was referring to the Halifax V, in a letter to Sinclair, as 'a deplorable aircraft'. By 30 December 1942, uninfluenced by the festive season, or perhaps influenced by its aftermath (he suffered from a stomach ulcer), Harris launched into a bitter attack on the Stirling and Halifax management, writing to Sinclair that:

> …The Stirling and the Halifax are now our major worries. They presage disaster unless solutions are found. I understand that the Stirling is to go in favour of the Lancaster as fast as the change over can be achieved. But it will not be fast – or achieved at all with good will and good intent – as long as HMG balk the issue of taking the Stirling management away from the incompetent drunk [Harris is referring to the Short Bros management] who at present holds our fate in his hands.

The Stirling Group has now virtually collapsed. They make no worthwhile contribution to our war effort in return for their overheads. ...There should be a wholesale sacking of the incompetents who have turned out approximately 50% rogue aircraft from S&H Belfast, and Austins, not forgetting the Supervisories responsible in the parent firm.

Much the same applies to the Halifax issue. Handley Page is always weeping crocodile tears in my house and office, smarming his unconvincing assurances all over me and leaving me with a mounting certainty that nothing whatever ponderable is being done to make his deplorable product worthy for war or fit to meet those jeopardies which confront our gallant crews. Nothing will be done until Handley Page and his gang are also kicked out, lock, stock and barrel. Trivialities are all they are attempting at present, with the deliberate intent of postponing the main issue until we are irretrievable committed...

Unless we can get these two vital factors of the heavy bomber programme put right, and with miraculous despatch, we are sunk. We cannot do this by polite negotiation with these crooks and incompetents. In Russia it would long ago have been arranged with a gun, and to that extent I am a fervid Communist.

If I write strongly it is because I feel strongly, as I know you do, for the jeopardy of my gallant crews and the compromising of our only method of winning this war.

These were harsh words indeed to be levelled at Sir Frederick Handley Page, who had been a pioneer designer and builder of aircraft, and a pilot himself; he had also earned immortality by designing the slatted wing to control the stall,'one of the most important safety devices ever invented for aircraft'.[38] Yet before we dismiss Harris' outburst (and there will be many, many more of them!) as dyspeptic, it might be useful to remember the comment of the official historian of the *Design and Development of Aircraft*, who in his draft had noted, as we have seen (on page 91) that the aircraft manufacturers did not exert themselves over new types or modifications when orders for the old ones were to be had; and we might also bear in mind the comment of the historian of *The Great War in the Air*, Walter Raleigh, that the two strongest motives of Englishmen in the aircraft industry were'patriotic devotion and commercial gain'.[39]

A further balance might be gained from an ORS report of 28 November 1942[40] which found that, with regard to the Halifax:

On this aircraft the extra drag of the duct [the exhaust shroud] reduces the normal cruising speed dangerously near to the minimum comfortable flying speed below which the aircraft becomes difficult to handle and cannot maintain steady cruising conditions.

The report estimated the speed loss due to the duct as 6–7 mph – surely very close to the bone! It estimated the visibility of the aircraft without the duct to be 1,100 feet to the rear – but, as we have seen, a Beaufighter pilot had reported seeing the Halifax's undamped exhaust flames 1$^1/_2$ miles away.

There was certainly a case to answer.

On 5 January 1943 Harris wrote again to Sinclair:[41]

...As I suspected, we are repeatedly catching up with Handley Page's performance promises only to find them to have been the usual Handley Page mendacities.

For instance, the unmodified Halifax II as claimed by Handley Page flies at 214 mph at 14,000 feet. Boscombe Down got 210 out of it. The cleaned up Halifax II (with turret) flies at 230 according to Handley-Page, and we got 218 out of it. So it goes on. Handley Page's promised performance of the Halifax 1A is 242 mph. We are quite certain it will not much, if at all, exceed 225 mph. I gave C.A.S. [Portal] a graph illustrating these claims and actualities yesterday.

It is a source of perpetual wonderment to me, as indeed to all flying personnel, that anybody ever believes Handley Page's performance promises. They have never come up to scratch yet and they never will.

When it comes to promising performance in order to obtain or maintain an order book, he will promise anything. He has got away with this for 25 years and it is more than time that he was taken at his real value and not at his face value.

We are now engaged in removing the dorsal turrets from some Handley Page aircraft in the hope that this practically unarmed machine will at least be able to meet aerodynamic and altitude requirements. This has great effect in making the aircraft more controllable, especially when jinking in searchlights or flak...

On 29 January 1943 Harris wrote again to Sinclair, giving him a summary of the hoped for improvements in the Halifax and the results. These results did not conform to the manufacturer's promises. The most significant changes for bomber defence were the removal of the exhaust shrouds, which left the aircraft highly visible at night; this was supposed to yield an increase of 8–10 mph, but this was not confirmed, and lighter exhaust shrouds were under development with reduced drag.

Handley Page had claimed that fairing the nose turret, while leaving it in place, would give 4–5 mph, but Harris pointed out that the removal of the whole front turret had gained 3–4 mph. An alteration to the radiator shutter had gained 3–4 mph, in line with the manufacturer's promise. An improved matt paint had yielded 3–4 mph rather than the 5–10 mph promised. Harris reported that, as the improvements had not yielded the gains promised, squadrons were now removing the dorsal turret, 'leaving the aircraft unarmed except for the tail turret'. 'This', Harris conceded, 'vastly improves the flying qualities of the aircraft and the ceiling.'

The greatest improvement lay in lowering the engine nacelles, which Handley Page thought would increase the speed by 10–12 mph. Harris commented that:

> …From all the information I have there appears to be a reluctance if not deliberate obstruction on the part of the firm to getting on with dropping the engines. As the alternative appears to me to be the one factor which promises adequate improvement, both in performance and reliability, every possible effort should be made to do this at the earliest possible moment. In fact I consider that as nothing but good can come out of dropping the engines, instructions should have been given four months ago, at least, to the firm to tool up their production without waiting for trials.
>
> You know the bad situation regarding the heavy bombers, and in my opinion it is time Handley Page should be told to produce what is required and not what they want to produce merely to keep up the production figures.
>
> Will you press for the immediate production of the dropped engine nacelles in the Halifax?

Sinclair replied on 18 February 1943:

> …The Air Staff have been working hard on this problem child …We shall push it forward as hard as we can and we shall not be intimidated – nor I am sure will Cripps [Sir Stafford Cripps, Minister of Aircraft Production] or Freeman – by Handley Page.

So a version of the Halifax was to be produced with no nose or dorsal turret. This would render the aircraft totally unsuitable for any daylight operations, if it was not already. Yet calls were still being made to increase the firepower of the heavy bombers and to move away from the rifle calibre turrets, and even, if that were not possible, to increase the number of .303" guns in the dorsal turrets. Indeed, Sorley and Harris had discussed an increase in firepower in the dorsal turrets in Stirling, Lancaster and Halifax aircraft by installing four .303" guns instead of the two with which they were armed. Sorley thought this was 'the only step we can take to improve the armament in these types, because of the very critical position of the centre of gravity in all of them, and also because we cannot afford to be continuously reducing the bombload and range for still heavier armament'.[42]

Harris had replied on 5 May, saying that he thought the four-gun dorsal turret should be proceeded with. He added:

> There can be little doubt that we ought to be able to achieve this with no reduction in speed by better streamlining of the new turret. Nothing, for instance, could be worse than the 2 gun turret at present installed in the Halifax for which, by the way, I hope that a new cupola is being developed.

On 31 August 1942 Sorley reported to Harris that:

> ...the trial installation of the [4 x .303"] turret in the Halifax has been completed and flight and firing trials are now in progress at the Aircraft and Armament Experimental Establishment. Introduction into the Halifax production line is planned for the 501st aircraft, which should be delivered in April 1943...

Sorley also added that the weight of the 20 mm dorsal turret for the Lancaster 'ruled it out at present', although he promised that development was 'being continued'.

Thus, not only was there nothing but infantry calibre weapons for the defence of the heavy bomber six years after they had been specified, but the Stirling had been found to be altogether lacking in the qualities required, and the Halifax had even had its small arms halved, rendering it absolutely unfit for day bombing without fighter escort, and thereby considerably reducing the flexibility of the bomber force. Harris argued that its exhaust shroud failure rendered it unfit for night bombing as well.

On 21 February 1943, Harris wrote to Sorley, taking issue with a previous statement of Sorley's, in which he had hoped to restore the Halifax 'to its original satisfactory state'.

'...It is not possible to agree with that statement,' wrote Harris, 'The Halifax never had an original satisfactory state.' He noted that its performance was too low, it had 'vicious habits', had very unsatisfactory exhaust flame damping, and attempts to make it carry the defensive armament required rendered it practically useless for operations.

On 16 March 1943 Sorley wrote to Harris that the new Halifax II Series 1A had gained 28 mph as a result of all the improvements. Harris replied on the 18th, writing that:

...I am not in any way impressed by your letter, dated 16th March 1943.

You may have increased the top speed of the Halifax by 30 mph. This might have been satisfactory in December 1942, when you held your conference, but today it still leaves the Halifax far behind the Lancaster in every way.

...Furthermore the improvement has been achieved by the sacrifice of the front turret, jettison pipes and many minor items, all of which the Lancaster has, and is still some 15 mph faster at *cruising speed*, which is the speed which matters.

Harris also noted that the Lancaster had a higher ceiling, and was also more economical on fuel. 'There really isn't any comparison between them', he wrote, 'the Lancaster is an aeroplane and the Halifax a failure.'

Harris referred also to the Halifax's rudder problems and its 'vicious characteristics', and pointed out that excessive engine vibration caused 'an enormous number of engine and radiator failures'. He went on:

Why we go on producing such an aircraft, I cannot understand. If my suggestion made last August, that all production of the Halifax should be stopped and turned over to Lancasters, had been followed...we should by now be much nearer to having good Lancasters in place of the bad Halifax.

Sorley's reply of 24 March pointed out that, during February 1943, the Halifax had dropped 108 tons for each aircraft lost, compared to 129 tons for the Lancaster; but the Halifax tonnage per loss rate from October to December 1942 had been only 30 tons, so the February rate was a very considerable improvement.[43]

However, in September 1943 Saundby, now Harris' deputy, would write to the Commander in Chief with figures which showed that the February loss rate had been something unusually favourable to the Halifax; in the six months March to August 1943 inclusive, the Lancaster had delivered an average of 103 tons per loss, the Halifax 42 tons and the Stirling 36 tons.[44] (Harris, in a note to the Under Secretary of State at the Air Ministry of 30 October 1943 had stated that the Lancaster delivered *five times* the weight of bombs per aircraft lost as the Stirling, adding that 'these results have been obtained over a period during which the Stirling was spared as much as possible the more difficult and dangerous targets'. This was a considerable difference to Saundby's figures, but Harris had not specified the period concerned.)[45]

Harris noted, in a letter to Sinclair of 13 May, that although the Halifax's nose was better, it was still without armament, and the engine nacelle modification had not been up to the fullest expectations – although it was hoped that modifications to the fin and rudder would prove satisfactory. He went on:

> We are losing, even on this side and therefore still more so on the other, large numbers of Halifax crews through accidents of the type which killed the investigating test pilots at Boscombe Down. Furthermore, we are also losing large numbers of Halifaxes because, even yet, only a part of the Halifax force is supplied with flame dampers.

On 9 September 1943 Freeman wrote to Portal, saying that 'Ludlow-Hewitt informed me that the operational casualties sustained by Stirlings were so great that he did not think that the aircraft could continue in operations over the western front after the end of the year'. Adding that the Halifax presented a similar problem, Freeman stated that he 'did not think that more can be done unless we replace the Halifax by the Lancaster'. He went on, 'This possibility was considered by the Defence Committee last winter, but was turned down owing to the great loss in bombers that must result…'

In September 1943 Portal wrote to Harris, saying that Sir Wilfrid Freeman expected that a modification to the Halifax, to round the wing tips, would increase the ceiling by 500–1,000 feet, noting that Handley Page expected 1,000 feet from the modification. This discrepancy could surely not have been expected to surprise Harris, who continued to criticise the Halifax, referring to it as 'almost as useless as the Stirling' and, understandably, continuing to call for its replacement by the Lancaster. Portal did not mention Freeman's reservations about the Halifax.

On 21 December 1943 the deficiencies of the Halifax and future policy on the machine were thrashed out at meeting at the highest level, including Portal, Freeman, Harris, Air Marshal Norman Bottomley (Deputy Chief of the Air Staff), Sorley, Air Vice Marshal Breakey (now ACAS(T)) and others.[46]

What was wrong with the Halifax? From the minutes, Harris, in unusually measured tones – perhaps modified more by the prudence of the author of the minutes than the presence of so many senior members of the RAF – gave the prime reason for the losses as the Halifax's low ceiling, as it operated at around 18,000 feet, and 'this was a most lethal height for flak'. The Halifax III might operate at about 19,500 feet, which was 'not nearly good enough'. Harris considered that a 'serious but necessarily unknown' proportion of Halifax losses in the past were due to the inherent vices of the aircraft. The modified tail of the Halifax would, he hoped, remedy losses from this cause, although it was still too early to say – but there remained an inadequate operational performance. It could never be made to carry the bombload of the Lancaster, and could not get a reasonable bombload above 20,000 feet, the 'critical height' for bomber operations over Germany. It could also not be used on as many occasions as the Lancaster 'owing to its inability to get high enough above the clouds'.

On the question of the performance of the latest version of the Halifax, the Halifax III, Harris told the meeting that it was too early to say if it would show 'a very great improvement' in its ceiling, but the modified flame dampers now seemed to be 'perfectly satisfactory'. But another serious shortcoming, which seemed to be even worse in the Halifax III, was its short range. This not only meant that the Halifax could not take the most evasive routes (see Chapter 7), but that the Lancaster crews were also sometimes confined to these routes in order to 'keep them company', causing additional casualties to the Lancaster.

Portal enquired whether the higher turnover of Halifax crews, due to heavier losses, had caused further losses by creating a 'lower standard of experience' among Halifax crews, and Harris agreed that this was the case.

Air Marshal Sorley, now Controller of Research and Development, reported that a further mark of the Halifax, the Halifax VI, would come out in May 1944, and that this version was expected to be a good deal faster and to carry a heavier load. However, all agreed that, whatever improvements could be made to the Halifax, it would never be so good a bomber as the Lancaster.

Portal now reported the Halifax losses, stating that there were now 1.5 Halifaxes lost to every Lancaster, that the Lancasters had dropped 1.75 times as much as the Halifax per aircraft attacking, and had lost only one third of the personnel per 100 tons of bombs dropped. It was therefore desirable that as much Halifax production as possible should be switched to the Lancaster. However, in the short term this would mean a loss of production equivalent to some five to six months for each factory changing over, and even though the Halifax was used against nearer targets it was still doing some good. Next year, 1944, he thought would be the critical year, for a numerical loss of aircraft would certainly mean fewer bombs on Germany in 1944. Much depended, therefore, on just when the war was going to end. If it would last into 1945, a changeover might be advantageous. In this respect it was noted that obsolescent types were still being produced, and perhaps Lancasters could be produced in these factories; it was left to MAP to see what could be done.

Three months later, on 28 March 1944, Harris returned to the charge, writing to Sinclair[47] that experience of the Halifax III had now been gained. He revealed that it had sustained a 30% higher loss rate than the Lancaster, which when combined with the smaller bombload meant that the relative usefulness of the two aircraft was 1:2.6 in favour of the Lancaster. Harris reiterated that these figures were in spite of the Halifax being favoured in operations – for instance, the Lancasters flew as both vanguards and rearguards, and were sent on the most dangerous routes. Harris added that, in addition to this, the dropping of strips of aluminium foil – code-named 'Window' – from aircraft, in order to confuse the German radar defences (which will be described later), was far more effectively done by Lancasters, which could fly at a greater height. Lancasters were thus able to protect the Halifax, without the Halifax being able to return the favour.

However, the expected date of the war's end, as we shall see, was miscalculated. In July 1944 it was expected that Germany would be finished by December 1944, and so the Halifax continued in production. After the great German offensive of December 1944 in the Ardennes, the 'Battle of the Bulge', estimates were revised to perhaps October 1945. The end, when it came in May 1945, was again unexpectedly early.

Yet, paradoxically, the Halifax, although a more dangerous aeroplane to fly in than the Lancaster, was found at the war's end to have possessed one compensating advantage for the aircrew, without which the Appendix to this book might not have been written. It was easier to escape from, once it was decided to evacuate the aircraft, some 25% of Halifax crews surviving compared with 15% in the Lancaster.

Harris could certainly not be criticised for having little interest in escape arrangements. After he had been in command just two weeks he had written to Sorley, saying that he had 'for years' been advocating the provision of adequate escape arrangements.

On 15 October 1942 Harris had written to Group Captain Bennett of the Pathfinder Force that the mid under escape hatch in the Lancaster was either filled with the FN64 under turret or covered over with a platform on which the flare chute was mounted. No. 5 Group, said Harris, were investigating whether the flare chute could either be moved inside the aircraft in emergencies, or jettisoned, to provide an escape hatch – but on Harris' copy of the letter is written the comment 'H2S may have to go there' – H2S being the downward-looking radar which will be encountered in a later chapter. 'Have to' of course meant without a serious stoppage or slowing of production by either making another place for the H2S equipment or another escape hatch.

On 14 October 1944 Harris wrote to the Under Secretary of State at the Air Ministry about the new types of heavy bombers which were being designed, saying:

> ...I see no indication whatever in projected types of heavy bombers that any serious attention is being paid to representations which have been made in the past that more adequate provision should be made for this vital requirement.
>
> It cannot be too strongly emphasised that when an aircraft is out of control crews will normally only get out of escape hatches provided firstly that the hatches are adequate in size and number, and secondly that the effect of centrifugal forces coupled with such aids as can be obtained from properly located hand-grips inside the aircraft, tend to facilitate rather than prevent the exit.
>
> It should now be clear to all concerned that only a small percentage of aircrew survive from a bomber aircraft which is brought down. That the percentage is so small is beyond a doubt due to a lack of adequate escape facilities.

Harris went on to mention two examples of a single crew member escaping – in each case, from a Lancaster – the first reporting that it was apparent that centrifugal forces prevented his comrades from escaping, the second an escape from the Bomber Command-inspired Rose-Rice turret.

Harris asked that the matter 'now be treated with all the urgency it deserves', calling for a special sub-committee to be set up in the Air Ministry.

On 14 February 1945 Harris was still minuting ACAS(T) pointing out that the new turrets were difficult to escape from. However Sinclair, the Secretary of State for Air, assured Harris on 23 February that a new back type parachute being introduced, which could be worn all the time, would 'considerably improve the gunner's chance of escape'.

But on 26 February Harris again returned to the charge, telling Sinclair that he had not even had an acknowledgement of his letter to the Air Ministry of 14 October 1944.

Sinclair's reply of 4 April was sympathetic, but in a way, damning. He pointed out that:

> ...although your Command were represented at all Mock Up Conferences during the design and development stage, no criticisms were made of the escape facilities of the turrets now coming off production. It was clear, however from the C.A.S.'s meeting that your personal views on the matter were not sufficiently stressed at the conferences...

Once again there had been a failure of communication in Bomber Command itself, and a surprising one in view of the energetic, forthright and dominating leadership style of Harris. Perhaps Harris too easily presumed that his views were so obviously correct that all of his Command would hold them. Perhaps his burden of responsibility was too great to allow him to check turret designs at every stage, or to meet with his officers at regular intervals to reinforce his views upon them. Perhaps his officers were too familiar with their counterparts in the turret firms and MAP, and looked at the problems of the manufacturers too sympathetically. Harris certainly knew the weakness of the armament design side, so it is curious that he so signally failed to impress his very strong views on his subordinates, although he obviously could not be expected to do their job for them.

Harris' reply to Sinclair on 6 April was not entirely convincing.

...As I have repeatedly remarked, and as I remarked after the last turret inspection [at Frazer Nash] it was quite obvious to me from the whole attitude of the manufacturers and others at the meeting, that there was not the slightest regard to our requirements for view and escape.

We were met at every turn firstly by the non possumus attitude, which is so familiar to us, that nothing at all could be done 'without interfering with production', and secondly by an atmosphere of nods and winks and asides which made it quite clear to us (as agreed amongst ourselves after the meeting) that those concerned with production had not the slightest intention of discommoding themselves by paying other than lip service to the requirements which we stated.

In any case the provision of adequate view and adequate escape facilities in a gun turret is a requirement so elementary and obvious that the Command cannot accept the passing of that baby to us, even if we had failed to stress these elementary requirements at any time. It should be well known as the very first requirement of turret design by anybody and everybody who has anything to do with the design and production of turrets. These requirements are in fact so elementary that there should be no more need to have to stress them to those concerned, than there is to remind them to put guns in the turrets...

However, Sinclair received a note from his Parliamentary Private Secretary on 21 April 1945,[48] saying that:

My main concern on the CinC's letter [of 6 April] is that I am still of the opinion that his past troubles have largely arisen because his own personal views have not always been adequately represented by his own staff at the meetings which they have attended.

Enclosed with the letter was a brief outline of the meetings between Bomber Command and the turret manufacturers concerning the latest tail turrets, the FN82 and the BP type 'D', both of which carried two .5" guns. These showed that the Command representatives, although criticising clear vision on the FN82, had seemingly made no mention of escape facilities, and indeed, on 9 March 1943 had 'expressed appreciation of the manner in which the firm had so successfully incorporated the changes in design suggested at the previous conferences'. On 17 March the 'Commander in Chief Bomber Command inspected the turret at his Headquarters and accepted it as an interim measure in order to equip the heavy bomber force with .5 turrets with the minimum delay'.

On the BP type 'D' turret, it was noted in the report that on 25 March 1943 'the Command representatives' made severe criticisms of the vision for this turret at the Mock Up conference. It was decided to send the BP 'D' and the FN82 to MAP for a 'side by side' comparison. In April 1943 a redesigned BP 'D' turret was accepted, subject to certain modifications, such as the sight support members, and the guns, being placed further apart, and the runners for the cupola doors being set higher. The chairman, Group Captain Spreckley, 'expressed his appreciation of the firm's efforts to provide a solution to the difficult problem, and said that the results reflected great credit on the designers. These remarks were endorsed by all present'.

There had been no mention of escape arrangements. However, adequate view had been mentioned repeatedly. The appreciations expressed for the turret firms perhaps said more for the good manners of the Command's representatives, and their positive attitude to the working relationship between themselves and the turret firms, than for the merits of the designs themselves. The note carried an implied suggestion that, as Harris himself had given interim approval to the FN82 turret, that he had felt the same appreciation for the firms' efforts at the time, and had now belatedly changed his tune. The bomber offensive was the main effort of the British Empire in the European War, and the gun turrets were a main determinant of the loss rate, and therefore, of the viability of the whole offensive itself. Had Harris simply bungled the communications within Bomber Command, and allowed the turret situation to drift until too late?

This was emphatically *not* the case; indeed, the whole potted history contained in the note seems to have owed more to political exculpation than any attempt to uncover an awkward truth.

Harris had written to ACAS(T) on 24 January 1943, some twenty-seven months before the note to Sinclair, clearly setting out the requirements for turret design as follows:

I have the honour to refer to the basic design of existing turret types, with particular reference to the position at present occupied by the gunner, which precludes effective search by reason of the conglomeration of guns, feed mechanisms, sight arch and turret support structure impeding his view, especially downward which is the most important sector...

The practice of placing the gunner's seat at the rear of the turret appears to have been accepted as standard in all existing types, a position which has been more and more obstructed with the introduction of added guns, servo feed mechanisms, and the armour plate considered necessary for the protection of the vulnerable equipment.

Harris additionally criticised the low status of armament at the Air Ministry and Bomber Command, although, as he pointed out, armament 'was the *raison d'être* of the Command'.

On 3 February 1943, twenty-six months before, Harris had written as follows to his Group Commanders.[49]

...the bad view from the FN20 rear turret [four .303" guns] coupled with the known fact that the majority of fighter attacks at night develop from underneath, presents a serious problem to which urgent solution is required.

I am taking up with the greatest urgency with the Air Ministry the redesigning of the FN20 turret to give an adequate view and suggesting an interim return to the FN4 turret which gave a reasonable view.

Meanwhile, however, No. 4 Group have provided an extra downward look out position by fitting what used to be the navigator's blister from the side of the control cabin in the Halifax into the floor. Using a look-out in this position they have seen and avoided a number of attacks which might otherwise have been successful.

I consider that the provision of such a downward look-out in all night bombers while the bad view from the rear turret persists, is a matter of the first importance and I wish all Group Commanders to give this their personal attention...

The next day Harris wrote to ACAS(T)[50] that:

The FN20 turret is a typical example of the introduction of new equipment of doubtful operational need at the expense of the sine qua non of tactical feasibility – vision.

Harris referred to technical and maintenance problems experienced with the FN20, and added:

But my main concern regarding the turret is the inability to see out of it by reason of the obstructions imposed, largely without reason, by a type of construction which can best be described as 80% angle iron and 20% scratched Perspex.

Harris went on to mention the attacks from astern and below which the Command was experiencing, adding that:

By reason of the conglomeration of gun cradles, servo mechanisms and armour plate it is impossible for the air gunner in the FN20 turret to maintain a satisfactory look out even when standing up... which is very tiring.

Asking for the return of the previous turret, the FN4, as an interim measure, Harris went on to ask for turrets mounting heavier calibre guns to be designed with a major regard to vision *'and not, as I understand is being considered for the FN82 turret by a re-hash of the grossly unsatisfactory FN20 type'*.

In the FN20 turret, Harris went on, *'Nothing has been left undone to destroy every advantage of vision accruing from the tail position'*. [Italics added.] In a letter three days later, Harris confirmed that his comments applied to *all* the turret manufacturers, and asked that a Directorate of Armament be instituted.

However, the report on the Lancaster I by the Air Fighting Development Unit at Duxford, dated 30 May 1942, clearly stated in a section on the tail turret that:

The FN20 turret in the tail is satisfactory and accurate...*The vision is naturally somewhat restricted by the armour and gun mountings, but it is impossible to have armour and perfect vision, and a reasonable compromise has been effected.*[51] [Italics added.]

It can be clearly seen, therefore, that although Harris had been dissatisfied with the plans for the FN82 turret, had stated that clear vision was 'a sine qua non', and had communicated these views very forcibly to the *Air Ministry*, there is no evidence that the AFDU report, which indicated clearly that the principle of vision was constrained by the principle of the armour defence for the gunner, was challenged at the time, and certainly that clear vision had been a sine qua non at the specification stage. Different Commanders in Chief had different policies, while the personnel in the Armament Department did not change at the same time. Harris had clearly not impressed the primacy of vision throughout his Command, although in fairness at that time he had only just taken up the reins – and the heavy bombers were not designed specifically for the *night* offensive.

On 4 February 1943 Harris wrote to Portal:[52]

> I must once again implore you to press for the establishment of an air officer as Director of Armament Requirements in the Air Ministry, supported by a staff of practical – if possible ex-operational – gunners and bomb aimers.

Harris suggested in this letter that:

> …It is symptomatic of the causes of all our armament troubles that after months of argument all the heads of my services, including even the accounting officer, have been upgraded to Air Commodore. Excepting only the Armament Branch. And this is <u>Bomber</u> Command! Bombs and guns! There is an Air Commodore in charge of Welfare in the Air Ministry while a Group Captain is in charge of Armament. As 'Boom' [Trenchard] remarked on hearing of the Welfare Air Officer appointment –'My Aunt did that in the last war!'
>
> You are well aware of the continuous streams of tactically and technically impracticable stuff that has been turned out in the way of bombsights, bombs and turrets. We are now up against a most serious difficulty with the FN20 turret. The whole idea of the tail turret was to give the gunner the maximum unimpeded view in the difficult problem of seeing fighters approaching from astern and underneath against a dark background. A study of the FN20 turret reveals that nothing which could possibly have been done to spoil the gunner's vision – short of building the whole turret solid with no outlook at all – has been left undone…

Harris mentioned to Portal that it would have been useful to remove the dorsal turret of the Stirling to improve the performance of that aircraft, as had been done with the Halifax pending new marks of the aircraft, but he had been:

> …up against adamant opposition from the Stirling crews who say that their tail turrets [FN20] are useless because the gunners cannot see out of them and that if the dorsal turret goes they are defenceless…

After referring to the 'interminable stream of mistakes which have signalised almost the whole of our production of bombs, guns, sights and turrets since the dim ages' Harris went on to say:

> Meanwhile, I hope (and I have written officially to that end) that in new 20 mm and 5 mm [sic] turrets the question of vision will be given absolute priority and not left – not so much as an 'also ran' but as a non starter…
>
> I have just had to order the Group Commanders to cut holes in the bottom of their aircraft, put in Perspex blisters and utilise an existing crew member, or an additional one, solely as look out in support of the blind rear gunner. This has already had gratifying results with the Halifaxes in avoiding action, but it still does not solve the problem of allowing the tail gunner in the FN20 turret to see, shoot at, or hit, anything…

On 19 February 1943 Portal replied to Harris' letter of 4 February, saying that when the turret was first considered the then Air Officer Commanding Bomber Command 'held the view that it was armour protection which must take first place', with view listed as 'best possible'.

Portal felt that 'the emphasis which each Commander in Chief puts upon various requirements changes with individuals and with the length of our practical experience'. Armour protection, low aerodynamic drag and weight, good view, comfort for the gunner, maximum field of fire – all were important. Portal added that the Director of Operational Requirements (DOR) had to balance turrets and the aircraft as a whole to get the best possible compromise. A high ranking armament officer would be in conflict with the DOR.

Although Portal refused to agree that the armament record had been 'an interminable stream of mistakes', he suggested that even with a Director of Armament there would be no reason to suppose that the personnel involved would change.

> If it is a question of the body of officers being up to date operationally, it is necessary that you release from the Command periodically suitable officers who can be fed into those positions, and I believe there has been some difficulty in obtaining them…

Portal ended with the suggestion that it was necessary that 'we should receive clear statements by your representatives when they attend mock ups of equipment with a full recognition that they cannot obtain everything in the same degree of perfection', and to 'never lose sight of the effect which a particular requirement would have on the performance of the aircraft as a whole'.

We have seen that Sir Edgar Ludlow-Hewitt had stressed the need for armour protection for the rear gunner. Peirse we have also seen writing to the Under Secretary of State at the Air Ministry in October 1940, stressing the need for a clear view panel in the rear turret. Indeed, Portal himself, who had just succeeded Ludlow-Hewitt as Commander in Chief at Bomber Command, spoke (with Harris' approbation) to the twenty-first meeting of the Air Fighting Committee on 5 April 1940 [see page 85 above] of the need for the rear gunner to be able to look 'straight out into the void', and that meeting had been attended by Operational Requirements, by the Director of Armament Development and by ACAS(T), at that time Sholto Douglas.

On 17 March 1943 Harris inspected the FN82 (two .5" guns) accepting it, as would be faithfully noted by Sinclair's PPS, as an interim measure. But Harris' letter to ACAS(T) was merely an acceptance under protest. He began by writing that:

> I have examined the mock up today and find that it in no way meets the requirements for the design of turrets contained in my letter …dated 24th January 1943.
>
> As a purely interim measure, in order to equip heavy bombers with .5 guns with the minimum delay, I am prepared to accept the FN82 turret, pending the urgent development of a design which will fully meet requirements.

Harris wrote again to Portal on 9 April 1943,[53] expressing 'the strongest suspicion that the present efforts to produce turrets [that] can be seen out of by night, and .5 and heavier armament, in combination with the required view, are by no means adequate to the seriousness of the situation', calling for the 'most extraordinary and exceptional steps' to put the matter right.

On the same day Harris wrote again to ACAS(T)[54] asking to be informed what action had been taken with regard to his letter of 6 February regarding the requirement for an unobstructed field of vision for the rear gunner.

> The delay in the receipt of any assurance that this vital operational principle is accepted, and evidence that the new turrets mounting .5 guns suffer from the same fatal defects as the 'old' types is most disturbing.
>
> I have repeatedly drawn attention to the shortcomings of our present turret types, the foremost of which is their blindness in all directions, and especially, downwards. I should welcome, therefore, confirmation that the question of improving the view of future designs is being given the urgent priority which is vital…

On 14 June Harris despairingly wrote to Freeman, the Chief Executive at the MAP, saying that:

> …There is a matter on which I would certainly ask your assistance. Our losses are mainly caused by the inability of gunners to see out of their turrets. In this respect, the turrets simply could not be worse. Rear turrets in particular might just as well not be there. I have harped on this theme until I am blue in the face at the Air Ministry, but there is complete inertia, lethargy, and a lack of drive over improving matters. This is directly due to the fact that there has never been an Air Officer in charge of Armament at the Air Ministry with the broadsides to put things over. Consequently, the whole armament side has become a depressed industry from which the few good fellows have done their utmost to escape, and most have.

After writing further on this theme, he went on to add the following damning comment:

> I saw Henderson (Parnall and Frazer Nash's turret designer) and he was astounded at the vehemence of my talk on the lack of visibility from the turrets. He said that apart from an occasional request for a bit of extra view here and there, or a clear vision panel, the point had never been seriously impressed upon him, or, as far as he knew, on any of the other designers. He said that the new .5 turrets would be almost as bad, but that if a real drive was made to put the first priority as view with everything else an also ran, which is as it should be, he saw no difficulty in meeting our requirements in due course.
>
> Will you really start a riot on this particular subject, because, try as I may, I can get no signs of life out of the Air Ministry, and in the present organisation of the armament side I cannot even find anyone to shoot at. It is of the most vital import, and until we can get turrets out of which a rear gunner can see properly, our losses are going to mount and may eventually be prohibitive.
>
> The two .5 tail turret which Rose's of Gainsborough are making in conjunction with Rice of No. 1 Group looks promising and I think should be firing within a week.
>
> In that turret everything has been sacrificed for view, and I believe the things which have been sacrificed will not themselves seriously affect our purposes.
>
> Please do all you can to help me over this, because the whole success of the bomber plan depends on the most urgent and exceptional pressure being put behind it…

On the next day Harris wrote to the Vice Chief of the Air Staff[55] reiterating the views expressed to Freeman, and asking for a conference on bomber defence. This took place on 24 June 1943. As a result of the conference, the two inner guns of the FN120 rear turret were removed and the ammunition limited to 500 rounds, in order to clear the view of obstructions. The next day Group Captain Crawford of Bomber Command wrote to Director of Bomber Operations at the Air Ministry, loaning him a copy of 91 Group Operational Training Unit's *Monthly Summary of Operations and Training*, drawing attention to the fact that, in exercises, 'although the crews are constantly reminded to search continually and to report all "enemy" aircraft, the interceptions are only a small fraction of the kills claimed by the fighters'.

Group Captain Crawford reported that he had interrogated captured German pilots of AI equipped Junkers 88 German night fighters,

> …and they constantly stressed that they could normally approach our aircraft well within gun range and even up to 50 yards without apparently being seen at all, as our aircraft took no evasive action and did not open fire. For some time they suspected a trap and expected our gunner to open fire at very close range…but this was not done and the night fighters therefore approached without any feeling of uneasiness.
>
> I took the pilot and the AI operator round to the stern of a Halifax, and the pilot said it was now obvious to him why we were losing so many aircraft, and why German fighters could not be seen at night.

After reporting that the German pilot had very helpfully suggested a means by which the underview could be improved (!), Group Captain Crawford ended by writing that 'on every occasion where our gunners did open fire before the Germans were in a position to open fire themselves, they found it wise to break off the attack. They have a good respect for our four gun battery of .303'.

On 6 July 1943 the Commander in Chief of Fighter Command, Air Marshal Sir Trafford Leigh-Mallory, wrote to Harris with the comment that the crews of night fighters intruding over German airfields '…have been appalled at the large number of aircraft they have seen shot down in flames', and suggested towing an explosive glider behind the bombers. This, of course, had already been thoroughly tried in the form of the Short Aerial Mine, and found wanting. In thanking him for this idea, Harris pointed out that the problem was not one of destroying the fighter, 'but of detecting the night fighter which approaches unseen even on bright moonlit nights…'

The overriding need for vision at night was leading to a very different set of requirements for day and night bombers. At night it was recognised by the leaders of Bomber Command that the greatest survival factor was vision, whereas by day, it was, if fighter escort were denied, firepower and accuracy. The Augsburg raid had shown that even the best heavy bombers were virtually defenceless against fighters by day, the fighters having stayed out of range of the .303" armament and used their cannon to devastating effect. As a result of this disaster, the Controller of Research and Development had placed an order with Nash & Thompson for a 20 mm mid upper turret, the FN79.[56] It was thought that these turrets could be used in conjunction with the heavily armoured Lancasters of No. 207 Squadron, either as a special daylight attack group or as a revival of the 'escort bomber' idea. However, Harris asked that they be installed in the Lancasters of No. 103 Squadron.

The Controller of Armament Operations thought that the two 20 mm cannon would give, with the standard reflector sight, a very low probability of hits. Whether this probability was lower than the probability of hits from the twin .303" turret which it would replace was not stated. More than five years after Dr Cunningham's paper which suggested that the lower probability of hits with the 20 mm cannon was more than compensated by the increase in the effective area of the target from its explosive bullets, and despite a further mathematical analysis of May 1940 which showed that, in a fighter, two 20 mm guns were the best of four options, and *eight* .303" guns the worst, the opposite was still maintained.

The very much greater accuracy which was promised by the gyro gunsight had made development of this sight a matter of great urgency. However, when the Mark 1C gyro gunsight was developed, it was found to be too bright for use at night. The shortened 20 mm cannon was also found to have a gun flash so great as to be absolutely blinding at night. It might be thought that the simple answer was to use the specially armed and armoured Lancasters by day, as had been intended; but Harris thought it uneconomic to keep bombers as specialist day forces only, and the FN79 turret was not easily interchangeable with the standard FN50 dorsal turret. Harris ruled, therefore, that the FN79 was of no use to Bomber Command. Harris had a reluctance to return to daylight raids, even late in the war, as we shall see, as he thought that the German day fighters would be concentrated against his Lancasters. Only Ludlow-Hewitt's speed bomber, 'Freeman's Folly', the Mosquito, which Harris had derided, could be used over Germany by day.

The increasing evidence of German attacks on bombers from below led to a conference on under defence (26 July 1943). The Chairman, CEW

Lockyer of the Bomber Development Unit at Feltwell (BDU) detailed a BDU scheme for under defence using either two .303" guns or one .5". A request that the Conference members should also inspect the FN220 rear turret, which with its improved vision might provide a useful under defence from the rear, was overruled despite the protests of its proposer, Group Captain Crawford, since the BDU scheme was available straight away. The under gun was developed as an urgent requirement from August 1943. The BDU scheme was indeed useful, as was recognised a year later in an intelligence report sent from the Air Ministry to the Deputy Director of Air Tactics on 12 September 1944.[57] But although it was recognised in the paper that the under guns and sighting point were a 'great help' in 'reasonably light search conditions', it recognised that under 'dark conditions with poor visibility' it was 'not adequate and of little value'. With no moon, it was estimated that the fighter could see the bomber from 4–500 yards away, whereas the bomber could not see the fighter beyond 150 yards. With no moon or stars, the fighter could see the bomber at 300 yards, whereas the bomber could not see the fighter beyond 100 yards. But it was realised later, as will be seen in Chapter 7, that visibility was much greater than this in the northern skies, especially in the summer months, when the sun lies under the northern horizon, and gives a perpetual twilight whose brightness increases with height.

With the heavy losses experienced at night, and survival being so heavily dependent upon the ability of the gunners, particularly in the tail turret, to see out into the night unimpeded by Perspex, glass, turret fittings or aircraft structure, it may seem incredible that the Air Ministry should contemplate a *reduction* in the minimum visual requirements for gunners. Harris wrote to the Director General of Medical Services on 24 February 1944 to say that the 'hexagon test', which determined visual acuity, and was set at a standard score of '8', was thought to be 'seriously low' anyway, yet he had been informed that, contrary to the opinion of the RAF consultant in ophthalmology, 'a further lowering of the standard was contemplated'. Harris, pointing out that, in the night, 'he who sees first lives longest', and that the safety of the whole crew would be jeopardised by a lowering of standards, insisted that visual standards be maintained. He demanded that such action should not be contemplated until and unless the entrants to all the services had been 'sifted out' in an effort to retain at least the existing standards. Also included in the proposals for a lower visual standard were bomb aimers.

This proposal may seem to be an almost unbelievable folly in any circumstances, let alone those prevailing in early 1944 – yet aerial gunnery had been almost completely neglected before the war. At a meeting of the

Air Fighting Committee of 7 December 1938 at which the discussion centred upon the 'fighting control' of aircraft, Ludlow-Hewitt had commented that 'one of the main difficulties of Bomber Command was that 'their air gunners were practically completely untrained'. On fighting control, the Commander in Chief had 'stressed the point that at present the Command was forced to rely upon the opinions of the air gunners (who, as he had pointed out, were practically untrained and not of superior mentality) on the future development of the gun armament of bombers'. In support of the Commander in Chief, it was pointed out at the meeting that on arrival at the Air Fighting Development establishment at Northolt, most had done no firing, and knew very little about sighting. The first cine films taken 'almost invariably showed that the gunners had shot the tail off their own aircraft…' It seems strange that the success of the legendary fighter pilots of the past – McCudden, Bishop, Coppens, Guynmeyer, Richthofen – should have been attributed by the RAF to their sudden recognition of the need to become expert shots, yet those gunners who were to oppose the legends of the future should be untrained – and then, when the training was finally satisfactory, that anyone could contemplate amid the horrendous dangers and losses of Bomber Command's night operations, that the standard of visual acuity should be *lowered*.

But if the gunner were possessed of good night vision, and were well trained in aiming his guns, then the Rose-Rice turret, where the gunner sat forward of the guns and looked out through a clear opening large enough to escape through, made full use of the few advantages which the bomber possessed by night. On 19 April 1944 Harris reported to Portal[58] on the trials of this turret, which was more or less a private venture between Rose Brothers of Gainsborough and Bomber Command. The turret, it will be remembered, mounted two .5" guns. Harris was able to inform Portal that the average gunner 'is scoring at least twice as many hits at twice the range with the two gun turret as compared with the old four .303 gun turrets', which Harris attributed to the 'excellence of view' from the turret and the heavier weight and higher muzzle velocity of the .5" bullet, 'which makes for a smaller deflection allowance'. Harris reported to Portal that the earlier violent vibration of the sight had been due to poor workmanship by Lucas, who supplied the mounting ring.

Portal replied to Harris on 21 April, telling him that Boscombe Down were 'enthusiastic over the turret', and 'very keen to be able to clear it'. However, on 27 April he told Harris that it had been found that the improvement in the vibration had been due not only to the correction to the component mentioned by Harris, but also to the .5" guns being de-rated from 750 rounds per minute to 450.[59] He added, perhaps mischievously in view of Harris' cynical comments on the motivation of Sir Oswald Short and Sir Frederick Handley Page and the turret manufacturers among numerous others, 'I tell you this because experts are not always candid about their products'. This surely tongue in cheek suggestion of the wise Sunday School teacher introducing his guileless and gullible pupil to the existence of individuals who were motivated by less than straightforward honesty brought the response from Harris that he was 'quite certain that the de-rating of the guns was not done intentionally or with any desire to mislead', adding that the problem was now solved, and asking for maximum production. But Rose Brothers of Gainsborough had earned Harris' undying gratitude – they had supplied the only British rear turret during the whole of the European war which was armed with machine guns larger than the rifle calibre .303", and from which the gunner could see clearly, and escape relatively easily.

On 22 April 1944 Harris asked the Director of Armament Development (Air Commodore Combe) for full production of the Rose-Rice turret, stating that Rose Brothers could supply fifty per month and insisting that 'immediate production should be undertaken on a far wider basis'. He also asked that Rose Brothers should be requested to investigate the possibility of equipping the turret with AGL(T). This, however, could not be done until after the end of the European war.

On 2 October 1944 Air Commodore Bilney of Bomber Command, in a file note for the attention of Saundby, referred to the iniquity of the manufacturer's 'turret ring', and Saundby agreed, suggesting a draft letter. Harris added on 9 October:

> I agree. We should say that the position is so unsatisfactory that we consider a board of enquiry should be held to determine who is responsible for the grossly dilatory and unsatisfactory procedures which have produced this deplorable state of affairs. Again we are told that 'nothing can be done'. We were told that before – and produced the Rose while Air Ministry achieved nothing.
>
> It is common property that the MAP head of Turret Development is a hopeless dud.

In response to Harris' pressure a very high level meeting on turret developments was held at the Air Ministry on 22 November 1944, under the chairmanship of Portal himself. Everyone in MAP and the Air Ministry concerned with turret development were present, including the MAP Chief Executive, Sir Wilfrid Freeman. At the meeting Harris stressed the usefulness of the Rose turret and its superiority to the .303" turrets so far produced. However, MAP confirmed that the Rose turret could not be put into mass production in under twelve months, because Rose Brothers were not equipped for mass production, each turret being hand made, and it would take *nine months* to produce tools and to complete new drawings. Further, there was a shortage of skilled labour in the turret manufacturers, and any dilution would result in reduced turret output as a whole.

It was noted at the meeting that 100 Rose turrets had been delivered, and a further 500 were on order, with a completion date of September 1945. Harris wanted these 500 completed, since although they would not be equipped with AGL(T) they would provide some insurance against the failure of the radar devices. Portal commented that all .5" turrets were required, and that the development of the Rose turret should be left to Bomber Command, as at present, rather than being handed to Air Commodore Combe, the Director of Armament Development. However, a suggestion by Harris that a controller of turret production should be appointed was overruled by Freeman.

So how good was the Rose turret, over which Harris and Bomber Command enthused so much? It clearly possessed superior visibility to any other turret. A Bomber Command Operational Research paper of 2 March 1945,[60] looking at the performance of the turret to end December 1944, concluded that, for night operations, the improved visibility had meant that the number of attacks by fighters on aircraft with the Rose turret had been 25% less than would be expected. This was a vindication of the design of the turret, and of the importance of clear vision in night operations. However, all was not well with the turret; the loss rate for aircraft carrying the turret was the same as for the others, despite their poorer vision. The reason for this discrepancy, which implied that, if attacked, the Rose turret was *less* able to defend the bomber, was to be found in the unreliability of the Browning .5" guns with which it was armed. Although the figures were taken from an analysis of only thirteen occasions on which the .5" Brownings had been fired, there had been eight stoppages, six of them involving both the guns – and in these latter cases the number of rounds fired had been just twenty-three. In an analysis of four-gun .303" turrets in which stoppages occurred in action, 62% involved one gun, 11% two guns and 27% three guns or more. Of all combats, the .303" Browning turrets were seriously incapacitated in 6%, whereas the .5" Brownings were out of action in 45%. 'It is thus possible', concluded ORS, 'that fighters who were able to make an attack had success above the average in shooting down aircraft with Rose turrets. Such a result might well follow from the apparently lower reliability of the Rose turret armament. Additional attempts to improve the armament are therefore highly desirable'.

Harris had written to ACAS(T) that:

…if it is the intention to perpetuate the use of the .5 Browning gun, serious accidents will occur unless steps are taken to overcome the defects of this weapon. It is well known that the .5 Browning overheats after a comparatively short burst of fire, and that the result is the 'cooking off' of the round in the chamber and the accidental discharge of the weapon. With the introduction of modern sighting technique, which calls for long bursts of fire, this is a serious matter, and one which must be tackled with vigour unless serious accidents are to occur…

Yet the Browning .5" was used in nearly all American fighters and bombers, and was noted for its reliability. This and the 20 mm Hispano cannon will be discussed later, when Harris' comments on the armament design staff of MAP are considered.

The clear advantage of the Rose turret in giving the gunner an unimpeded view into the night raises the question of the value of armament to the night bomber – would it have been better to merely keep a look-out in the rear turret with no armament at all, as has been suggested by Max Hastings.[61] If this were so, then firing a few rounds before the gun jammed would advertise your presence to a fighter who *may* not have seen you.

The controversy over whether to fire first or not had troubled Bomber Command. Saundby had raised the issue in June 1942.[62] The classic bomber manoeuvre on seeing a fighter, or coming under fire, was the 'corkscrew'. This consisted of a steep dive of about 1,000 feet, followed by a climb of about 700 feet. The dive might be to either port or starboard, and the climb might be in the same or the opposite direction, No. 5 Group favouring a dive to port and a climb to port, whereas the usual method was a climb to starboard after a dive to port. The mid upper and rear gunners would need to know in which direction the corkscrew was to be made, so that they could keep their guns on the target. But would it be better to just corkscrew on seeing the fighter, given that he might not have seen you, or should you open fire and corkscrew at the same time?

It had been the policy of Bomber Command not to open fire until attacked, but in June 1943 No. 5 Group decided to instigate a policy of attacking the enemy fighter (and corkscrewing) on sight. Noting that the policy of not opening fire first had been due to the fear of giving the bomber's position away, Air Vice Marshal RA Cochrane, the Group Commander, pointed out in a letter to all No. 5 Group squadrons that enemy radar developments now meant that the fighter was vectored on to the bomber stream, 'where they will either see a suitable target or if they are equipped with AI will get a reading on their instruments'. Noting that the all round view from a fighter was poor at night, Cochrane suggested that the fighter might not be aware that he had approached within range of a bomber. This gave the bomber an opportunity of shooting the fighter down, or at worst scaring them off, since fighters, once fired on, rarely made an attack, but looked for easier targets, a fact which had been confirmed by reports from prisoners of war. But if, on the other hand, the bomber withheld his fire, the fighter would have an increased chance of success by firing first, and would become emboldened to concentrate on the target in front – *and lower casualties among night fighters would mean a steady increase in the skill level of German night fighter crews.*

Cochrane ordered that his letter was to be brought to the notice of all aircrew and was to be the subject of a talk at Conversion Units, where crews were training on heavy bombers.

In August 1943 Bomber Command's Operational Research Section (ORS) produced a paper on tactics to counter enemy night fighter, searchlights and gun defences which noted, in a section considering the possibility of German infrared detection devices, that these were unlikely to be developed 'in view of the accuracy of the German Ground Control Interception (GCI) radar and the relatively great distances at which aircraft are visible in silhouette or by exhaust flame'. There could surely be no greater confession of vulnerability than to confess that the enemy did not *need* infrared detection!

ORS reported that 76% of attacks on bombers were from astern, and increasingly from below, 'which at present are most difficult for our rear gunners to see in time for effective action to be taken'. Attacks were more frequent in moonlight, or in conditions of a strong aurora borealis, for which it was most important to keep a meteorological watch.

Entering into the 'fire first' debate, ORS recommended that:

> ...while the primary purpose of the bomber is to bomb and not to fight, there is no doubt that a spirited engagement considerably embarrasses enemy fighters. Enemy fighters that are in range should be engaged immediately, concurrently with evasion tactics.

ORS recommended that the evasion tactic should be an 'extended corkscrew', which was a straight dive converted into a 60-degree turn for 1,800 feet and climbing at full power in the opposite direction – a manoeuvre which could not be followed by AI radar.

On 2 October 1943 Bomber Command Headquarters circulated a discussion paper to all groups,[63] suggesting that 'the primary rules of night tactics are to avoid combat or break off combat as soon as possible by manoeuvring', but added that 'it is considered important that defensive manoeuvres should be planned with a view to allowing the gunner the best chance of using his guns when an attacker is identified'. It was noted in the paper that:

> …the bomber's gunner is at a great visual disadvantage to the fighter pilot…in fact, so poor are the gunner's chances of seeing an attacking fighter at all that we find that the majority of 'successful' attacks are unseen. Therefore the bomber's chief defence at present is to shorten the time between seeing [a]fighter and the beginning of a defensive manoeuvre.

On 13 October came a comment from No. 8 (Pathfinder) Group, who thought the paper unnecessarily alarming to bomber crews unless it is pointed out that conditions are never 'similar'. Agreeing that the fighter had the advantage of smaller size, and also, if radar controlled, of knowing in which direction to look, they pointed out that new radar devices made it also possible for the bomber to know where to look. Their argument ran:

> Although the bomber was visible at greater ranges than the fighter the respective conditions of search are very different, and it is by no means the same thing as saying that the bomber is ALWAYS SEEN [capitals in original]. Consider the following points:
>
> a) The fighter pilot has to fly his aeroplane, to which task he must devote some of his concentration; the gunners on the bombers have nothing to do but search for fighters.
>
> b) The fighter pilot has night vision snags in the form of luminous instruments in front of his eyes, a thick bullet proof windscreen to look through (which *may* be covered oil from the propellers as ours sometimes are) and possibly sparks or flames from his exhaust; the bomber's gunner looks straight out into thin air without any such obstructions.
>
> c) The visibility from any single engined aircraft is badly restricted by the engine and the wings; there are practically no restrictions to visibility from a turret, apart from the limits of a turret's movement.
>
> d) The fighter pilot has only one pair of eyes; most heavy bombers have 2 lookouts.
>
> It is therefore suggested that official tactical papers, especially those containing information and instructions to be passed to the bomber crews, should assume a less pessimistic tone than has been

the case hitherto, and that tactics should allow for the fact that the Hun makes quite as many blunders as the Englishman, the Hun also has inexperienced pilots and radar operators etc., and should avoid giving the impression that all the advantages are always with the enemy fighter.

However, it was suggested that 'it would be unwise to allow the virtually unrestricted use of guns', adding that 'A Mosquito, for example, looks very similar…to an Me210, and the surest way of antagonising our own fighters is to shoot at them without provocation when they are trying to protect us.'

Unfortunately for the aircrews of Bomber Command, none of the disadvantages listed applied to enemy twin-engined fighters, excepting the thick, bullet proof windscreen.

Eventually the question became the subject of a specific enquiry by Bomber Command Operational Research Section, who produced 'A Note on Offensive Defence against Night Fighters' on 12 November 1943.[64] The report grimly noted that 'Like all analyses of combats it lacks the important details of the combats in which the fighter was successful'. Noting that No. 5 Group had attacked fighters on sight since June 1943, the report showed that the number of 5 Group sorties engaged in combat after June had increased both relative to 5 Group before June, and to No. 1 Group over the whole period March to 31 October 1943. However, it was noted that:

> …the percentage of 5 Group sorties attacked before starting the policy of opening fire was higher than the corresponding figure for No1 Group and some influence additional to that [of] opening fire may affect the comparative records of the two Groups.

The report went on:

> Since the missing rates of 1 and 5 Groups have been the same in spite of the greater proportion of 5 Group aircraft attacked, it seems likely that the lethality of the attacks made has been on the average lower for 5 Group than for 1 Group…

The proportion of attacks causing damage had been less for 5 Group, but because 5 Group were attacked more often suggested to ORS that 'the nett effect has been that 5 Group aircraft have been in greater danger from fighters than 1 Group aircraft'.

It was also noted in the report that most of 5 Group Lancasters were equipped with the backward-looking radar night fighter detection system code-named 'Monica', whereas most of No. 1 Group's Lancasters possessed 'Boozer', a system which emitted no radiation but would let the crew know when the aircraft was being tracked by ground or AI radar.

However, ORS observed that 'if any difference between the effect of these two devices has existed, it has originated in the stimulus given by "Monica" to 5 Group's gunnery against distant targets.'

However, in July 1944 a Junkers 88 night fighter landed in error at Woodbridge in Suffolk, and was found on inspection by British scientists to be equipped with a device which enabled the aircraft to track 'Monica' transmissions from over 100 miles away and to be sufficiently accurate to bring the fighter to within 1,000 feet of the 'Monica' transmissions. Harris stopped the use of 'Monica' by heavy bombers immediately. However, just when the first sets were actually installed into German fighters I have been unable to discover. It must surely have been introduced gradually. It is tempting to reflect that the use of this equipment against 'Monica' might have been a factor in the 'greater danger from fighter attack' noted by ORS for No. 5 Group's Lancasters during the period ending 31 October 1943. The Germans, after all, had been aware of the existence of 'Monica' since March 1943[65] and a device was produced by July 1943[66] and was therefore possibly coming into operation in the same period as that covered by the ORS report.

In February 1944 Cochrane commented on the ORS paper after fully consulting with ORS themselves. First, he made it clear that he had never encouraged opening fire on a 'suspected' night fighter, but an identified fighter which was within range, and this was unique to No. 5 Group. Cochrane felt that the question was one of 'the degree of emphasis to be given to armament in the defence of the heavy bomber in relation to manoeuvre'. He pointed out that while manoeuvre 'requires some seconds to build up, firepower is instantaneous'. If the crew were 'taught the doctrine of evasion', the pilot would 'consider that the defence of the aircraft primarily depends on the manoeuvres which he undertakes', which would therefore be violent and would prevent the gunners from any chance of hitting the fighter. The manoeuvre should give the gunner the opportunity of a known deflection shot, as he knew the direction in which the bomber would be going, whereas the fighter did not, and would be faced with an unknown deflection shot. Cochrane pointed out that No. 5 Group had shot down fifty-eight fighters during the period of the ORS review, and with better training could do better – and further, all this would exert a deterrent effect on the fighter. If all Groups adopted the policy of attacking an identified fighter first, it would be reasonable to expect to shoot down thirty to forty fighters a month, and damage many more, and these could crash on landing.

Bomber Command confirmed to Cochrane that it was policy to fire on every identified fighter; however, identification was very difficult on a dark night, and spending time on this would delay manoeuvre.

The problem of target identification could have been aided by 'Monica', which could have been used in conjunction with more gentle manoeuvres to see if the aircraft behind was actively tracking you, or was just a bomber who happened to be in the vicinity. But 'Monica' was now banned from the bombers.

As has been seen, AGL(T) was afflicted with the same problem of identification, and this was not solved before the European war ended. Unfortunately, this system had offered the best hope of a gun defence for the night bomber. It was estimated[67] that some 30% of shots aimed at the night fighter using AGL(T) were within a 1 degree cone, and would enable the AGL(T) equipped bomber to secure hits on a fighter at from 700 to 400 yards distance. This meant that at 700 yards 0.22 bullets per second would hit the fighter from the four .303" guns, rising to 2.6 per second at 200 yards and 10.5 per second at 100 yards, although at 700 yards there was little chance of .303" bullets penetrating armour. It was estimated that, if the fighter was closing at 30 mph (some 15 yards per second), the bomber could secure some four hits on vulnerable areas of the fighter. But the areas of a fighter which were vulnerable to .303" fire varied considerably, from 8,520 square inches for the Junkers 88 with two Jumo 211 liquid-cooled engines to just 684 square inches for the Focke Wulf 190 single-seat fighter. The Focke Wulf, however, was roughly four times as vulnerable to fire from .5" machine guns, while the Jumo-engined Junkers 88 was about 1.2 times as vulnerable. Given the low chances of the .303" bullets penetrating armour at the longer ranges it was proposed to use a higher proportion of incendiary bullets with .303" guns.

The AGL(T) equipment had another drawback in that it could be tracked by fighters, and therefore give away the position of the bomber stream, other members of which were not so equipped. However, although they could be tracked, in No. 1 Group they suffered a loss rate of 1.3% to end September 1944, compared with 4.1% for the rest; in No. 5 Group they had lost none from eighty-five sorties, compared with 1.8% of other No. 5 Group aircraft. The discrepancy between the losses of unequipped aircraft from No. 1 Group compared with No. 5 Group was not commented on, and these were not, perhaps, strictly like for like. However, it is tempting to suppose that the difference in their respective 'fire first' policies had some influence.

On 14 July 1944 Harris wrote to the Air Ministry asking for the Mark IIc gyro gunsight to be fitted retrospectively to turrets which could accommodate it, but was told that, since it took some 200 man hours for each turret it was impracticable to do this.[68] Gyro gunsights were fitted to all Lancasters coming off the production line from 21 October 1944, but

Harris had not been informed in time, and training was therefore 'behindhand'. In December 1944 FN121 turrets with gyro gunsights became available, and these were fitted retrospectively to No. 3 Group aircraft for daylight operations. By the end of the war 450 aircraft were equipped with the sight.

By the end of the war, therefore, the means of defending the bomber were becoming available, but had been overtaken by other factors – fighter escort, both in daylight and with the 100 Group intruders at night, the defeat of the German Air Force by the Americans, the shortage of fuel for the German fighters caused by the targeting of oil by the heavy bombers and the advance of the Allied armies through France and Belgium, which deprived the Germans of most of their early warning system. Why had the bombers not been better equipped for defence before these other factors came in to save them from the slaughter?

For Harris there was no doubt. In his *Despatch on War Operations* he speaks of 'an unending series of technical difficulties and failures', and adds 'The armament design side, as evidenced by the stores issued to my Command, showed throughout a standard of incompetence which had the most serious repercussions on the efficiency and effectiveness of the bomber offensive'. Included in Harris' comments were the bombs themselves, which we shall see detailed in a subsequent chapter. The designers of turrets incurred the specific comments that 'Throughout, those responsible for turret design and production displayed an extraordinary disregard of the requirements of the Command'.

But the faults ran deeper than a simple failure of the armament design side, although fail they certainly did. Despite the known limitations of .303" armament since 1925, virtually nothing was done to develop a .5" machine gun. The Air Fighting Development Unit at Northolt produced a largely fallacious argument to justify the retention of .303" guns in the rear turret of the bombers, based on the relative motions of the fighter and the bomber.

ORS accepted this argument, which meant that the new heavy bombers were designed around .303" turrets, but later accepted that larger guns would prove to be necessary. Yet even then, in a move intended to bring the armament fully up to date, they by-passed the .5" machine gun in favour of the 20 mm cannon. But it was then thought to be too late to fit these cannon into the new bombers, because of their effect on the centre of gravity of the aircraft. This problem was not, of course, insurmountable, for the extra weight aft could have been balanced by heavier guns forward – but what was wrong with 20 mm cannon in the nose as well? These moves would, of course, have led to the necessity of strengthening the airframe, and thereby, adding yet more weight.

Here was the crux of the matter. A somewhat simplistic argument was maintained by some, that 'it was the purpose of the bomber to carry bombs, not guns'. Any deduction from the bombload was to be deprecated. This thinking was a hangover from the days of the RAF rearmament programmes in the 1930s, when parity with Germany in the number of bombers was found to be impossible to attain, and the new aim became parity in bombload, to be achieved by the use of four-engined heavy bombers. This was acceptable, of course, if the bomber was always going to be able to get through.

But there was a saner, more scientific method of judging the success of a bomber force than a simple count of bombs dropped. It was propounded by Tizard and by Ludlow-Hewitt, that the criterion of success was not numbers of bombs dropped, but the number of bombs dropped *on target per aircraft lost*. This, with the removal of Ludlow-Hewitt, seems to have been lost sight of. When unbearable casualties were sustained in daylight, there was a move to night operations, which greatly eased casualties; yet such was the inaccuracy of this method, that by the criterion of Tizard, perhaps fewer bombs were actually put on target per aircraft casualty. But the move to night bombing only provided a short breathing space, before the fighter found the bomber in the night skies over Germany. When that happened, when the bomber was seen by the fighter, it stood less chance by night than by day. The fundamental problem was still there.

It had been considered by Professor Melville Jones that the only really effective place to put guns in the bomber was the front and rear turrets (and American experience was to show the necessity of heavy frontal armament in daylight). The Professor had believed that the bomber was doomed if it allowed the fighter to close, and thought that, because 20 mm cannon could not be placed in the front and rear for centre of gravity problems, two .5" guns should be planted in the rear at least. However, because it was thought that 20 mm cannon would soon be necessary, and these could not be put into the rear turret, Operational Requirements Section decided that they should be put in upper and lower amidships turrets. Then it was thought that .5" guns could be allowed in the rear turret as well. And then, the design of turrets mounting 20 mm and .5" guns was suspended when the MAP was created amid the crisis of 1940, and Lord Beaverbrook took over at its head.

As to the guns themselves, the .5" machine gun and the 20 mm cannon, it had been decided in July 1936 that 'all possible efforts be made to expedite the trials of larger calibre guns'.[69] Yet the .5" Browning gun in the Rose-Rice turret was not fully effective – indeed, was unreliable – even at the end of 1944, despite the use of .5" guns in some American aircraft supplied to the United Kingdom, and despite the full information on .5" guns given to the Tizard Mission by the American representatives.

The 20 mm cannon was a different proposition to the .5" machine gun, for although it was well known as a fighter weapon, it consisted only of a barrel and breech block fixed rigidly into the fighter and mainly firing through the shaft. It had never been mounted in a turret, or put on any ring or swivel mechanism. It was, of course, very much larger than the .303", and the barrel would be in the slipstream of the aircraft when fired to the quarter from the rear turret, exposing it to heavy forces. It needed a power operated turret.

However, the bomber offensive was, until the invasion of Normandy, Britain's main effort towards the defeat of Germany, and it seems incredible, in view of the huge importance of this offensive and the vast industrial effort involved, that the problem was not solved by the end of the war. Because four .303" machine guns were held to be more effective at long range than two .5"s or 20 mm cannon, there was always an argument against developing heavier weapons without developing better sights. Since the number of hits obviously decreased with range, it was held by some as a doctrine that the greater volume of fire from four .303"s gave them greater range. Yet these arguments ignored the better trajectory following from the greater energy and higher speed of the larger calibre weapons, which meant a smaller deflection for the gunner. They ignored the increases in the vulnerable areas of the target to higher calibre weapons, which even in the .5" could increase the effective target size by up to four times. And even if the .303" guns were to be retained, papers on the development of weapons with a higher rate of fire, and perhaps more promising still, weapons with much higher velocity .303" bullets, with all their advantages of trajectory and hitting power for not much more weight, seem to have lain dormant. In all this, the voice of Bomber Command was neither clear nor united in the critical early period, and the armament development section, incredibly dilatory, given the sheer importance of the task, were given no clear directive from above.

This process can be clearly seen at work on the question of visibility from turrets. Harris himself mentions that a turret designer had been unaware of the priority that Bomber Command needed to be given to the factor of vision from the turrets at night. His own staff seemed to express satisfaction over designs which Harris later execrated for their lack of vision and ease of escape. Turret effectiveness was obviously of vital importance to the bomber, and thereby, to the bomber offensive, and thereby to Britain as a whole. But a Commander in Chief cannot closely and continually supervise squadron leaders in matters of quality control liaison. He could, however, ensure that the very best and most experienced of Bomber Command's men were installed in key liaison positions in the MAP – yet we have seen Peirse's continual refusal to release a man who was thought by MAP to be the best for this position.

What seemed to be missing was a clear policy and clear understanding and clear statement of the requirements by all concerned; but there were too many fingers in the pie, and the Commander in Chief himself was continually receiving instructions from junior officers at the Air Ministry on how to run his Command. This was not only a complaint of the irascible and outspoken Harris, but of the more cerebral and calm Ludlow-Hewitt. The fundamental requirements for the armament which was to defend the bombers was never clearly agreed, and the 'Augean Stable' of the Armament Department – indeed, of armament in the RAF as a whole – which was so severely criticised by Tizard, by Tedder and by Harris, was never properly cleaned out.

The consequences for the defence of the bomber will never be fully known. Would the provision of 20 mm guns, or even of .5" guns, have made a big difference? Certainly, had bomber armament consisted of 20 mm guns, the casualties would have been reduced, and with gyro gunsights earlier on, or with the radar-controlled AGL(T) turrets with proper friend or foe recognition arrangements, casualties would have been considerably reduced, and German fighters would have suffered much more, and would have had to increase their armament and armour protection very considerably. All this extra firepower would certainly have been at the expense of bombload. But as Tizard pointed out, the size of the bomber force was a factor both of the production rate and the loss rate. Some 5,000 bombers were lost between February 1942 and June 1944 alone. Had both this loss and the bombload per aircraft been halved, Bomber Command, which in June 1944 numbered some 1,000 aircraft, would have numbered 2,500, and total bombload would actually have increased. The crews would have had more experience and therefore been more effective. Daylight bombing, which was certainly more accurate over this period, might have been resumed, and this would have increased the impact of Bomber Command on the European war, which was very considerable anyway, much more. Even if these measures had failed to produce significant results, and the night offensive had continued, the simple provision of clear visibility from a satisfactorily heated rear turret would have made full use of the bomber's only compensating advantage compared with the formidable weighting towards the fighter in night combat.

Notes

1 Karl von Clausewitz, *On War*, Penguin Books, London, 1982, 133.

2 PRO Air14/60.

3 PRO Air14/232.

4 See also AHB BD/GRO/12.

5 PRO Avia13/879.

6 See also Vincent Orange, *Slessor*, p90, re the RAF's 'random posting policy'.

7 These hopes were soon dashed, for the Defiant was hopelessly vulnerable to the German Me109 fighter.

8 PRO Air41/39.

9 PRO Air 41/39.

10 Martin Middlebrook and Chris Everitt, *The Bomber Command War Diaries*, Midland Publishing Ltd, Hinckley, 1995, 31.

11 PRO Supp22/33. A 15" naval shell weighs 2,000 lbs, but contains only 60 lbs of high explosive. With so much energy required to burst the case, the equivalent weight of explosive is 25 lbs. The bomb, having a much gentler delivery system, requires no such thickness of case. A British GP (general purpose) bomb, weighing 1,000 lbs, carried a charge of 344 lbs – a MC bomb 475 lbs.

12 Denis Richards, *The Royal Air Force 1939–1945*, Vol 1, The Fight at Odds, HMSO, London, 1974.

13 Martin Middlebrook and Chris Everitt, *The Bomber Command War Diaries*, 42.

14 PRO Air16/504.

15 PRO Cab102/207.

16 PRO Air 9/105.

17 Haig's heavy tanks could reach 4 mph, his light tanks 8 mph.

18 See eg PRO Avia10/212, MAP letters to suppliers.

19 IC B/Tizard/7.

20 PRO Avia 10/26.

21 CA G250/1. The note does not specify to whom it is addressed.

22 RAF H91/1.

23 PRO Air 1/2387/228/11/50, RAF Staff College Notes of War Experiences, 1924.

24 PRO Air14/63.

25 PRO Air14/2175.

26 PRO Air14/607.

27 Adolf Galland, *The First and the Last*, Methuen, London, 1955, 231–2.

28 PRO Air15/742, AFC 130 report 47 dated 30-5-42 produced by Air Fighting Development Unit at Duxford and sent to No. 16 group Coastal Command (Chatham) which did not operate Lancasters. I am uncertain as to who pencilled the comment on 16 Group's copy, and upon whose authority. The comment is cross referenced 5025/44 OPS, which relates to the report on the Halifax of 3-6-41.

29 PRO Avia46/102, Official History, report to Prof. Postan by Squadron Leader Ellison.

30 RAF H16.

31 RAF H78.

32 RAF H16.

33 RAF H66.

34 RAF H81.

35 RAF H16.

36 Harris is sometimes blamed for not caring about the Halifax, eg in Ben Shepherd's *A War of Nerves*, 288.

37 RAF H81.

38 Christopher Chant, *Aviation*, 119.

39 Walter Raleigh, *The Great War in the Air*, Vol 1, 111.

40 PRO Avia7/1991.

41 RAF H79.

42 PRO Air14/607.

43 RAF H17.

44 RAF H82.

45 RAF H67.

46 RAF H83.

47 RAF H79.

48 PRO Air19/165.

49 RAF H49.
50 PRO Air14/607.
51 PRO Air15/742.
52 RAF H82.
53 RAF H82.
54 RAF H67.
55 PRO Air14/607.
56 PRO Air14/607.
57 PRO Air 14/632.
58 RAF H68.
59 Curiously, neither man commented on the strange fact that two guns firing a mere 450 rounds per minute could be superior in hits to four guns firing 1,100 rounds per minute each. Either the test was wrong, or the guns were a lot better than even Harris thought.
60 PRO Air 14/4535.
61 Max Hastings, *On the Offensive – Bomber Command*, Pan Books, London, 1995, 164.
62 PRO Air14/103.
63 PRO Air14/631.
64 PRO Air14/631.
65 Alfred Price, *Instruments of Darkness*, Greenhill Books, London, 2005, 142.
66 Price, 150.
67 Air14/3017.
68 Sir Arthur Harris, *Despatch on War Operations*, Frank Cass, London, 1995, 111.
69 Air 20/3605, AFC, sixth meeting.

CHAPTER SIX

Defence by Fighter Escort

O Wedding-Guest! this soul hath been
Alone on a wide wide sea:
So lonely 'twas, that God himself
Scarce seemed there to be.
Samuel Taylor Coleridge, *The Rime of the Ancient Mariner*

The question of fighter escorts for bombers had fallen into a doctrine-induced slumber until the use of escort fighters by both sides in the Spanish Civil War provoked a further injection of doctrine, and a renewed slumber. On 23 November 1936 Group Captain Peirse, the Deputy Director of Operations, who four years later would head Bomber Command, minuted the Deputy Chief of the Air Staff, Air Marshal Sir Christopher Courtney, through Sholto Douglas, the Director of Staff Duties, noting that fighter aircraft had escorted bombers in that war, 'particularly on Franco's side'.[1] Peirse drew attention to the 'poor leadership' and 'indifferent formation flying' in Franco's air force, but added 'nevertheless, these operations provide the only examples of modern air forces in actual conflict with each other since 1918'.

Peirse stated that 'we must not overlook' the 'possibility of German and Italian influence', and added that 'This possibility becomes a probability when one bears in mind recent reports from Germany of the intention of the German High Command to use fighters either as escorts or as a sort of advanced guard for the bombers'. But Group Captain Peirse hastily absolved himself of any leanings towards heresy by adding:

While, therefore, I still feel that it would be a confession of weakness and a waste of effort on our own part *even to contemplate* the use of fighters in this way, I cannot help feeling that we ought to be prepared for such an eventuality.

I recommend therefore that the question should be raised in either the Bombing or Fighting Committees and that you should instruct DDOR [Deputy Director of Operational Requirements] to produce a specification for a fighter which could be used in much the same way as the distant patrols of 1918 or as a sort of defensive fighter accompanying the bombers...

Sholto Douglas minuted the Deputy Chief of the Air Staff (DCAS) on 30 November, saying that:

> *...my own feeling in the matter is that the bombers should be able to look after themselves without the addition of an escort of fighters,* [italics added] although certain of the bombers might be more heavily armed than the remainder at the expense of their bomb load. They would be placed at the more vulnerable points in the bomber formation (ie at the rear and flank) to cover the remaining more lightly armed aircraft.

Douglas suggested to the DCAS that the matter should be discussed at the next meeting of the Air Fighting Committee, and that a paper by Flight Lieutenant Pharazyn, which put forward 'rather different' views from his own, but was 'supported by quite reasonable arguments'.

Flight Lieutenant Pharazyn's paper had been presented to both Douglas and the DCAS. In it he gave the opinion that:

> ...it is unlikely that optimism will ever reach such a pitch that bombers will seriously expect to win air battles against fighters or to destroy AA guns in their stride. The most they can expect is to evade or ward off the one, and to avoid the fire from the other.

Pharazyn thought that escort fighters 'fitted magnificently' into the picture of formations of bombers as a defence against fighters – but the escort fighter was not a true fighter, but was in reality just Douglas' more heavily armed and armoured bomber, 'indistinguishable in outward appearance' from the other bombers. He added the important rider that:

> If the competition between gun calibre and thickness of armour plate spreads to the air, the gun is bound to win; the Escort Fighter is not an Aerial Battleship, for there would be no difficulty in fitting the ordinary fighter with a gun capable of shooting it down. Nevertheless, if it becomes necessary to fit fighters with extra large guns for this purpose they will not be equally suitable for attacking un-armoured bombers, and even in its moment of destruction the Escort Fighter will afford protection to its family.

Unfortunately, a continuation of this point, that the extra large gunned fighter would be incapable of dealing with a single-engined escort, even if carrying extra fuel, was not made.

Sir Christopher Courtney, having thought about these points, minuted Douglas on 1 February 1937 with a clear restatement of orthodoxy:

> ...Fighter aircraft designed for escorting bombers would have the effect of detracting from the potential weight of air bombardment capable of being carried exerted by an air force of a given size.
>
> I have no doubt whatever in my own mind that the whole conception of fighter escorts is essentially defective, and though I do not wish to cramp free discussion of the question in the Fighting Committee, I think that someone should bring up the arguments that I have advanced above.
>
> ...[During] my recent visit to Germany...When I referred to the use of fighters in Spain for escorting bombers, they replied quite reasonably that the circumstances of that war were quite peculiar and very unlike the circumstances of a war between air powers; in the latter case the bombers would be operated at long ranges where escorts would be impracticable.

With these seeds from above planted and manured in fertile ground, Air Commodore Douglas chaired the ninth meeting of the Air Fighting Committee on 9 June 1937. He described the consideration of Fighter escorts as a 'hardy annual', implying cleverly that it was in reality a weed, uprooted annually by doctrine. Referring to the Spanish Civil War, Air Commodore Douglas noted that reports indicated that that fighter escorts were used in large numbers, 'in some instances even outnumbering the bombers'. Air Chief Marshal Dowding, the Commander in Chief of Fighter Command, suggested that this was because fighter aircraft were 'cheaper and easier to obtain' than bombers, and that the close proximity of the contestants to each other's bases 'rendered it easy for single seat fighters to accompany the bombers'. There was no mention of its *effectiveness* in protecting the bombers – Air Chief Marshal Sir Edgar Ludlow-Hewitt would not assume the mantle of Commander in Chief until November 1937, and its current head – Air Chief Marshal Steel – was not present at the meeting, Bomber Command being represented by Douglas Evill, an Air Commodore.

The Committee had before them a paper entitled 'The Question of Fighter Escorts for Bombers', which was divided into two sections – the first written 'by an advocate of the principle', the second representing 'The opposition viewpoint'. However, the escort fighter which was discussed was simply Sholto Douglas' bomber, 'indistinguishable in outward appearance from its family of bombers', but a bomber which would carry extra guns instead of bombs, armed with perhaps eight machine guns and

20,000 rounds of ammunition – that is, exactly the same guns as the projected B36 heavy bombers which would be shot out of the sky with appalling frequency between 1942 and 1945 – although the escort bomber would carry more ammunition. These escort 'fighters' might be used, it was thought by their advocate, 'as a rallying point where a long raid passes from cloudy to fine conditions and requires to change its policy from evasion to mutual support', although if it was 'indistinguishable' from the standard bomber it is difficult to see how this could have been achieved in the heat of action.

The 'opposition viewpoint' was that:

> …fighter escorts to bomber formations are justified only if they enable the bombers to reach a vital objective otherwise unattainable or if in certain circumstances they enable a given number of aircraft to deliver a very considerably greater weight of bombs on the objective than would otherwise be possible.

No mention of loss of crews, no mention of imposing casualties on enemy fighters, just the maximum bombload delivered onto the enemy!

The 'opposition viewpoint' also mentioned that the escort 'fighter', because its performance was analogous to that of a bomber, 'is always likely to be inferior to that of a local defence fighter', and would 'be unable to deal with the attacking single engined fighter, which could deliver a 'lethal density [of fire] at 300 yards range in 2 seconds'.

This ninth meeting of the Air Fighting Committee was, therefore, not discussing the escort fighter as it became known later in the war, but rather a heavily armed adaptation of the standard bomber. Air Chief Marshal Dowding pointed this out clearly by saying that, if single seat fighters were intended as escorts, they could not be 'close escorts' – ie fly in the formation – but must be 'distant escorts' – ie flying above or behind or on the flanks of the formation. It would be easy, he went on, to draw a 'distant escort' off from the bomber, 'thus permitting the main formation to be attacked at leisure'. Dowding considered therefore that a single-seat fighter escort could be ruled out at once, a view which met with 'general' agreement. This very one-sided view of the situation seemed to ignore the corollary – if the single seat-single engine escort fighter was 'drawn off' from the bombers, it could itself be envisaged as 'drawing off' the attacking fighters from the bombers. This separation of enemy fighters from your bombers, indeed, could be said to be its main purpose! Here, as mentioned before, was the main weakness of separate commands – the officers of Fighter Command were concerned with defence, with fighters shooting enemy bombers down, and not with being 'drawn off' themselves into the offensive, by protecting Bomber Command. Bomber Command needed the voice of its Commander in Chief, Air Chief Marshal Steel, at this *vital* meeting, and he was not present.

So it was considered at the meeting that multi-seat fighters 'with their fire power mainly aft' could actually accompany the bombers and form part of the rear of the formation, and thereby 'the need for superior performance would largely disappear, as the aircraft in question would virtually be a converted bomber, which would not leave the formation'.

Air Commodore Douglas Evill, for Bomber Command, thought that, rather than a 'distant' or a 'close' escort, a multi-seat fighter might be better termed a 'roving' escort, which would come to the aid of any part of the bomber formation. It is difficult to see how this could be done by a converted bomber whose performance was the same (or worse, as it was later suggested) than the standard bombers, which would presumably be flying at maximum speed under attack.

Wing Commander Davis, the Assistant Director of Research and Development (Armament) at the Air Ministry, pointed out at this point that fighters would probably be armed with 20 mm cannon or even larger calibre weapons, which bombers simply could not carry in any equivalent number, and which would mean that the bomber's defence would become inadequate. In these circumstances, some form of escort would be 'just as necessary for bomber formations as it was in a composite fleet'.

The Chairman then pointed out that a 'fairly strong feeling' existed that some form of escort was necessary, and '*since a single seat fighter could be ruled out*' (italics added), a 'multi seat fighter with a 'roving commission' was needed.

But once again the argument circled round to simply arming some of the bombers with more guns and more ammunition, and increasing armour protection. And once again it was stated that an aircraft with a performance superior to the standard bombers would be required. But Operational Requirements pointed out that additional gun turrets would *decrease* the performance to *below* that of the standard bomber which it was to escort. Even sacrificing bombload for defensive armament (and it could be imagined that some officers genuflected furiously when this heresy was aired) did not lessen the aerodynamic penalties of extra turrets. (The American YB40, a converted B17, would later, after heavy American bomber losses, be built on this principle, and would carry extra armour and some twenty machine guns and cannon. However, although virtually invulnerable, it could not keep pace with the standard bombers, and was reconverted later.)[2]

Now Air Commodore Garrod, the Air Officer Commanding the

Armament Group, stated 'with the support of several members' that 'distant escorts, where escort aircraft left the formation', should be ruled out, and 'if it was considered necessary' to increase the defensive powers of the formation, it should be done by adding guns and armour to the bomber, if necessary reducing the bombload. He 'deprecated the principle of providing fighters to hang around the bombers', and considered that the bombers should be able to 'fight their way through'.

But Operational Requirements now simply repeated their assertion that extra guns and turrets would reduce performance. The Chairman, perhaps sensing the completely circular flow of the discussion, suggested that the simplest solution would be to give the standard bomber more armour and more ammunition.

Thus the constantly revolving arguments came to no real solution of the problem of bomber defence. Any 'roving' or 'distant' escort would involve being 'drawn off' the bombers by enemy fighters. So the escort had to stay in the formation. It had to have extra guns and turrets, which would so reduce its aerodynamic performance that it could not stay in formation. It could, however, have extra armour and ammunition – but then, suppose fighters were armed with 20 mm cannon or larger. The bomber would then need escorts, but…and so on. The bomber, the soul of the doctrine, the mainstay of the logic of an independent RAF, remained defenceless, while electronic eyes became ever more capable of leading heavily armed fighters to them.

Sholto Douglas, referring to the minutes of the above meeting, sought – and obtained – the approval of the DCAS to fend off the idea of fighter escort. He had done well by the doctrine.

It may be of some interest to the reader, therefore, to leave the smoke of the committee room for a while, and transfer his or her thoughts to the alarms and excursions and terrors and sudden deaths on the Western Front in the Great War. The year is 1917, and an old man is recounting his thoughts of that year when, as a young twenty-three-year-old fighter pilot and squadron commander in the RFC, he observed the terrible attrition of the bombers. He wrote in 1963:

> I came to believe that Trenchard was wrong in his opposition to fighter escorts for bombers. He believed that the bombers ought to be able to fight their way through on their own, but time and time again we found that the bombers suffered tremendous casualties when they ran into a strong force of enemy fighters. But that conflict of views persisted even after the First World War, and it was to provide a lesson that we had to re-learn in the early days of the

second war. Even as late as 1942 the Americans…followed Trenchard's line of thought…He [Trenchard] was unquestionably a great man, but…not infallible…[3]

The old man was Marshal of the Royal Air Force Lord Douglas of Kirtleside; the young man was William Sholto Douglas. In the interplay of memory, of doctrine and of ambition, it is difficult to detect the precise influence of each. All that seems certain is, that the doctrine – and progress in the RAF – were closely linked; and that if a talented and brave airman, as Sholto Douglas undoubtedly was, felt confident that he would benefit his country further by serving it in a higher capacity, then incense had to be burnt on the altar of the doctrine of the relentless offensive.[4]

The escort fighter was again discussed, in passing, at the seventeenth meeting of the same Committee, which took place nearly two years later, on 31 May 1939. It was again chaired by William Sholto Douglas, now an Air Vice Marshal and Assistant Chief of the Air Staff. The aim of the meeting was to 'clarify views on the role and characteristics of the Field Force Fighter'. This was the fighter which would operate, not for home defence over the United Kingdom, but over the fighting area on the Western Front.

It was generally agreed that the purpose of the Field Force Fighter was to destroy enemy aircraft in the air. This was agreed 'in principle', but there was some 'divergence of opinion' as to which enemy aircraft were to be shot down primarily, bomber or fighter? Air Chief Marshal Dowding, again present for Fighter Command, stated that the primary target of the fighter was the same as that of the home defence fighter, ie the bomber, and he 'deprecated any tendency' which would detract from this; provided the fighter had enough speed to catch enemy bombers, its manoeuvrability could be sacrificed, as its speed would enable it to evade combat with enemy fighters. But Group Captain Chapel, of No. 22 Group, said that the fighter should be of sufficient performance not only to attack enemy bombers but to shoot down enemy reconnaissance and fighter aircraft, and thereby gain air ascendancy. He later reiterated his view that army co-operation aircraft should be able to operate freely, and this required that the Field Force Fighter must be able to deal with enemy fighters.

Dowding agreed that the Field Force Fighter would frequently meet enemy fighters, and thought that all fighters should be back armoured to protect from surprise attacks. He pointed out that, in the Spanish War, fighters did not often catch enemy bombers, which were escorted by fighters. 'The bombers flew away from them, leaving the fighters to have a dog fight with the escort fighter.' In this respect, Dowding went on, the

Field Force Fighter might be 'a bit handicapped' in manoeuvrability, against enemy fighters, or even against army co-operation machines if the enemy were content to make them 'slow and manoeuvrable'.

These comments of Dowding's on escorts seemed to show the reverse of the coin of his earlier comments in 1937, that the escorts would be 'drawn off' by enemy fighters, leaving bombers unprotected. At that time nobody had cared to point out the corollary to the Air Chief Marshal.

However, since the previous discussion on escorts at the November 1937 meeting, the very astute and far sighted Sir Edgar Ludlow-Hewitt had been appointed Air Chief Marshal and Commander in Chief of Bomber Command, and, as we have already seen, he was well aware of the bomber's weaknesses against the fighter. He had not missed attendance at the meeting like his predecessor, and now commented that, although he thought that bomber escorts should be drawn from other sources than the Field Force Fighter, he was 'impressed that, in all recent wars, escorts had been used very considerably'. He thought [and Dowding agreed] that 'so long as we had bombers which were inadequately armed against modern fighters, *the adoption of some sort of fighter protection, in certain circumstances, might be imposed upon us'.*

However, having secured this point, Ludlow-Hewitt went on to say that the question at immediate issue was whether this protection should be provided by the Field Force Fighter. If a fighter designed primarily to destroy bombers was also suitable for working in conjunction with bombers, then so much the better.

The Chairman now reminded the meeting that, despite its willingness to discuss escorts, the question was, what was to be the role of the Field Force Fighter? This was agreed to be the destruction of enemy aircraft in the air – 'to insist upon the requirements of escort in its design might prejudice entirely its suitability for its primary role'. He felt that '*the right answer to the escort question was that in paragraph 10 of the Commander in Chief's letter AFC60, ie a suitable bomber type with additional armament, and not a new type.*' [Italicised in the minutes of the meeting.] He pointed out that 'a similar conclusion had been reached at the ninth meeting of the Air Fighting Committee'. This had been two years before! However, he concluded with the sop that the Air Ministry had recently re-opened the question of escorts for consideration 'with a view to its re-discussion by the Committee *in due course*' [italics added]. Yet Sholto Douglas would write to Ludlow-Hewitt on 12 August 1939, 'I am directed to refer to the conclusions of the ninth meeting of the Air Fighting Committee, at which the question of escorts for bomber formations was discussed' – but there was no mention of *fighter* escorts at all.

Hindsight is, of course, the weapon of the auditor, whose duty has been often likened to that of walking the battlefield after the fighting has ceased, bayoneting the wounded. It is easy to forget that the American triumph in the air war with the Lightning, Thunderbolt and Mustang escort fighters was five years of battle and change and experience into the future, and the war had not yet begun. Even so, for the Chairman to override a thriving current discussion, and to point back two years, like a mediaeval churchman, to the *timeless* doctrinal conclusions of past synods and conclaves, might be considered to be one of those fatal steps which led inevitably to catastrophic bomber losses by day, and thereby to the initially inaccurate and comparatively ineffective night bombing offensive.

Thus the bomber, which was the primary arm of the RAF, although considered by its most capable and intelligent commander to be 'inadequately armed', would be left to defend itself, or seek protection from other, more heavily armed bombers, a strategy about which doubts had already been expressed on aerodynamic grounds. If this were not enough, the examples of fighter escort provided by the Spanish Civil War were dismissed in 1937 as due to 'a surplus of easy to obtain fighters', and in 1939 discussion was referred back to 1937.

But the Field Force Fighters themselves – which were to be Hurricanes – were, despite the increased production forced on the Air Ministry by the wisdom of Sir Thomas Inskip, still utterly inadequate in numbers. In 1917, the copy of the Smuts report which was sent to Field Marshal Sir Douglas Haig was endorsed with a comment that the argument that a war can be won in the air as against the ground was 'a mere assertion unsupported by facts'. That it could be *lost* on the ground was almost proved when the German Army, with close air support and fighter escorts, conquered Norway, Denmark, Holland, Luxembourg, Belgium and even great France itself, and drove Britain from Europe, narrowly missing capturing her entire field force. But for the subsequent heroism and skill and technology of Fighter Command, and for a torrent of Russian blood, it might well have been lost. Then the doctrine, which had failed so completely by 1940, would be implemented in full because it seemed to many to be all that was left. For years to come until the British return to France in 1944 Bomber Command, with its terribly vulnerable aircraft whose few advantages had served merely to draw attention from its many weaknesses, unsupported by fighters and inadequately armed for defence, would attack the enemy's head directly, while the enemy's teeth and claws were deep in Russia, and while the Royal Navy attempted to keep the monster in its European cage, and the Army worried and snapped at the enemy's flanks.

As we have seen, before the war no faith had been placed in fighter escorts for the hopelessly vulnerable bombers. Fighter escorts were condemned by the doctrine of the relentless offensive, since it had been believed that all effort should be put into the bomber attack. Despite radar, despite the voices of reason and intelligence heard on the vulnerability of the bombers, fighter escort was still ruled out. How could a long-range fighter dispute the skies with a single-engined short-range interceptor? This question was not so often asked of the slow, cumbersome, heavily laden bomber – yet if a long-range fighter was generally accepted as too vulnerable, what odds could be placed on the bomber's chances?

By 3 October 1939 the French General Mouchard had reported that:

> The fact that our fighter aircraft have been frequently surprised by enemy patrols can be explained by the fact that they have been employed almost entirely on escort duties up to now, and by the increasing difficulty of this type of duty owing to the speed of modern aircraft [ie, slowing down to the bomber's speed].
>
> The conclusion appears to be one of the greatest reasons for discontinuing the use of modern aircraft for escort duties.

By 16 October it was noted of the French that:

> The French have relied to a great extent on escort in their tactical doctrine, probably influenced by events in Spain. Our view on the other hand has been that the practical difficulties in operating it, particularly as regards fixed gun fighter escorts, appears to be insuperable. It is therefore interesting to note that French doctrine may be completely revised and that their experience has shown that our views on this subject were well founded.

In a note on Franco–German fighter versus fighter combats of 6 November 1939 it was calculated by the French that:

> It is quite clear nevertheless that a close escort of fixed gun fighters cannot be a real protection to a bomber or reconnaissance aircraft. As soon as the enemy fighters are encountered the escorting aircraft ceases to be an escort as they cannot participate without fighting, while if they fight they cannot continue to protect...A fixed gun fighter escort can only be regarded as a means to an end. The aircraft it is escorting becomes in effect a sort of decoy...

To liken the escorted bomber to a decoy was a curious analogy – a hunter might use a goat as a decoy for a tiger, which is not very nice for the goat – but surely better than being simply left unprotected by the hunter!

'Fools think they profit by experience', said Bismarck 'I prefer to profit by the experience of others.' American doctrine provided for close escort of bombers by fighters – and the American bombers, ill armed before the war, were upon analysis of British experience, armed with the much heavier Browning .5" machine gun, and furthermore, had more of them. Yet at first, even thus heavily armed, they had encountered the same difficulties. The escort fighter, to keep station with the bomber, had to weave in and out of and around the formation, a manoeuvre which considerably reduced its range. This close escort did not prevent attacks by German fighters, and indeed, by tying them to the bombers, put the escorting fighters at a disadvantage – although it did, of course, mean that a fighter attacking an escort was not attacking a bomber, and it imposed a much greater loss rate on the attacking fighters. The main aim of the attacking fighters was to impose such heavy losses on the bombers, or threaten them to such an extent, that they restricted or even abandoned their bombing, or to ruin the bomber's aim and, perhaps, the morale of the crew. Any combat with a fighter was a distraction for the bomber, especially over the target.

To look further ahead, the victory of the American fighters over the *Luftwaffe* was due to three main factors; the first, numbers – the huge productive power and efficiency of American industry, and the high quality and vast output of the pilot training schools; the second, the design and production of fighter types which possessed both the necessary range (with the design and provision of jettisonable extra fuel tanks) – the Republic P-47 Thunderbolt, the Lockheed P38 Lightning and, above all, the P51B North American Mustang with a Rolls-Royce Merlin engine; and thirdly, a strong yet flexible will to overcome difficulties and carry on with daylight bombing (despite counsels of despair from the RAF), and to change tactics when appropriate.

The tactical change was to fly a detachment of the escorts with the bombers for a time, to be replaced by other escorts which flew straight to the bombers; eventually three relays of fighters escorted the bombers, with P-47s replaced by Lightnings and finally by Mustangs. The returning escorts made what trouble they could, striking targets of opportunity on the ground. Later, some escorts flew with the bombers, while others sought out the fighters who were on their way to the bombers, or who were returning to the airfields, while yet others ranged ahead of the bombers looking for trouble. These tactics imposed a heavy burden of attrition on the German fighters, who had to fight their way to the bomber, and if they arrived, had little time to engage them before being hit by the escort fighters.

But the American use of the .5" heavy machine gun in their bombers[5] had a considerable effect on the air war. Although unescorted heavy bombers suffered severely at the hands of the German fighter force, their formations still inflicted losses on the fighters, and imposed on them the necessity for heavy armour and armament. As George Volkert had pointed out in 1937, whatever armour or armament was carried by the bomber, the fighter could always carry more, so neither the 20 mm nor the .5" gun could ever have assured the safety of the *unescorted* bomber. Provided that the fighter need only contend with the bomber, armament and frontal armour could be piled on with impunity. Indeed, a Focke Wulf 190 fighter, the FW190A *Sturmbock* (battering ram) fighter, equipped with two 20 mm and two 30 mm cannon, and carrying extra frontal armour, could afford to close with formations of B17 Flying Fortress and B24 Liberator heavy bombers and blow them from the sky. But all this extra weight for vastly increased firepower and frontal armour (in the wrong place for fighter versus fighter combat, where it needed to be in the rear) converted the fighter into a bomber destroyer, which was itself vulnerable to enemy fighters.[6] An extraordinary example of this is given by Richard G Davis' *Carl Spaatz and the Air War in Europe*. On 27 September 1944, a group of forty-eight *Sturmbock* FW190A-8 fighters came across thirty-seven temporarily unescorted B24 Liberator bombers and before their escorts could return shot down twenty-six bombers in three minutes, despite the ten .5" machine guns with which each bomber was armed. The blood of the bomber crews did not go unavenged, however; when the American Mustang fighter escorts returned, they shot down eighteen of the *Sturmbocks*.[7]

However, as we have seen, RAF doctrine was not in favour of fighter escort. Even Ludlow-Hewitt confessed himself 'no believer in close escort by fighters' in a letter to the Secretary of State for Air, Sir Samuel Hoare, of 7 January 1940.[8] However, he added the significant comment:

> ...but I do believe in fast long range fighters being used to operate in conjunction with bombers, as the Bristol was used most effectively in the last war...The advantage of long range fighters, given that they have the performance, is that the bombers provide them with the means of making contact with enemy fighters under terms which may be favourable to our own fighters. Our fighters in this way may be able to have the security and advantage of both high altitude and surprise, and, though they may not be able to prevent losses to our bombers, they will make the operation more expensive to the enemy by causing greater casualties to his fighters. I strongly recommend that a suitable fighter be developed.

Here was the positive view of the bomber as a decoy.

Ludlow-Hewitt had unfortunately given the example of the twin-engined German Me110 as an escort fighter; this aeroplane was found, in the Battle of Britain, to be so inferior to the Hurricane and Spitfire in performance that it needed a single-engined fighter escort itself! When the reply came from the Air Ministry to Ludlow-Hewitt's letter, it suggested that the twin-engined Beaufighter be considered 'to co-operate with bombers on important missions'. It was pointed out that it was more heavily armed than the Me110. Eventually the Beaufighter, equipped with AI radar, would be used in the intruder role as a night fighter in support of the bombers, but although its firepower was indeed shattering, it lacked range and speed.

Tizard, in a note to Brooke-Popham in August 1940, suggested that 'everyone was agreed about the need for a long distance fighter'[9], adding that he thought it should be equipped with radar. Tizard was no great believer in the Mosquito as a fighter, regarding it as a stopgap before the development of the jet fighter, which he believed should be concentrated upon much more. He also believed in the jet bomber, a concept which, had it come to fruition in the RAF in the Second World War, might have avoided the necessity for an escort fighter altogether.

Although the Mosquito was being developed with all energy as a fighter, Fighter Command itself wrote to Operational Requirements as late as March 1942[10] that they did not expect it to hold its own with a single-seat fighter in daylight. Nor indeed could it. In trials against a Spitfire, although slightly faster, it was easily out-turned. While they now accepted that the single-seat single-engined fighter could provide an effective escort for short distances, they wrote that 'We feel in Fighter Command we shall never have a fighter capable of escorting bombers on long raids in daylight, and suggest that the old horse dealt with in the attached paper may be pulled to its feet and flogged again'.'The old horse' was the heavily armoured escort bomber, with .5" machine guns and 20 mm cannon. In the attached paper, Fighter Command suggested that 'many bomber pilots do not appreciate the moral and physical effectiveness of their power operated turrets and the tremendous concentration of lead which a section of three aircraft can turn onto a fighter trying to attack them'. They felt that flak was a greater danger to bombers than opposing fighters, and cited the Battle of Britain as having shown the ineffectiveness of escort fighters, whether single- or twin-engined. They also pointed out that in the RAF fighter sweeps over France in the summer of 1941, 'determined Huns managed to pierce through' and 'occasionally' claimed a bomber. In the blind adherence to doctrine which seemed to characterise the RAF attitude to fighter escorts before the more energetic Americans tried it out, there was not a question raised on what would have been the fate of *unescorted* bomber sweeps. It was even accepted by Bomber Command Operational Research that, although fighter escort was most effective in protecting the bomber, its range was too limited and the numbers required too great.[11]

Sir Charles Portal concurred in the feeling that a long-range fighter was a non starter, on the logical grounds that anything that carried extra fuel and fuel tanks could not compete in manoeuvrability with a single-seat home defence fighter. He employed this argument in a reply to Churchill on 3 June 1941, and in arguments with the Americans in 1943. In an appendix concerned with Portal's involvement with the fighter escort question, John Terraine made the telling statement that General Arnold, the USAAF Commander in Chief, 'found the spectacle of a fighter force which Portal stated to consist of 1,461 aircraft with crews remaining inactive while his bombers were being shot out of the sky both incomprehensible and unacceptable'.[12] To prove his point Arnold, the British Official History noted, specially equipped some Spitfires and flew them across the Atlantic. The official historians were unimpressed with this, for 'to be able to get there is one thing and to be able to fight when there is another'.[13] But the more vigorous and enterprising Americans were surely proved right.

Harris wrote to the Commander in Chief of Fighter Command, Air Marshal Sir Trafford Leigh-Mallory, on 17 June 1943,[14] asking that intruder aircraft attack three important *Luftwaffe* night fighter sector stations, and adding that he hoped Fighter Command 'will shortly be adding bombing to the very useful work already carried out by your cannon fighters'.

However, much to Harris' disgust, Leigh-Mallory's reply, although he agreed to attack the three stations, put the support of Coastal Command as his first priority. But 141 Squadron, equipped with Beaufighter MkVIs, were assigned to intruder operations. They were equipped with AI radar, which enabled them to locate enemy aircraft. They were also equipped with 'Serrate', the code name for a device which tracked the radar emissions of German night fighters on the same visual display tube as the AI radar, and which was effective at a distance of 80 to 100 miles. However, the British Official History reports that between 14 June and the beginning of September 1943, 1,180 'Serrate' contacts resulted in just twenty combats, with thirteen enemy aircraft claimed as destroyed. The principal lesson of the experience, wrote Webster and Frankland,[15] was that 'the Beaufighter was inadequate to the task'.

On 3 July 1943 Harris wrote to Portal,[16] asking for more support from Fighter Command, and Portal replied on 9 July, saying that any conflict of priorities between Bomber Command and Coastal Command should be referred to the Air Ministry for resolution. Portal told Harris that 'arrangements have been made to provide two more Serrate squadrons' equipped with Mosquito night fighters, although it would take two to three months for them to become operational. Mosquito fighter-bombers were 'coming along reasonably well', reported Portal, and it was intended to use them against German night fighter airfields. Portal added that two squadrons from No. 2 Group (which had been transferred from Bomber Command to a new force, the 2nd Tactical Air Force under Leigh-Mallory) were to be used on intruder work against German airfields.

Needless to say, Harris was not satisfied. On 31 August he wrote to the Deputy Chief of the Air Staff (Sir Norman Bottomley) saying that the intruder operations carried out by Fighter Command were 'excellent as far as they go, but they do not at present exercise more than a minor effect upon the enemy's powerful defensive organisation...'. Harris added that:

> It is not unreasonable to conclude that air offensive action, on the scale required to give fair prospect of success against the German defensive system, is unattainable so long as the responsibility remains with Fighter Command whose primary and essential function is something entirely different, namely the ensuring of the defence of Great Britain against any probable scale of enemy air attack. The defences of Germany are far too powerful and well organised to be dealt with as a side issue...
>
> I therefore suggest that the Night Fighter and Intruder squadrons should be transferred to Bomber Command and formed into a Group whose specific duty it would be to conduct co-ordinated offensive measures in support of bomber operations...

Harris thought that four night fighter and two intruder squadrons would initially be required, and also wanted a radio countermeasures squadron. Acknowledging that this would reduce the strength of Fighter Command below the minimum necessary for defence in the event that the Germans renewed their air offensive, he added in true Trenchardian style that 'the success of the Bomber Offensive is the best possible insurance against any such renewal...'

Surprisingly, Harris got his way. No. 100 Group was formed at the end of 1943 and included both Mosquito night fighters and radio countermeasures aircraft.

Nor content with this, Harris wrote to Douglas Evill, the Vice Chief of the Air Staff, on 18 November 1943,[17] stressing the vital need to get No. 100 Group going as soon as possible, and asking in addition for further support from Fighter Command's Typhoon single-engined fighters, fitted with long-range fuel tanks, for attacks on the Ruhr. Harris wrote:

> Urgent development of the Counter-Measures Group and extended use of our large fighter force to help the bombers are, at the moment, operational requirements of the highest importance. It is time Fighter Command took some interest in the Bomber Offensive. At present they run an entirely private war on their own…

Harris' request for the Hawker Typhoon to escort his bombers to the Ruhr eventually found its way to Leigh-Mallory, who thought that navigational difficulties at night for a single-seat fighter might be too much, and that there were other problems of identification at night, including the difficulty of distinguishing the Typhoon from the Focke Wulf 190, to which it bore some resemblance. Harris accepted this.

No. 100 Group began operations in November 1943 under Air Vice Marshal Edward B Addison, an electrical engineering specialist with degrees from both Cambridge and Paris.[18] The Group had two broad functions – night fighting, and radio countermeasures.

We have already seen that the Bristol Beaufighters of 141 Squadron carried both AI radar and the 'Serrate' equipment. The 'Serrate' patrols, homing in on the enemy's 'Lichtenstein' AI radar emissions, began in June 1943. As we have seen above, contacts with enemy night fighters were disappointingly few, one successful combat resulting from every nine sorties in the first three months, falling to one from every thirty-five in the second three. The AI MkIV radar with which the intruders were equipped suffered from severe interference, and the Beaufighter, as the official historians had noted, was not really a match for the enemy night fighters – although, of course, at night victory went to he who saw the other first, as Harris had always maintained. As in all night fighting, 'kills' were very disproportionately spread, the most skilful accumulating great numbers. Of the twenty-three Beaufighter successes, one pilot alone had nine, while two others had five each.

With the advent of No. 100 Group, three 'Serrate' squadrons were re-equipped with Mosquito Mk IIs, with both backward and forward-looking radar.[19] At first, enemy contacts were sought over the target area itself, but too many bombers were present, and this was also the case when the night fighters tried to fly with the bomber stream as close escort. Enemy fighters could be intercepted either approaching or leaving the stream, but once in, they were lost in the mass of signals from the bombers. Another method still was to visit the beacons where the enemy tried to assemble their fighters, giving them a known position from whence they could attack the bombers – but here, navigation to the beacons themselves presented a problem, although after 6 June – D-Day – the Germans began to assemble their fighters in beacons over France, and here the No. 100 Group patrols were more successful. Later, the fighters of No. 100 Group would attack airfields directly, or lie in wait some distance away for enemy fighters to attempt to land, at which time they were very vulnerable indeed. Nevertheless, between December 1943 and April 1944 thirty-one enemy aircraft were shot down by No. 100 Group fighters, one for every fifteen sorties.

Harris wrote to Sir Douglas Evill, Vice Chief of the Air Staff, on 7 April,[20] asking for a minimum of ten night fighter squadrons. Pointing out that 'as a result of the losses suffered in the air, on the ground and at production centres from the Combined Bomber Offensive, the defensive strength of the Luftwaffe is no longer adequate to meet its commitments in full'. Harris went on to warn that 'The Germans have therefore cut their coat to suit their cloth', and 'they will give priority in defence against the night bomber offensive', adding that 'there is evidence that this policy is already in operation'.

Harris expected that concentration against the night bomber would be 'maintained and intensified' because *'Day bombing as practised by VIIIth Bomber Command, except under clear weather conditions, is not a very serious menace to Germany'.* [Italics added.] Harris pointed out that *factories* destroyed by the VIII United States Air Force could be replaced more easily than the *cities* destroyed by RAF Bomber Command. Suggesting that the Germans only opposed the USAAF in strength when clear weather conditions promoted accurate bombing, Harris went on to say that 'Unescorted night bombers can be destroyed with a smaller relative loss of fighters than can escorted day bombers', thus reducing *Luftwaffe* wastage and enabling them to 'maintain a fighter force which at least has some chance of disputing local air superiority during the first few critical days of any premature allied invasion in the West'. This was hardly a consistent argument, since in poor daylight weather, bombs which missed factories but destroyed the city area surrounding them was just what Bomber Command were doing, save that Bomber Command were intending to destroy the city in which the factory lay, whereas the USAAF accepted that destroying cities was an inevitable result of missing precise targets. It has been said that the difference was between area bombing of precise targets, and precision bombing of area targets.

At the time of writing this letter Harris had suffered major defeats; in the period from 18 November 1943 until 31 March 1944, in what was called the 'Battle of Berlin', 1,117 bombers had been lost, 3.8% of those attacking; a further 113 crashed in England. In the Nuremberg raid of 30/31 March 1944, ninety-six bombers were lost, 10.1% of the attacking force.[21] Harris had said to Churchill that, if the USAAF joined in this offensive, it would cost Bomber Command 500 bombers, but would cost Germany the war. These defeats Harris attributed to the ineffectiveness of the .303" armament and the poor view from the turrets, although he felt that:

> ...even if AGL(T) were to become effective soon enough to be used in the war against Germany (which is improbable) the chances against the bomber would still be too great to give a reasonable chance of success against the enemy defences...remedial action is therefore an urgent operational matter which cannot be deferred without grave risk.

Harris pointed out that since even the Lancaster could not fly in formation by day above 18,000 or 19,000 feet, at which height:

> ...flak would be lethal and would more than compensate for the losses which the fighter escort might be expected to save,[22] [the] only remedy was night fighter support on a substantial scale, and it is considered that a total minimum of ten night fighter Mosquito squadrons should forthwith be placed at the disposal of 100 Group to satisfy this requirement. This force would be used both for night fighter support and in attacks on enemy night fighter bases.

Harris continued:

> Finally, it may be said that a major decision of this kind could not be made effective quickly enough to have a worthwhile effect. But if this were seriously urged, we should compare very poorly with the American performance in providing their day bombers with long range fighter escort within a few weeks of the necessity for this step becoming apparent; though the difficulties which confronted them were far greater than those with which we are now faced.

Harris had originally intended to end the letter with the comment that:

> ... support for the Bomber Offensive within our available resources has all along been put on low priority, compared especially with defence against a comparatively non existent menace and against almost any and every other fancied or real requirement.

However, this was crossed off Harris' copy.

But later in April Harris had some success, although far from the ten squadrons demanded. He was given two squadrons of night fighters. On 22 April 1944 he wrote what was, for him, an unusually subtle letter[23] to Sir Roderick Hill, the very talented Commander in Chief of the Air Defence of Great Britain, the new organisation which now encompassed the old Fighter Command. Harris began by sympathising with the squadrons who were being transferred to his command after earning glory in their own, pointing out that:

> …the existence of a separate air force has justified itself in two major directions during this war alone, firstly by the saving of this country during the Battle of Britain and secondly by the Bomber Offensive against Germany which has been the preponderating means of reducing Germany to her present parlous position at home and on every front. But while the existence of a separate air force could never be justified on a purely defensive basis its offensive potentialities are now at last realised as our major source of strength against the enemy. To that end, as always in war, it is essential for the defensive to utilise the least practicable proportion of our resources and for every effort to be made to apply the maximum effectively…

Hill replied on 24 April, saying that Harris' points were 'so rightly made', and that he would give Harris 85 and 157 Squadrons, the former of which was equipped with the latest AI MkX radar, while the latter was equipped with AI MkIV. These squadrons began operations on D-day, starting with low-level airfield intruder operations. However, with the launching of the first flying bombs against London in June, they were used as interceptors to shoot the bombs down, being allocated that task full time from 21 July. They did not return to their bomber support duties until the beginning of September 1944, when the flying bombs' launching sites were captured by the advancing Allied armies. But in their preliminary prowling of the German airfields they had destroyed ten enemy aircraft in 176 sorties.

Norman Bottomley, the deputy Chief of the Air Staff, was pressing for another approach to the problem – that of a return to daylight operations with fighter escort, conceding that this would result in an average loss to fighters of 5%, a little over twice the American rate due to .303" armament and the lack of training in formation flying, with a further 1.4% lost to flak.[24] But this would still be less than the 6.5% sustained by Bomber Command in night operations over central Germany in the period March to May 1944. 'In view of the developments in night fighter technique,' wrote Bottomley to Portal on 10 July, 'we may well have to sustain losses higher than 6.5% when deep penetration by night is again possible.'

But the liberation of France and Belgium transformed the air war both by night and by day, by depriving the *Luftwaffe* of their early warning system and by providing fighter bases within France itself. Attacks on German oil supplies, coupled with the loss of the Rumanian oilfields due to Soviet advances in the east, crippled the *Luftwaffe* operations by imposing a fuel rationing so severe as to restrict not only operations, but training as well. The Americans had achieved air supremacy in the west, and Bomber Command operations, escorted by Spitfires, were being carried out by day, at less cost in casualties than by night. However, Harris pointed out to Portal[25] that, as the days grew shorter, 'daylight work…was severely circumscribed …by the refusal of our fighter escort to take off or land in the dark', adding that 'otherwise their co-operation is excellent'.[26]

Harris added pessimistically:

> So far, we have got away with daylight attacks simply because the Boche fighters have never attacked us. The reason is that we hide behind Eighth Air Force operations and feint attacks. This is too good to last and one day soon the Boche will ignore the Eighth Air Force attacks and concentrate on us.

Harris continued:

> With our small number of fighters and their short range (not even all our Mustangs have yet built in long range tanks, and the requirement is urgent) we shall take a tremendous beating. Thereafter, once the Boche have discovered how easy it is, we shall take plenty more. It takes 600–800 fighters to keep Eighth Air Force alive, and their bombers have heavy armament…

Harris could be most persuasive and forceful, and although he seemed often to get nowhere with the Air Ministry and its tortuous bureaucracy, he sometimes did better when dealing directly with other commanders. On 19 September 1944 he attended a conference at Versailles held to discuss fighter escort for Bomber Command with the commanders of the 2nd Tactical Air Force and the Deputy Supreme Commander, as well as Norman Bottomley, the DCAS, and others. The minutes record that 'Air Chief Marshal Harris put forward an impassioned plea for Bomber Command to be given a priority call on both Mustang wings to escort Bomber Command on strategical missions into Germany'. Harris pointed out that Mustangs were long-range escorts, yet were frequently used for ground attack duties which might be carried out by shorter-range aircraft. The reason he had not begun day bombing sooner was the lack of a long-range fighter escort. His bombers, with their .303" armament, were virtually unprotected. Although little opposition had been encountered by day so far, he feared that the Germans might divert some of their night fighters against his daylight raids. He felt that daylight raids with escort might incur fewer casualties than raids by night. In all this he was supported by Bottomley.

In a letter read out at the meeting in his absence, Air Marshal Coningham, Commander of the 2nd Tactical Air Force, pointed out that the Mustangs had been invaluable for ground attack when lack of fuel, due to the rapid advance of the armies through France, had grounded his Typhoons and Spitfires. However, Harris pointed out that static airfields near to the front line enabled these shorter-range aircraft to do the job. He also pointed out that the American Mustang escorts took bombers into Germany, and strafed ground targets on the way back.

Harris got both wings, six squadrons in all, and he further secured an agreement by the Air Defence of Great Britain to train them to take off and land in darkness. However, he undertook to let 2nd Tactical Air Force know in time of occasions when these squadrons were not required, so that they might be employed in the tactical role.

However, small raids could not get escorts by day, and even the Mosquito needed an escort since the advent of the Me262 jet fighter. Bennett had written to Harris on 17 December 1944 with a paper on the use of small numbers of Oboe-led (see Chapter 8) Mosquitos for attacks on oil targets. Saundby replied for Harris that such escorts were reserved for heavy bomber operations – however, said Saundby, when high icing clouds in the Ruhr area prevented these, only Mosquitos and fighters could operate anyway, so such days could be used, and also the Mosquitos could:

> …take advantage of large scale operations by the Eighth Air Force, especially when they are routed close to the Ruhr on their way to targets deep in Germany, or weather conditions such as fog and very low cloud which would severely hamper the operations of fighters in North West Germany.

Harris never really felt that his bombers were safe at any stage of the war, even at the very end. When strategic bombing was abandoned in April 1945, Portal proposed to publish a message to the world, saying that 'henceforward the main tasks of our Strategic Air Force will be to afford direct support to Allied Armies in the land battle and to continue the offensive against the sea power of the enemy…' Harris objected strongly to such a public announcement as this, because the Germans would then be enabled to simply ignore feint attacks against cities – and they were especially sensitive about Munich and Hamburg – and also transfer flak guns. Evasion – by feint attacks and other means – was still, day or night, the most effective defence of Bomber Command, despite fighter escort, despite No. 100 Group intruders, despite AGL(T) and gyro gunsights and .5" gun turrets, and it is to this method that we will turn for a final chapter on the defence of the bomber.

Notes

1 PRO Air2/2613.

2 John Killen, *The Luftwaffe: a History*, Pen and Sword, Barnsley, 2003, 236.

3 Sholto Douglas, *Years of Combat*, Collins, London, 1963, 180–181. In Volume 2, *Years of Command*, Lord Douglas wrote that, before the war 'there even persisted a conviction that the bomber would have little or no trouble in bombing Germany in daylight without fighter escort' (p58).

4 In June 1939 Douglas and Courtney, then AOC Reserve Command, were on a flight to Northern Ireland which crashed. Courtney, due to take Dowding's place at Fighter Command, was injured, and Dowding carried on until after the Battle of Britain, to be succeeded by Sholto Douglas. See *Years of Command*, 40–42.

5 And in their fighters, most being armed with six.

6 Series editor Philip Jarrett, *Putnam's History of Aircraft – Aircraft of the Second World War*, Chapter 3, Dr A Price, *Fighter Development Mid 1941 to Mid 1945*, London 1997, 65.

7 Richard G Davis, *Carl Spaatz and the Air War in Europe*, Smithsonian Institute Press, London, 1992, 511–12.

8 PRO Air14/251.

9 IMP B/Tizard/3/9.

10 PRO Air14/154 & Air2/2613.

11 Sir Charles Webster and Noble Frankland, Official History, *The Strategic Air Offensive Against Germany*, Vol I, 'Preparation', The Naval and Military Press Ltd., Uckfield, 2006, 449.

12 John Terraine, *The Right of the Line*, Wordsworth editions, Ware, 1997, 704.

13 Sir Charles Webster and Noble Frankland, *The Strategic Air Offensive Against Germany* Vol II, The Naval and Military Press Ltd., Uckfield, 2006, 44 (Fn 1).

14 RAF H67.

15 Sir Charles Webster and Noble Frankland, *The Strategic Air War Against Germany 1939–1945*, The Naval and Military Press Ltd, London 2006 (1st pub 1961) 141.

16 RAF H82.

17 RAF H16.

18 Jonathan Falconer, *Bomber Command Handbook*, Sutton publishing, Strand, 1998, 180.

19 PRO Air14/2911, a history of 100 Group.

20 PRO Air14/735, RAF H68.

21 Bomber Command War Diaries.

22 In *Bomber Offensive* p183, Max Hastings quotes Harris as considering a return to daylight attacks of 'lightly defended' targets in central Germany (letter to AOC 4Group, 11-12-'42).

23 PRO Air14/735.

24 RAF H57.

25 RAF H47.

26 Bennett, the Pathfinder leader, had complained to Harris on 14 September 1944 about the fighter escort, but Harris had asked all the groups concerned, who all expressed their satisfaction with the support of the fighters. Harris presumed that the pathfinders, being always 'in the van' of the attack, saw less of them.

CHAPTER SEVEN

Evasion

If you cause opponents to be unaware of the time of battle,
you can always win.

Sun Tzu[1]

When Stanley Baldwin had made his famous comment in the House of Commons that 'The bomber will always get through', he had adduced, as the reason for this assumption, the 'hundred cubic miles of sky covered with cloud and fog'. But then came radar, which could penetrate the murk and give an increasingly accurate picture of the position, height, speed, number and direction of approaching aircraft. Yet throughout the war, despite the pulsing eyes of radar, evasion was not only the first, but the most successful, of the strategies by which the bomber could arrive unscathed at the target. You may see the conjuror's hands and still be deceived; you may concentrate on your opponent's straight right which you see, and be knocked out by the left hook which you don't.

If you arrived at the target, you had evaded but one arm of the defence, for you were then subject to anti-aircraft fire – the famous German *Flakartillerie*. A heavy flak gun could fire a shell which could reach out to 30,000 feet above, taking eight seconds to reach 15,000 feet, twelve seconds for 20,000 feet and eighteen seconds for 25,000 feet. The danger area from the fragments thrown out by the explosion of a heavy flak shell was 100 feet across. There were two general methods of anti-aircraft fire – predicted fire, which was aimed to hit a specific target by visual or radar aim, and barrage fire, which was aimed at the formation as a whole and intended to render the whole area dangerous. Each flak shell was fused to burst at a certain height, so it was essential for the gunners to estimate height correctly, either visually or by radar. When allied to a predictor, which could calculate the future positions of the aircraft and the shell and ensure their meeting, flak was deadly. At low levels, the German cannon were even more to be feared, rendering this form of attack even more dangerous.

When operating at night, the flak gun had allies in the searchlights, which could pick up a bomber by scouring the sky, or by radar, and 'cone' it – catch and hold it in the light of three or more searchlights, making it terribly vulnerable both to flak and to prowling night fighters.

As we have seen, the first daylight bombing efforts directed against North West Germany and Norway, and against France and Germany, in 1939 and 1940 had met with a disaster which amply demonstrated the defencelessness of the current bombers. Ludlow-Hewitt had said in October 1939 that 'there is no more valuable ally in air operations than surprise – followed by clouds'.[2] He was indubitably right about the first, but to use cloud cover for day bombing was to court disaster, for even today, when the nations aid each other in it, and reconnaissance aircraft and equipment are not attacked, and results are calculated on electronic computers, weather forecasts are often inaccurate, and the clouds may disperse, leaving the attacker in the open. And cloud cover was fickle, for icing clouds could bring an aeroplane down. Even this hazard was solved by evasion; Air Marshal Brooke-Popham had asked Harris on 20 February 1943[3] whether icing 'was still a problem', and Harris had replied that:

> The problem of icing is nothing like as bad as it is painted. It is much more a matter of avoiding icing conditions by correct flying or, on a limited number of occasions, by cancelling operations, rather than one of competing with it technically. In particular, now that it is no longer necessary to see a target in order to bomb it the actual restrictions in operations due to icing is no longer a very serious matter, although icing conditions still give us occasional and very welcome nights in bed.

If, of course, they were forecast.

Night, as we have seen, provided the bomber with an invaluable cloak, more reliable than clouds, for the night was lit but dimly by the stars, with the moon in its regular phases giving a much more variable light. Although, as will be related, night bombing brought very serious problems of bombing accuracy and navigation, at first the only real dangers were searchlights, flak, and the accidents which were an inevitable result of taking aircraft heavily overloaded with high explosives and incendiaries up into the night sky with primitive methods of navigation and maintained by heavily overworked fitters.

German air defence radar, which was technically in advance of the British, consisted of two main sets. The first, code-named Freya, was an early warning radar which could see approaching aircraft some seventy-five miles away, but which could not give their altitude. The second was

Wurzburg, which could accurately locate the position of aircraft at a distance of twenty-five miles, and which was used at first for directing the anti-aircraft batteries in the Ruhr.

Between the start of the war and August 1940, of some 6,800 night bomber sorties over Germany, just 1.7%, 155 aircraft, were lost. This compared with some 6% of sorties by day. Of all these night losses, only ten were confirmed by the Germans as due to night fighters.[4] The method of night fighting used by the German fighters was to take off when warned by Freya of a British raid, circle radio beacons in the area of attack, and watch for bombers caught by the searchlights. This method, called *Helle Nachtjagd* (illuminated night fighting) used Me109 single-engined fighters.[5] The heavy flak guns allied to the first Wurzburg radars were much more formidable, but by August 1940 there were just 450 of these, mostly concentrated in the Ruhr.

From May 1940, after the German bombing of Rotterdam, the RAF had begun its bombing of Germany proper, and Hermann Goering was concerned enough to assign a special force of night fighters to the defence of Germany, appointing Josef Kammhuber to command it. Kammhuber believed that the most effective form of night fighting was what he called 'long range nightfighting', intruder patrols which prowled the enemy's land, attacking bombers during take-off and landing. This was carried out for a year, although all attempts to increase the strength beyond a few aircraft failed. In August 1941 Hitler ordered the intruders to be sent to the Mediterranean theatre, nor would he relent when the night bombing became a major problem, for he considered that the place to destroy the bombers was over Germany, where their tangled and bloody metallic remains might inspirit the German people.

Kammhuber instituted a searchlight line from Schleswig to south of Liege, with another line to defend Berlin. The night fighters were placed behind the line to avoid interference with the sound detection apparatus, the *flugwachen*, prowling the sky at between 12,000 and 18,000 feet waiting for the lights to illuminate a target.

Intense competition developed between flak and fighters over possession of the new Wurzburg radar sets, which were being produced at a rate of twenty per month. Later, Wurzburgs would be available for the flak, and new 'Giant' Wurzburgs, with a 25 foot dish instead of the original 10 feet, were to operate in pairs, one tracking the bomber while the other tracked the fighter, which was directed towards it by a controller. This was 'dark' night fighting, otherwise known as Ground Control Intercept (GCI). If this failed, and a bomber passed unscathed through the line, it entered the radar-controlled searchlight zone. Here, one radar-directed master searchlight pointed straight up into the sky. When the radar locked on to a bomber, the searchlight would hold it until four ordinary searchlights were switched on and took the bomber over, upon which the master light would await the next 'customer'.[6]

The 'Kammhuber Line' thus formed divided sections of the sky into 'boxes', each one of which could only handle one fighter at a time, although as more radar sets became available a 'reserve' searchlight line was formed. This system began to enjoy some successes, and British bomber losses rose accordingly. Yet, as was the case with the German jet fighters, apparent victory lulled Goering into a very false sense of security, and his suspension of projects which might not prove to be of immediate benefit extended to the field of radar. The Wurzburg gave its information in the form of range and bearing co-ordinates. Bill Gunston in his book *Night Fighter* reports that the development, which was already advanced, of a Plan Position Indicator (PPI) for the Wurzburg Giant, which would have given the fighter controller direct visual information in real time of the movements of the bomber and fighter, was not thought worth development. The information was therefore plotted on to a Seeburg Table, where an operator, given the range and bearing figures of the bomber by telephone, played a red spotlight up onto a table, while a second operator similarly moved a blue spotlight to represent the fighter. 'The mind boggles', wrote Gunston, 'at the number of places where errors and inaccuracies could be introduced'.[7]

The extension of the Kammhuber Line gradually made it impossible for bombers to avoid it, except for flying very low, which exposed the aeroplane to the deadly German light flak. According to Kammhuber, the dark night fighting of the GCI system and the 'illuminated' night fighting with the searchlights enjoyed equal successes in shooting down the bombers – until the spring of 1942, when Hitler, to Kammhuber's chagrin, ordered all but one searchlight regiment to be used in conjunction with the flak to protect 'special objects within the Reich', which included the Ruhr. This, writes Alfred Price, was a more effective system anyway, and even Kammhuber himself later admitted that it was an improvement.[8]

If this system was to be defeated, it was necessary first to establish just what the system was, and what equipment it was using. The Freya sets had been identified, but the Wurzburgs were an unknown quantity. When an object suspected to be a Wurzburg was located at a Freya site on the French coast at Bruneval, it was decided to investigate it by the delightfully straightforward, but dangerous, method of simply going in and looking at it, taking whatever parts were thought useful to the investigation, and carrying them back to Britain. In February 1942 a remarkably daring group were parachuted onto the site, taking not only samples but expert German radar operators as well, and retreating by sea. The Bruneval raid yielded much vital information, not only directly, but because the Germans subsequently protected all their other exposed sites with quantities of barbed wire, enabling them to be readily identified by Photo Reconnaissance aircraft. It was also thought prudent to move the Telecommunications Research Establishment inland, lest this more literal approach to information gathering should prove too tempting to the enemy.

Bomber Command raids were usually a matter of each aircraft navigating to the target and returning by its own route, a method which spread out the attack over a number of hours. This suited the Kammhuber system admirably, since entering many boxes at staggered times enabled the German fighter controllers to use more boxes at a time, and gave individual fighters time to engage more than one aircraft. It also permitted the flak guns to concentrate more on individual aircraft over the target. The solution seemed to be to concentrate the attack both in time and space. However, it was only with the improvements to navigation made possible by the introduction of the radio aid 'Gee' that, in June 1942, individual routeing was abandoned, and concentration became the order of the day.[9]

However, the value of all aircraft taking a common route to the target was not undisputed. Guy Gibson, then a squadron commander in 5 Group, thought that route planners should consult with squadron commanders in each case, because, as he put it, '…Bombing technique is changing every day, and so are the defences of Germany'.[10] Saundby's response (on 21 August 1942) was that:

> …a careful check is kept of all casualties in relation to routeing and every endeavour is made to alter routes to counter the enemy's defences. Ideas from Groups on routeing are always welcomed. It will, however, be appreciated that it is almost impossible to reconcile all the Groups to any given route, let alone all the squadrons.

However, Saundby pointed out that 'in taking the law into their own hands on the question of routeing, [squadron commanders] may be jeopardising the safety of the force as a whole…'

It had originally been thought that if aircraft were more concentrated together they would be better targets for both fighters and flak. Later, when the German GCI system was better understood, it became clear that concentration would flood the defences and, although it might make it more likely that a fighter in a particular box would find a target, the fighters in the other boxes would be searching in vain. It was a similar phenomenon to the introduction of the convoy system for merchant ships, when the German U-Boats seemed suddenly to be sailing an empty sea. But the bomber convoys, of course, had no protective escorts.

In 1941 the bombers arrived at the target at a rate of around forty an hour; by 1943 it was ten a minute. Later, as we shall see, when the German GCI system had suffered a considerable defeat, the night fighters adopted a different method, that of interception over the target. This made an even shorter time over the target, illuminated as it was by flares and fires, more desirable for the bomber, and the bombing rate was increased to thirty per minute.

With this degree of concentration came other problems – collisions. This risk could be reduced by bombing at different heights, which also made it more difficult for the flak – but here again was a new danger – the bombers were themselves in danger of being hit by falling bombs, some of them from a much greater height and travelling at high speeds. Small incendiaries, in particular, were showered from aircraft at a high rate. The answer was to cluster the incendiaries, but this, as will be seen in the next chapter, was handled by the same Armament Department which had failed so signally over the defence of the bomber.

Concentration also meant that the number of shells which the flak guns had time to fire was very considerably reduced, although barrage fire, that is, fire aimed at no particular aircraft but at the area in general –'browning' fire – was made more effective as the sky became thicker with aircraft. To counter this aircraft were dispersed in breadth as well as in height.

An Army Operational Research paper of March 1943 had arrived at the conclusion that 'the effect of avoiding action in mitigating the risk of anti-aircraft fire…is shown to be small compared with that of adopting suitable formations'. However, an article in the Air Force magazine *Tee Emm* at around the same time incurred the wrath of Bennett, the Pathfinder chief[11], since it advocated violent manoeuvres and 90-degree turns to avoid flak, which would have made both bomb aiming and gun defence against fighters impossible. In defence of the article, it was pointed out that the magazine was for the Air Force as a whole, and that, in the Middle East, bombers would spend much longer over the target, as flak was considerably less than over the cities of the German homeland. Harris himself became involved, supporting Bennett's view and pointing out that evasion in heavily defended areas was futile – indeed, Harris pointed out, in an operation by No. 5 Group,'…The AOC issued an experimental order that on no account was evasive action to be taken in the target area, everything was to be subordinated to a dead straight run and to accurate bomb aiming.''The results achieved,' Harris went on, 'were outstanding in regard to concentration of bombing' and his losses were described by Harris as 'infinitesimal' compared with the normal losses to be expected in such an operation.

With the arrival of fighter escorts by day, and the defeat of the German fighter force by the USAAF, it eventually became safer for bombers to bomb by day than by night; between June 1944 and April 1945, of 341 Bomber Command aircraft lost by day, 62% were shot down by flak, with a further 14% due to unknown causes.[12]

Flak defences were, of course, strengthened for particular groups of targets when it became obvious that they had become priorities for the bombers. When oil targets, for instance, became priorities, flak defences were deadly; in one raid on Gelsenkirchen on 11 September 1944, 77% of the attacking aircraft sustained flak damage.[13] There had to be deception over target systems, as well as targets, and this led to the continuing area attacks on cities – although Harris was committed to these anyway.

Concentration on the route did not mean that all bombed, or returned, at the same height. The height at which aircraft returned was dependent upon each Group. The return flight over the North Sea seemed to present different dangers at each height. British intruder aircraft reported to Bomber Command on 24 August 1942 that large numbers of bombers returning over that sea in bright moonlight flew at heights between 2,000 and 6000 feet, and that they were visible at that height for a distance of ten miles. This prompted Bomber Command to ask each Group at what height their bombers left the Dutch coast. The replies showed a wide variation, from the 10,000 to 12,000 feet of No. 1 Group to the 200 to 300 feet or lower of No. 5 Group. No. 3 Group flew low over the sea in the summer months to prevent being silhouetted against the aurora borealis, the northern lights, but thought that aircraft should avoid flying *too* low over both cloud and water, 'both of which reflect the moonlight, and against which the aircraft would be plainly visible'. 'The astonishing differences of light and shade obtained in the sky, even at night', the report added, 'make any definite ruling as to which height to fly in moonlight when over the sea to avoid detection, quite impossible'.

The return flight was always dangerous, as the defences were certain to have been alerted. But however low the return over the North Sea, the aircraft had to climb to a height of 2,000 feet when thirty-five miles from the English coast in order to establish their identity with Fighter Command on the IFF (Identification Friend or Foe) automatic recognition system. Below that height, the system would not work in time, and they would trigger off the formidable night defences of the RAF.

Over heavily defended areas of Germany it was certainly safer to fly high in order to make things as difficult as possible for the deadly heavy flak guns. Yet height itself in Northern latitudes could be dangerous in the summer. An attack on the synthetic oil plant at Wesseling near Essen in the Ruhr on 21 June 1944 suffered 27.8% losses, due, in the words of the ORS report, to 'the excellent visibility prevailing at high altitudes on this, the shortest night of the year'.[14] It was later confirmed that visibility against the brightest part of the sky at a height of 20,000 feet at that latitude on that night at *midnight* on British Double Summer Time (2200GMT), *with no moon*, was over ten miles, dropping to 5.5 miles $1^{1}/_{2}$ to two hours later, and then returning to more than ten miles by 0315 BDST. At 10,000 feet the distance fell to a high of five miles and a low of two miles at the same times. The attack had taken place at 0130 BDST, when visibility was at its lowest. Even in the darkest part of the sky, however, it had been two miles at that, the darkest hour. The bombing height had been between 17,000 and 20,000 feet.

On 29 June, just eight days after the carnage at Wesseling, Bomber Command ORS produced a paper which stated that at 52 degrees north (which is just south of Berlin):

> During the mid-summer months the depression of the sun below the northern horizon is so small …that a condition of twilight prevails throughout the night, even at ground level, and the brightness becomes greater both with increasing latitude and with increasing height above the ground...

The paper noted that, in the absence of the moon, visibility depended upon five factors; the angle of depression of the sun below the horizon, the bomber's height, the weather, the azimuth, or horizontal angle which the direction of observation makes with the sun, and the angle of elevation of the direction of observation above the horizon. Of these factors the observer, the fighter pilot, could control only the last. At different times, between 30 degrees and 90 degrees – a quarter of the horizon – was illuminated.

These dangerous nights were far from being confined to midsummer itself. The 'normal' visibility range of a heavy bomber on a clear moonless night was very roughly 1,800 feet, but could rise to 3,000 feet. Even at a latitude of 48 degrees, over Munich and southern Germany, there were fifty-five days in the year when this visibility increased to 5,000 feet for a four-hour penetration of enemy territory at a height of 20,000 feet, and the visibility was above 10,000 feet for twenty-four of those days. For the Ruhr and the oil plants, a penetration of even two hours would give a visibility of 5,000 feet for thirty-eight days, and a four-hour penetration further east would give this degree of visibility for eighty days. For the Baltic, for 100 days of the year the visibility range is 5,000 feet. This imposed quite severe limitations on Bomber Command's flexibility in the summer months, for even at a height of 10,000 feet the restrictions were not much less.[15] Despite the shorter penetrations of the summer months, Bomber Command's losses had increased in each year, and this had been partly due to this increase in visibility. The question was far from being merely academic.

But how visible you were in the night was a secondary part of evasion, for even with ten miles' visibility range the fighter had still to be placed within a ten-mile circle of the bomber, and the skies over Germany and the occupied territories were vast, and the fighters relatively few. The primary aim of evasion was to bomb the target without the GCI fighters being alerted and directed at all, or if alerted to have them sent to the wrong place, or if they were directed and alerted to the right place, to be gone before they arrived. To achieve this, three interrelated methods were used – to interfere with the enemy's radar, to block his communications and to make 'feint' attacks so as to send his forces elsewhere.

When the Wurzburg radar equipment captured at Bruneval was analysed and other intelligence on the German defensive system was brought together, it was decided to attempt to 'jam' both the radars themselves, and the German night fighter radio communications. But it was the Freya early warning system which was jammed first. A system with the code name 'Mandrel' jammed the Freyas by noise transmissions, while another, code-named 'Moonshine', received signals from Freyas and then amplified and re-transmitted them, giving the impression of a close formation of aircraft. This, however, could not fool the Freyas at night, for the enemy knew that no such close formation could be adopted.[16]

German radio communications between control and the fighter were jammed by a device code-named 'Tinsel', an operator simply identifying the frequency used for the messages and then obligingly entertaining the enemy with the ear-shattering sounds picked up by a microphone located in the bomber's engine.

Another fate was in hand for the deception of the Wurzburg and Giant Wurzburg radars. It had been suggested before the war that to drop strips of metal from aircraft would confuse radar operators, and by 1941 scientists at the Telecommunications Research Institute (TRE) began to experiment with these strips; by March 1942 they had demonstrated that they could confuse and deceive a radar system. But this deception was a spear with a poisoned tip at each end, which could easily be used by the enemy. Portal, who had ruled in favour of its use in April 1942, was dissuaded by Lord Cherwell, who felt that British defences should first be tested for their vulnerability to this disruption. They were found to be wanting in some respects.

But by April 1943 advances in British and American radars enabled Portal to feel that it was now safe to initiate this form of deception, and recommended its use to the other Chiefs of Staff – who felt that it might be safer to delay things until after the Allied landings in Sicily, scheduled for July, in case it was used against them by the *Luftwaffe*. Portal concurred. The stage was now set for the defeat of the Wurzburg radars, and thereby the German GCI and flak systems, by this method, which was code-named 'Window'.

At the end of 1942 it was discovered that German fighters were using AI radar in the 490 megacycles range. In May 1943 the crew of a German night fighter, equipped with the latest Lichtenstein AI radar apparatus, deserted to Britain. Soon, a device code-named 'Serrate', which could home in on the emissions of Lichtenstein, was devised by TRE. 'Serrate' did not make any emissions itself, and could not, therefore, be tracked. It was also discovered that Lichtenstein was vulnerable to Window.[17]

The paper-backed metallic strips, each cut to a length equal to half the wavelength of the radar system to be deceived, were dropped by bombers in bundles, each bundle giving identical reflections to those given off by a heavy bomber. The bundles separated immediately after release and formed a dense cloud, falling at a rate of some 3–400 feet per minute. Bundles were dropped over enemy territory at a fixed rate, usually every two minutes, although the rate was increased over the target, where the flak relied on the Wurzburg radar close by, and the Lichtenstein-equipped night fighters prowled for prey.

Window was first used in a series of attacks on the great port city of Hamburg which began on 24/25 July 1943, and resulted in the German GCI system being rendered completely ineffective, as were the searchlights and the flak. The only resource open to the guns was barrage fire, aimed at the general area of the bombers, which was much less effective than aimed fire, although occasionally a searchlight picked up a chance target which could be aimed at.

Perhaps the greatest value of Window was that it enabled a few aircraft, furiously dropping bundles of Window, to give the appearance of a large force of bombers.[18] This was the 'spoof' raid, which was ineffective in the face of a perfectly functioning GCI system. Spoof raids would 'feint' at a target, drawing the defensive fighters to the wrong place, while the real target lay elsewhere. Sometimes spoof raids would take place when no real raid was intended at all, just to keep the defenders guessing.

But by the end of 1943 the German defences had staged a remarkable recovery. A *Luftwaffe* Major, Hajo Hermann, suggested to Kammhuber that the hard pressed twin-engined night fighters might be supplemented by single-seat day fighters with flame dampers fitted to their exhausts, manned by bomber pilots, who were used to flying at night. These would attack bombers revealed by the searchlights and by the flames from the burning cities, in a similar fashion to the former 'illuminated night fighting' technique. Kammhuber's refusal was simply by-passed, Hermann going above his head and getting permission from his superior, *Generaloberst* Weise. On 3 July 1943 he and his men shot down twelve bombers over Cologne, despite the flak – he had not contacted them to inform them of his presence. This method of night fighting became known as 'wild boar', and it came just in time, for Kammhuber's system would soon be overwhelmed by Window.

Soon, raids began to be tracked by the emissions from the bombers – the IFF (which the bomber crews sometimes left on in the mistaken belief that it confused the flak guns), the H2S scanners and the 'Monica' rear defence radar. The German night fighters, having identified the bomber stream, would then infiltrate it, and losses again began to mount steadily. A new German AI set, the SN2, immune to Window, was being installed as rapidly as the electronics industry, hard pressed by the production of the foolish and wasteful V2 rocket, could make them. These began to take a toll. The Wurzburg radar sets were modified to detect any Doppler effect in order to see whether the Window cloud was moving (although this did not work if the cloud itself was moving at 13 mph in the wind, or if real bombers were flying an oblique course. Skilled operators could also detect the modulation to the echo due to the bombers' propellers. Harris' series of raids referred to as the 'Battle of Berlin' ended with the Nuremburg raid, when the stream was infiltrated (it was actually routed over fighter assembly beacons) and ninety-five bombers out of a total of 795 were lost. In the 134 days up to and including this raid, Bomber Command lost 1,117 aircraft, with a further 113 crashing on their return to England. This loss was inflicted on 3.8% of the sorties in this period.[19]

A temporary relief to the sufferings of Bomber Command came when the strategic bomber forces were placed under the 'strategic direction' of General Eisenhower and his Deputy, Sir Arthur Tedder.[20] The main targets now became the French railway and transport systems, in preparation for Operation *Overlord*, the invasion of North West Europe, and finally of Germany. On 6 June American, British and Canadian forces secured the

Normandy bridgehead in one of the most famous operations of the war. The Army was feted for its historic achievement; but Harris pointed out to Sir Douglas Evill, the Vice Chief of the Air Staff, on 30 June that in May and June 1944 the Army had lost 2,500 killed, while over the same period Bomber Command had lost 4,047.[21]

On D-Day itself began the use of the airborne 'Mandrel' screen, to jam the Freya (and the supplementary 'Mammut' and 'Wassermann') early warning radar sets. The screen, formed of jamming aircraft flying a 'Racecourse' pattern, a series of flattened circuits which gradually advanced towards the enemy coast, obscured all movement behind it from electronic eyes. It was developed and used extensively for the rest of the war, sometimes intentionally split to allow the enemy to 'see' a Window force behind, or a spoof force of training aircraft which later turned back, and sometimes hiding nothing at all, but causing the enemy to presume that a force was there, and adjust their fighter forces accordingly.

But the greatest aid to evasion was the advance of the Allied armies to the German border, which deprived the German defences of their early warning altogether. In October 1944 came 'Dina', an airborne jammer of the SN2 radar, which was used on aircraft equipped with 'Jostle', an airborne jammer of *Luftwaffe* VHF radio communications.

At the time of the German surrender, the deception measures undertaken by Bomber Command were in the ascendant, but German countermeasures were on the way – new systems more difficult to jam with the existing equipment. No doubt measures against these would have been found, for in the electronic war, in the expert opinion of Dr Price in *Instruments of Darkness, all* victories are temporary.

The temporary ascendancy in the electronic war, gained by Bomber Command in late 1944 and early 1945 at such a huge expense in intellectual and electronic resources, should not obscure the dreadful fact that all of the wizardry, all of the effort in route planning, in spoof raids, in feints, in Pathfinder marking of spoof targets, in 'Windowing', in 'Mandrel' screening, was because the ill armed bomber, to the very end, was almost defenceless when it was caught.

Notes

1 Sun Tzu (trans. by Thomas Cleary), *The Art of War*, Shambhala Pocket Classics, London, 1991, 46.
2 PRO Air14/232.
3 RAF H35.
4 Edited by David C Isby, *Fighting the Bombers*, Chapter 3, 'The Development of Nightfighting' by Josef Kammhuber, Greenhill Books, London, 2003, 63.

5 Bill Gunston, *Night Fighters – A Development and Combat History*, Sutton Publishing, Stroud, 2003, 94.

6 Gunston, *Night Fighter*, 98.

7 Gunston, *Night Fighter*, 98.

8 Alfred Price, *Instruments of Darkness*, 58.

9 Slessor, commanding No. 5 Group, had already issued instructions on 10 November 1941 to adjust take-off times so that concentration over target was achieved, both to defeat flak and searchlights, and for the morale effect.

10 PRO Air14/233, 14 August, 1942.

11 RAF H90.

12 PRO Air14/3932.

13 PRO Air14/2050.

14 PRO Air14/3012.

15 PRO Air14/3012.

16 Alfred Price, *Instruments of Darkness*, 101.

17 Alfred Price, *Instruments of Darkness*, 124–154.

18 PRO Air14/3012.

19 Middlebrook and Everitt, *Bomber Command War Diaries*, 488.

20 Official History, Vol III, 20.

21 RAF H15.

CHAPTER EIGHT

Bombs and Navigation

The bulk of the scientific information in the department had been obtained by regarding the German attacks on this country as a large scale experiment carried out for us by the enemy.

AJ Astbury, History of the Research and Experiments Dept, Ministry of Home Security.[1]

…intellects vast and cool and unsympathetic
…slowly and surely drew their plans…
HG Wells, *The War of the Worlds*

The Director of Armament Development (D.Arm.D.) at the MAP worked sometimes in direct liaison with armament firms, and sometimes through the Armament Design and Research Departments of the Ministry of Supply. This Department was huge, dealing with the armaments of all three services, and was controlled by the services themselves, each taking it in turn to appoint the Department's head.

This Department had acknowledged failings, which were detailed in the Guy report of August 1942.[2] In his report, Dr Guy quoted, as an aim, Trenchard's dictum that 'It is as much the duty of the technical departments to anticipate requirements as of the Air Staff to put them forward'.

The Committee recommended that a new highly paid 'Chief Engineer and Superintendent of Armament Design' be appointed, with a high salary and status, in charge of a section of 'highly trained and experienced mechanical engineers'. They also recommended that promotion be by merit, rather than seniority. The evidence given to Dr Guy's Committee (on which sat Air Commodore Pidcock, the D.Arm.D.) suggested that the department worked in an office atmosphere far removed from the roar of engines, the spitting crackle of machine guns and the urgency given to life by danger and fear. One man, a soldier, had been quoted as saying that 'Gun design is a closed book, and I will bloody well keep it closed'. Evidence was also given by Group Captain Sealy, Superintendent of the Bomb Section. Sealy was in charge of draughtsmen, whom he supervised and instructed. But the senior draughtsman in the bomb section thought the others had 'no real interest in their work' and he did not like working with serving officers who 'could not begin to understand their technical problems'.

But the gravest shortcomings identified in the report were the 'failure to make adequate financial provision for research, design and development in the years preceding the war'. Nowhere did this seem more glaringly evident than in bomb design.

The bombs used by the RFC and Royal Naval Air Service, and inherited by the RAF, were a 'mixed collection of bomb designs and bomb stocks which bore no relation to a fixed policy of any sort'.[3] The designs, the shapes, the fusing and the construction were varied, a result of meeting the immediate short term requirements of the services.

After the peace, the shrinking of the RAF precluded any policy on bombs; the Deputy Director of Research (Armament) – DDR(Arm) – also thought it prudent to await details of aircraft design before embarking on the design of bombs. This, thought Miss D McKenna,[4] was a result of the inferior status of the Armament Department, which from 1926 to 1936 was an Assistant Directorate only. Miss McKenna wrote:

> Bombs were designed so that they could be carried conveniently in existing aircraft, instead of aircraft being designed to carry bombs designed to do the maximum damage to the enemy.

However, even after the war was over, as late as November 1946, fifteen months after the atom bomb had been dropped, the report of the British Bombing Survey Unit's 'Weapons Effectiveness Panel' could write (of bombs) that:

> It may be mentioned that the unsatisfactory state of affairs prevailing in 1939 was no reflection on those responsible for armament design; bomb design must of necessity be governed by general policy and the carrying capacity of aircraft.

This observation touches on a fundamental flaw in RAF thinking before, and during, the war. As Tedder had observed, the gun and the bomb were the sole reasons for the existence of the RAF – artillery observation and reconnaissance alone could have better been left to the Army. When the doctrine of the relentless offensive was formulated, it was intended to attack industries and cities directly to ruin the enemy's capacity to make war, and to pin them to the defensive in order to save your own cities. This would be achieved if you dropped 'bombs' on their cities and industries. But the type of bomb was unspecified, its effect implied rather than scientifically calculated, because the 'destruction', any destruction, would crack morale. The aeroplane was thought of as the weapon. But the aeroplane is not a weapon, but a weapon carrier. 'My job is transport', said Harris in a foreign broadcast in July 1942, 'The transport of bombs in the right quantity at the right time to the right place'.[5] The bomber was analogous to a merchant ship, and the defending fighter to a submarine, which had the job of preventing it from delivering its cargo. In practice, of course, the bomber differed mainly from the merchant ship in that it was expected to travel in convoy without escort, nor was its self defence treated with the energy it deserved.

Had the first approach to the destruction of industries been to study exactly what design of bomb was necessary to achieve the object, and where to place them, and what the aiming error would be expected to be, and therefore, how many bombs must have been dropped to achieve whatever was the desired probability of the target's destruction; or what the effect of fire was on a city, and how best to incinerate its factories, its houses and its infrastructure, the result would have been appalling both morally and for the sheer scale of the effort involved. All this could have been worked out in 1918, for the explosives and the combustible fillings were known.

But the devil was morale. Chess games may be fought until a pawn and a king remain to each player, and the attrition, or even the sacrifice, of rooks and bishops, of knights and queens, is easily tolerated in order to secure a favourable position. But if the pieces were alive, and could reflect on their individual fates, and the loss of their comrades, and could seek salvation by flight, or by deserting their captain, the game would be utterly different, and incalculable. Even if the pieces were given a Spartan training from birth, it would not really resemble chess as we know it. And many of the German pieces had taken flight in 1918…

The RAF was cut down to a size the treasury could tolerate, and relied on pilots and aircraft to drop whatever was available on the enemy on the supposition that their morale would be suspect, while that of Britain would be, save for the 'aliens' in the east end of London, intact.

In 1921 the DDR(Arm) decided to proceed with a standard bomb design that would be useful against any type of target, which became known as the General Purpose (GP) Bomb. New bomb fillings were investigated. The maximum amount of energy which could be released from a chemical reaction was estimated to be about twice as destructive as those used in the Great War.[6] Chemists knew, therefore, that no chemical explosive would be discovered that would transform war itself – but nevertheless, an explosive of double the power would yield a significant advantage to the user.

It should first be stated that the standard high explosive consisted of a mixture of TNT and ammonium nitrate called amatol. TNT (trinitrotoluene) alone was rather more powerful than amatol, but much more expensive.

A new filling which seemed to offer promise was a TNT/CE (trinitrophenylmethylnitramine) mixture, with a blast effect described by the official narrative[7] as '30% greater than TNT or amatol alone' (although, as has been stated above, TNT alone is more powerful than amatol). This explosive, however, was found to be difficult to obtain in sufficient quantities, and too sensitive. The next explosive tried was hexanite, a mixture of 60% TNT and 40% hexanitrodiphenylamine, but this could not easily be prevented from exuding through the fuse hole joints of the bomb. This left amatol as the standard filling until the arrival of cyclonite, cyclotrimethylenetrinitramine. This substance, first made in Germany in 1899, was originally patented for medicinal purposes. The Research department at Woolwich developed it as an explosive before the war, calling it RDX (Research Department Explosive). A pilot plant to manufacture RDX was set up at Waltham Abbey in 1938.[8] RDX was a considerable advance on amatol, 1 cubic foot of the explosive giving the same blast impulse as 1.541 cubic feet of amatol 60/40. However, production in 1940 was only 60 tons per month.

The last great improvement in high explosives used for bombs in the Second World War came to Bomber Command much later than it might have done, the reasons for which are still partly hidden. It had been known since 1905 that the addition of aluminium powder to high explosives gave a greater blast impulse to the explosive. The Royal Navy had developed two aluminised explosives; Minol, a mixture of ammonium nitrate, TNT and aluminium powder in the proportions 40/40/20 and Torpex 2, a mixture of RDX, TNT and aluminium in the proportions 42/40/18.[9] The power of Torpex underwater was known to the RAF at least by May 1943, since it was the high explosive used in the 'bouncing bomb' in the famous raid on the dams of 17/18 May 1943. It was also known to Air Commodore JW Baker, Director of Bombing Operations and Chairman of the Bombing

Committee by 14 January 1942, for Torpex was mentioned at a meeting of the Bombing Committee on that date as being better at starting fires on merchant ships, although this was disputed. Also present was Air Vice Marshal Saundby of Bomber Command.[10] And experiments by the Road Research Laboratory in Richmond Park from 8 to 10 July 1942 showed that hexanite was much superior to amatol and even to Torpex in forming craters, although hexanite was ruled out for other reasons. However, it was noted that Torpex craters were some 76% larger than those caused by the same amount of amatol.[11]

The power of aluminised explosives in air was brought to light in a rather dramatic way. On 14 September 1943 the War Cabinet's Defence Committee (Operations), under the chairmanship of the Deputy Prime Minister (and future Prime Minister) Clement Atlee, discussed the German Long Range Rocket and its expected impact on London. Herbert Morrison, the Home Secretary and Minister of Home Security, had put before the Committee an estimate of the likely damage from the impact of the German Rocket, based upon a 2,500 kg German bomb which had fallen at Hendon on 12 February 1941. No warning had been given, and no warning of the rocket's arrival could be given, so the effect on casualties might have been thought to be comparable. But Lord Cherwell, the Paymaster General and, it will be remembered, Winston Churchill's scientific advisor, thought that the effects of the Hendon bomb had been exaggerated, since the serious damage caused by large British bombs was in the order of three acres (14,520 square yards) 'seriously affected' to the ton. However, a Ministry of Home Security report on the power of large British bombs, written in November 1943, gave the area of 'destruction' of a British 12,000 lb bomb filled with amatex (ammonium nitrate, TNT and RDX in the proportions 51/40/9) as a 'demolition' area of 9,100 square yards, an area of permanent evacuation of 21,000 square yards, an area of temporary evacuation of 50,000 square yards and an area of damage not causing evacuation of 235,000 square yards. The corresponding acres *per ton* (2,240 lbs) were 0.35, 0.8, 1.9 and 9. It is therefore only by including areas of damage which did not cause evacuation, which could hardly be classified as 'serious', that a figure of three acres per ton for the 12,000 lb bomb could be achieved, a curious discrepancy.[12] Even a Torpex-filled 12,000 lb bomb yielded figures of 0.5, 1.3, 3.2 and 15.3 acres per ton respectively. The 12,000 lb high capacity bomb was more destructive, per ton, than any bombs of lesser weight.

Lord Cherwell was asked on behalf of the Committee to undertake an enquiry into the apparent discrepancy between the power of German and British bombs, which he undertook to do on the understanding that he would establish facts, not apportion blame.[13] Lord Cherwell's enquiry established that German bombs were of greater power because, unlike British bombs, they were filled with aluminised explosive. A subsequent enquiry by Sir Walter Monckton, which was told to spend 'no large amount of time' and to complete in no more than three or four sittings, reported in February 1944 that the problem had, in the main, been caused by a failure of communication between departments responsible for strategy, for raw materials and for research. The departments concerned had, however, acted with 'zeal and energy'.

The fact that the Admiralty had produced Torpex and Minol, both acknowledged to be greatly superior to non aluminised explosives under water, had not suggested to the Static Detonations Committee (on which sat the Director of Armament Development (D.Arm.D.) of the MAP) that it might prioritise tests of its power in air or underground, nor had the memory of the still famous detonation of the nineteen huge mines which had blown the Messines Ridge skywards on 7 June 1917, each of which had contained ammonal, an aluminised explosive. The Committee had not prioritised experiments with aluminised explosive for the RAF because aluminium was in short supply. An experiment in June 1941 had not shown aluminium fillings to be superior in inflicting irreparable damage on a target. Given that Torpex was some 80% more powerful than amatol, it seems to say little for the experimental method. Later experiments would use piezo-electric gauges, but these were in short supply. Later, the results for Torpex and Minol were compared with a German mine which contained aluminised explosive. They were found by the Committee to be only half as effective. The Monckton report recognised that the test result was 'unreliable', due to the difference in the casing and in the shapes of the bombs.

But by November 1942 aluminised explosives were shown to be superior in air. A written report was considered by the Static Detonations Committee on 4 January, 1943. On 27 January the Static Detonations Committee made recommendations as to the most effective explosives for bombs. Aluminised explosive was omitted on the grounds that aluminium was not available. Tests continued, but were given low priority because of the shortage of aluminium. On 23 July 1943 a representative of Directorate of Armament Research informed the Static Detonations Committee that 20 tons of aluminium had become available, and that supply was easing.

On 6 August 1943 the Static Detonations Committee recommended that a full-scale trial be carried out 'as a matter of urgency'. Tests began at the end of September and were discussed by the Committee on 16

October 1943. Results showed 80–100% improvement over amatol. 'Meanwhile,' the Monckton report stated, 'Lord Cherwell had been informed unofficially by Dr Guy as to the way the tests were shaping.'

On 28 October the Scientific Advisory Council formally recommended the use of aluminised fillings for bombs, and bombs containing Minol were deposited upon Germany by the end of 1943. Churchill made perhaps the best epitaph on the affair by summarising the activities of the Static Detonations Committee as 'more static than detonating'.

Sir Charles Portal, Chief of the Air Staff, noted on 30 September 1943 that the bomber offensive 'is being heavily handicapped by inferior material'. In his *Despatch on War Operations*, Air Marshal Sir Arthur Travers Harris wrote in unusually measured words that 'In the middle of 1943, improved fillings became available for High Explosive bombs. ...No troubles were encountered with any of these fillings and their increased power over amatol fillings proved of great value...' Had that irascible and judgemental leader known of the true history of the matter – and of the close involvement of his *bête noir*, the Armament Department of the MAP – the letters might still, with not a little justice, glow with sarcastic fury; but there is, as Ecclesiastes tells us still, 'a time to every purpose under the heaven', and Sir Charles Portal well knew the 'time to keep silence'.

Whatever the efficiency of the Armament Department, Bomber Command was supported by high science in the shape of its own Operational Research Section, and above all, by the Ministry of Home Security. The beginnings of the latter were unobtrusive. In 1935 an Air Raid Precautions Department was formed, and in 1939 this became the nucleus of the Ministry of Home Security. Originating in the Home Office, a Research and Experiments Branch became the Research and Experiments Department of the Ministry of Home Security. Throughout the war the two ministries were under one head, the Home Secretary and Minister of Home Security, first Sir John Anderson and second, in 1940, Mr Herbert Morrison. The Research and Experiments Branch was formed to apply 'scientific enquiry to the many new problems arising out of the effects, on the life of the civil population, of air attacks'. One section dealt with 'fundamental research on the effects of high explosive weapons, blast, fragments and earth shock'.

'Theory, experiment and experience were gradually assembled to bring a rational understanding of the relation between weapon and effect.'[14] Examination of all the data from German raids was undertaken; the enemy bombs themselves were identified from a minute examination of their fragments and their blast effect. Traces of their explosive filling were analysed, and damage plots and casualty surveys made. The overall effects of the raids on 'morale, factory production, transport etc were examined in the department's social survey'. The Department then began to examine enemy structures on the basis of the knowledge gained from the German raids. They accumulated a very large knowledge of the material damage which could be expected from any type of bomb and bombing technique.

The mathematical work of the Research and Experiments Department enabled it to assist Bomber Command in many ways, liaising closely with Bomber Command's Operational Research Section, especially in the statistical methods used to calculate the weight of attacks necessary to achieve various probabilities of the destruction of a target, given certain levels of accuracy of bombing. *The History of the Research and Experiments Branch*, by AR Astbury, noted above, recounted the Department's trials of full sized British bombs, and contained the following comment:

> The Department collaborated with the services in many ways; thus, it supplied estimates of the effectiveness of the larger light case bombs (4,000 lb – 12,000 lb), and urged their use in area attacks. *Its early appreciation of the great blast damage done by German parachute mines made it an advocate of the early use of aluminised explosives.* [Italics added.]

In 1941 the Department provided Lord Cherwell with a thorough analysis of the effects of the German attacks on Hull and Birmingham, including damage done to industry both through direct damage and morale. They concluded that the greatest damage to morale arose from having your house destroyed by bombing. The experience of Harry Winter, recounted in the Appendix, may provide an example of another reaction altogether to being 'bombed out'! However, this led Lord Cherwell to his famous 'de-housing' memorandum to Churchill, which seemed to provide some scientific justification for the all out bomber offensive which had already begun. It would be strange if Professors Bernal and Zuckerman of the Research and Experiments Department of the Ministry of Home Security failed to convey the information to Lord Cherwell that German bombs were aluminised, and just as strange if Lord Cherwell did nothing about it – presuming, of course, that the 'early' appreciation of, and 'early' use of aluminised explosives meant before July 1943. The true facts behind this strange affair do not yet seem to be on record.

One lesson that *was* learned from the analysis of the German attacks was the great effectiveness of the German thin case blast bombs. It was realised that the use of the British General Purpose (GP) bomb, with its relatively thick case and low charge/weight ratio, was simply, in Cherwell's words, 'carrying scrap iron to Germany'. It was also shown by the Department that large bombs were, ton for ton, more effective than small bombs. This began a process of building larger and thinner walled bombs, the so-called medium capacity (MC) and high capacity (HC) bombs. By 1944, the use of bigger, thinwalled bombs filled with aluminised explosive had raised the destructive power of British bombs from the 2,500 square yards per ton of the amatol-filled GP 500 lb bomb with which Bomber Command started the war to the 9,500 square yards per ton for the Torpex-filled HC 12,000 lb bomb, an increase of 3.8 times. The 4,000 lb GP bomb containing amatol 60/40 would create an area of demolition of 870 square yards, and an area of permanent evacuation of 1,940 square yards. The 4,000 lb HC bomb filled with amatol created 3.7 times the demolition area, and 3.1 times the area of permanent evacuation. The 4,000 lb GP bomb contained some 27.1% filling (Type I) and 29.8% (Type II). The 4,000 lb MC carried 57.6% HE (high explosive), and the 4,000 lb HC 72.8%.

In June 1942, in consultation with the Air Staff, Department RE8 of the Ministry of Home Security was formed. It studied the application of British experience under air attack to assess the effects of Allied attacks on Germany, '…giving importance to the principal (sic) that improvement turns on scientific measurement'. The German attacks on Britain were coldly surveyed and analysed, not in a spirit of revenge or retaliation, but simply as a scientific enquiry, to see what lessons could be learned in the business of industrial damage by demolition and demoralisation. They displayed no sympathy even for British casualties, but simply observed the effects of bombing as coldly as they did on the unfortunate baboons upon whom the effects of blast were measured.[15]

As we have noted, these calculations revealed that factory absenteeism following raids was small, but was 'closely proportional to the proportion of buildings destroyed in a town'. There was no guarantee that German morale would be the same – but it was thought that, mathematically, 'the uniformity of the British response suggested that, whatever the German reaction was, it would not be, say, more than twice as much or half as much as the British, and certainly not ten times as much or ten times as little'.

It was necessary to measure the damage on Germany scientifically, and for this reason careful aerial and ground photos were taken of the British towns damaged, to establish precisely how damage on the ground related to the aerial photos, and how these should best be interpreted. It was found that the damage to industrial plants could be seen on the photos, and it was possible to distinguish between structural damage and mere damage to the roof. Housing damage was carefully categorised: Category 'A' – House demolished; Category 'B' – House partially demolished and having to be pulled down; Category 'Cb' – House damaged too severely to be habitable without major repairs; Category 'Ca' – House uninhabitable until minor repairs are carried out; Category 'D' – House habitable, but slight damage to roofs, windows etc.

'A' and 'B' damage could be distinguished from the air, but 'Cb' could not. However, the mathematicians discovered that ratios between 'A'+'B' damage and 'Cb' damage were constant for fire and high explosive attacks respectively. The fall of bombs of above 250 lb GP could be plotted on aerial photos, and damage to the utility distribution system could be related to the density of high explosive strikes per given density of streets. A standardised casualty rate was established for high explosive bombs of different sizes for a given population density. However, what could *not* be measured from British experience was the cumulative effect of *very* heavy attacks, where a very high proportion of the city or its industry were destroyed, since the cumulative effect was greater than a simple sum of the damage to each area.

The Department trained observers for the United States 8th USAAF in photographic interpretation, and maintained a close quality control check on both the 8th USAAF and Bomber Command interpreters. But 'improvement turns on scientific measurement', and the measure applied to both attacks on individual factories and area attacks was the 'man month' of industrial effort. Here, the 'total effects of an area attack were distributed among the industries represented in the town'. These effects, and the effects of USAAF attacks on individual industries, were then distributed over the subsidiary industries which made goods for, or replaced damage to, the individual industry attacked.

Department RE8 also examined the effects of the weapons used, and the resistance of the targets. The effects of incendiary attack were carefully noted, and the 'general principles of the vulnerability of targets to incendiary bombs emerged'.

This information led to a pre raid study of targets. From photographs of the city a 'Structural Intelligence Group' studied the relationship between buildings' dimensions and roof shapes seen on aerial photographs so that the construction type and strength of the buildings could be assessed. A 'Target Vulnerability Note' was then prepared, detailing the most effective bombs to be used in the attack, and what result might be expected.

In order to 'predict the extent of damage, and to compare the effectiveness of different kinds of HE weapon and to compare the powers of resistance of different kinds of structure it is necessary to employ the concept of vulnerable area', wrote F David and F Garwood,[16] noting that 'similar considerations apply to the damaging of service mains (gas, water and electricity)'. They drew attention to the 'elegant' paper by LBC Cunningham on the concept; it has already been noted that Dr Cunningham's recommendation, using the concept of 'vulnerable area', on the use of 20 mm cannon for aircraft *defence* had not been thought elegant, if it was even noted, by the Armament gurus.

Department RE8 noted, after inspecting the German cities attacked, that huge bunker shelters, housing some 4,000 people, were constructed – but that after 1942 'shortage of labour and materials' cut short the building programme. They also noted that 'the State did not undertake the provision of dispersed shelter for the population at large'. This was, of course, an option, a conscious decision of the German authorities that guns came not only before butter, but before the safety of the civil population. This should be borne in mind when the cost of underground factories, particularly those that were constructed to make the 'V' weapons with slave labour, is considered.

The Department worked closely in conjunction with the Operational Research Section of Bomber Command, which was staffed by civilian scientists. Together, they worked out a technique of 'Raid Analysis and Forward Planning'.[17] For raid analysis, data was obtained from Photo Reconnaissance pictures of craters, and photographs taken at the time of bombing.

Craters were difficult to plot, due to variations in the ground type, or the presence of water. If more than one high explosive bomb was released from a bomber, craters would tend to show an elongated pattern along the track of the bomber. With pictures taken at the time of bombing, the camera was set up to take a photograph of where the first bomb would have fallen; at night, the frame was exposed for four seconds, and a flash bomb was dropped at the same time – thus, the bombs were still in flight when the picture was taken. Errors resulted from the aircraft being banked over at the time of release, and also, perhaps, being at the wrong height.

When the series of dots that represented the fall of the bombs was finally established, the statisticians got to work. Immediately, a proportion of the dots was excluded as 'gross errors'. Then a mean point of impact (MPI), the arithmetical centre of the points, was established. The distance of the MPI from the aiming point (AP) was called the systematic error. The measure of the scatter of bombs about the MPI was called the random error. However, an added difficulty in calculating these errors was that as marker bombs burned out, others were dropped, and so the AP changed during a raid. If the distribution of the dots was roughly circular, it was possible to draw a circle round the 50% nearest to the MPI, and the radius of this circle was the 'probable radial error'. The most useful figure to the planners, however, was the 'radial standard error', which was the square root of the mean of the squares of the radial distances. In practice, the random and systematic errors and radial standard errors were averaged out over a series of similar raids, so that a fairly reliable figure could be gained.

This figure was then used in the forward planning of raids, enabling the number of bombs required to achieve a certain density per acre to be calculated with varying degrees of probability. The result was indicative of the huge penalty for inaccuracy, which was much larger than common sense might suggest. Thus to achieve a 75% chance of unit density per acre at the aiming point, with a radial standard error of 400 yards, 400 bombs were required. With an error of 600 yards, 960 were required.

As an example of what this meant in practice, Harris, in June 1944, wrote to the Air Ministry[18] listing ten oil targets in the Ruhr, varying from a size of 45 acres (Dortmund) to 270 acres (Sterkrade-Holten). It was calculated that 0.75 tons per acre would be necessary to disable these heavily defended targets, which totalled 1,350 acres. It was calculated that even with the accuracy provided by blind bombing aids, 32,250 tons of bombs would be necessary to achieve this (it would have been less if the targets could have been marked from low level).

It might be thought, therefore, that given the central doctrine of the relentless offensive, and given the heavy penalty which large aiming errors gave, that in its first twenty-one years the RAF would have devoted a large effort to navigation and bombing accuracy. However, the problems involved in bomb aiming and target identification did not really become evident until the advent of the high-speed monoplane. Navigation itself was not a high priority – in January 1933, of 1,346 officers between the ranks of flight lieutenant and group captain, only thirty-eight had passed an ordinary specialist course in navigation.[19] In 1934 it was confessed by the officer in charge of the Air Defence of Great Britain that the bomber's ability to fly by night in all weathers 'compared unfavourably with Lufthansa', who operated a service between Cologne and Croydon.[20]

In January 1937 Group Captain MacLean, who we have already met in connection with bomber defence, wrote a paper on 'The Problem of Bombing at High Speeds'. His conclusion was that '…even under conditions of maximum visibility on the clearest days bombing anything but an area target would be an impossibility, while in conditions of poor visibility, and at night, the problem becomes completely impossible'.

On 1 April 1938 the AOC No. 2 Group pointed out that the fall times of bombs released when the aircraft was travelling at 200 mph was 37 seconds at 20,000 feet, which meant that the bomb must be *released* $1^7/_8$ miles from the target. Added to this, since one minute was required for a run up to the target, the minimum distance from the target at which it must be identified was $5^1/_4$ miles.

To some, the answer to the problem created by the airspeed of the bomber lay in killing the forward speed of the bomb, either by a parachute or by some form of rocket, so that the bombs could be released directly over the target (Harris pointed out that this would solve the problem of the AA gunners!).

On 28 March 1939 Sir Edgar Ludlow-Hewitt chaired a conference at Bomber Command HQ. Present were Watson-Watt and Air Vice Marshal Sholto Douglas. The former introduced an idea, that not only could terrain tracking radar differentiate between land and sea as an aid to navigation, but might be able to distinguish between agricultural and industrial areas. Radio direction finding (RDF) was also suggested as a means of navigation, and this would bear much fruit later. It will be remembered that Sir Henry Tizard thought that the real criterion of bombing was the number of bombs on target per bomber casualty. One side of the ratio, the question of bomber defence, was only 'solved' by the banishment of the bomber to the night sky, where it was inaccurate. But the other side was all but solved in the mind of a genius, a committed pacifist; but before introducing Alec Reeves, we must return to 1939, and to see Ludlow-Hewitt's fears fully borne out.

Between 25 and 28 July 1939 Sir Henry Tizard visited stations in Bomber Command to see if he could provide assistance in solving problems. Tizard thought that navigation by sextant observation should enable an aircraft to approach within ten to fifteen miles of a target, but saw that 'no one could guarantee finding an objective unless they could see the ground and pin point their position'. He foresaw the need for RDF to assist in navigation, and also the need for a gyro stabilised automatic bombsight, although he preferred low level bombing for accuracy [for which Ludlow-Hewitt wanted the speed bomber], high level bombing being too long and too expensive in bombs – although he recognised that in low level attacks the bombs might not have sufficient velocity to penetrate their targets. He pointed out, however, that 'at present night bombing of selected targets is hopeless', although it was generally felt that 'self illuminating' targets, such as blast furnaces, might be located and attacked at night.

But as has been seen, night bombing became the only recourse of Bomber Command after the heavy losses experienced in bombing the German Navy, and in the Norwegian and French campaigns. When the bombing of specific targets at night was found to be all but impossible –

an aiming error of 300 yards was expected and, it was very over optimistically thought, 1,000 yards achieved – area bombing began. But even this was hopelessly inaccurate – Lord Cherwell, closely in touch with the situation and also closely in touch with the Ministry of Home Security – induced the War Cabinet to investigate, and the Butt Report was produced in August 1941. This concluded that'…of all the aircraft recorded as having attacked their targets, only one third had got within five miles of them'.[21] Over the French ports, two thirds were within five miles. Over the Ruhr, with its heavy defences and industrial haze, this reduced to one tenth within five miles. In full moon (when losses to fighters were more likely to spoil Tizard's ratio) two fifths of the aircraft reporting that they had found and attacked the target were within five miles. With no moon, when they were safer, only one fifteenth were within five miles. Once again Sir Edgar Ludlow-Hewitt had been correct, although he seems to have been blamed partly for the inaccuracy, and partly for continually pointing out its likelihood.

But the scientists were now mobilised, and the first of the radio aids to navigation was introduced. Called 'Gee', derived from 'grid', it was first thought of by Robert Dippy, a Government scientist, in 1937, but due to the concentration on the defensive use of radar at the time, it received little attention until 1940.[22] It consisted of a pulsed radio signal from a 'master' ground station and two 'slave' stations, which were transmitted into the night. On board the aircraft, the signals from each source were received and displayed on a cathode ray tube, which showed the differences in the receipt times of the signals. From this the relative distances of each of the slave stations from the master was calculated, each distance giving a range of possible locations which were plotted onto a grid as a hyperbola. The intersection of the two hyperbolas gave the aircraft's position.[23] It was realised by Bomber Command that the system would eventually be jammed by the Germans, although even when it was, it provided a useful service for bombers over the North Sea and the French coast, and for bombers returning from Germany.

The first jamming of 'Gee' on 4 August 1942 left night navigation once again inaccurate – but now the idea of Alec Reeves entered the stage. Alec Reeves[24] was born in 1902. He attended Reigate Grammar School, won a scholarship to the City and Guilds Engineering College and, in 1921, entered Imperial College. On graduation he joined International Western Electric, and stayed with the company for fifty years. Reeves was described by Frank Metcalfe, a former bomber pilot, as 'a lovely, lovely dreamy man' with 'an inventive mind, and you felt it when you were in his presence'. His method of solving a problem was to relax, 'ruminate for a time', and then let ideas come into his mind, until 'an exciting moment, one of intense intellectual pleasure' – and a solution occurred.[25]

Reeves was interested in all aspects and properties of the brain, including telekinesis, telepathy and communication with the dead, feeling that he was guided on occasion by Michael Faraday. Certainly, by whatever inspiration, Alec Reeves had an extraordinarily powerful mind. His formulation – in 1937 – of the principles of pulse code modulation laid 'the foundations for all of today's digital and multimedia technologies'.[26] Electronic switching systems, semi conductors, even the use of light to carry information, were all aided and seeded by him.

The impact of Reeves' ruminations on blind bombing – navigating to by night, and hitting, unseen targets – was to be felt throughout Bomber Command, and throughout Germany. Reeves' system was called 'Oboe' from the noise of the main transmission. In Oboe there were two ground tracking stations, a 'cat' and a 'mouse'. Each sent radio pulses towards the Oboe-equipped aeroplane. A receiver in the aeroplane amplified the pulses and returned them to the ground stations. This enabled the precise distance between the aeroplane and the tracking stations to be calculated. When the aeroplane was at the same distance from the tracking station as the target was, this distance was precisely maintained, the pilot receiving dashes from the cat station if he was too far away, and dots if he strayed too near. On course, a continuous signal was received. The aeroplane therefore flew in an arc, which would pass exactly over the target, whose position had been ascertained from a careful study of maps and a precise alignment of their grids. The 'mouse' station calculated just how far down the arc the aeroplane had travelled, since it received both the 'cat' station's signals and its own from the aircraft. When the bomber was ten, eight, six and three minutes from the target the 'mouse' would send the letters 'A', 'B', 'C' and 'D' respectively, and would signal the precise moment for bomb release, allowing for wind, height and speed, so that ideally the bomb would fall precisely on the target. It was this system which enabled the bombers to hit the ten Ruhr oil plants with some accuracy.

The system had some weaknesses. Firstly, the Oboe-equipped aeroplane had to fly in a direct line with the transmitter stations, and due to the curvature of the earth, this limited the range. The effect of this limitation was mitigated to some extent by the use of the Mosquito bomber, which flew at some 28,000 feet and could therefore reach the Ruhr. The use of Mosquitos also, because of their great speed, reduced the extra risk from night fighters which was incurred in flying along such a predictable path.

The second limitation was that only one aeroplane at a time could be so controlled. This could be obviated by the aircraft bombing together, or by the use of target marker bombs, at which the following heavies would take visual aim. This latter method became the norm; with the formation of the Pathfinder Force (PFF), which was strongly opposed by Harris (he wanted each Group to create their own Pathfinders to avoid the creation of an elite), came great accuracy – but with the limitations of range. The marking of the target by Mosquitos, whether by ground markers or, in dense cloud, by sky markers, would be aimed at by the heavies, following a set line of approach. Markers were also placed along the route to mark turning points, although these were, as has been noted, used by German night fighters to infiltrate the bomber stream.

To overcome the limitations of range with 'Gee' and Oboe, a downward-looking centimetric radar code-named H2S was devised. This could enable a skilled operator to distinguish built up areas and coasts, estuaries and broad rivers and, independent of range, also aided in navigation. However, it has already been noted that the German fighters carried a tracking device, called Naxos, which enabled them to follow aircraft with H2S radar systems turned on, and when this was discovered eventually, the sets were switched off until fifty miles from the target.

The limitation on the number of aircraft that could use Oboe was also solved, to an extent, by using a system that Harris called 'Oboe in reverse',[27] the aircraft transmitting first to two ground stations, which re-transmitted the signals back to the aircraft.

A further system, with a range of 1,400 miles, was called 'Loran'. This used a 'Gee' type system with a much lower frequency – but it was easily jammed.

The use of these systems gave Bomber Command a fair amount of accuracy, and were a vast improvement on the old systems. However, as has been noted, even an error of 600 yards requires a very large number of bombs to be dropped to achieve a great likelihood of just one per acre over the target area. It was this central fact, even in 1944 and 1945, that provided area bombing with its rationale, for a miss would still hit other targets in a city. This was 'precise bombing of an area target', as against 'area bombing of a precise target'. The effect on the city was often little different.

By July 1944 the Research and Experiments Department, after contacting the Operational Research Sections of the various commands, came up with the following levels of accuracy, giving three percentages of bombs falling in circles of 500 feet, 500–1,000 feet, and 1,000–1,500 feet of the aiming point respectively.

For Bomber Command at night, at a height of 12,000 feet, the figures were 8%, 21% and 46% respectively. For the United States 8th USAAF, at 18,000 feet, the figures were 15%, 23% and 48%. For medium bombers, by day, they were 22%, 30% and 42%. Dive bombing, at 4,000 feet, achieved 26%, 45% and 28%. Proving Tizard's point about low level bombing were the fighter-bombers, at minimum altitude, with 87% and 13%, which the US 9th USAAF claimed was still improving.[28]

But the most destructive weapon of all was an area weapon, the incendiary bomb, for it could start devastating fires, causing the incineration of everything in whole areas of a city, destroying its houses, its factories and its utilities while cremating or asphyxiating its inhabitants.

The complex science of burning down cities consists mainly of chemistry, of aerodynamics and of statistics. Great minds were harnessed to achieve this destruction but, as with the defence of the bomber, little energy seems to have emanated from the Air Ministry and the Armament Department at the MAP. As in blast bombs, the Ministry of Home Security was closely involved in the mathematics and in the science, although the early work was carried out by the Civil Defence Research Committee.

In 1935 an Incendiary Bombs Committee was set up under the Home Office, concerned with methods of defence against incendiary bomb attacks. They distinguished three types of incendiary bomb – single effect, where the bomb rested on inflammable material; multiple effect, by the expulsion of incendiary units; and oil or phosphorus bombs, whose liquid contents caused an effect somewhere between the two.

Tests at the Research Department at Woolwich listed the calorific value of each incendiary material. Magnesium (780 calories/gram) burnt quietly at a temperature of 1,100 degrees centigrade, radiating much heat, for approximately ten minutes, but produced very little flame. Thermite (780 calories/gram), a mixture of aluminium and iron oxide, burnt independently of the air supply, at a temperature between 2,000 and 3000 degrees. The molten iron 'ensured good contact with the underlying materials'.[29] Thermalloy (770 calories/gram) was similar to thermite, but contained 25% sulphur, and burnt with a large, hot flame, hindering inconsiderate attempts to extinguish it by the sulphur dioxide which the combustion produced. Oil (11,000 calories/gram) relied on its flames for igniting materials. Phosphorus and carbon disulphide (5,700 and 3,250 calories/gram respectively) was not as efficient an incendiary agent as oil, but when put out, re-ignited. They also produced gases which rendered approach difficult.

Tests in 1937 showed the great value of the 2 kg magnesium bomb. By 1939, experiments were taking place at the Forest Products Research

Laboratory at Princes Risborough (where Department RE8 was eventually located) and here the emphasis changed to initiating, rather than extinguishing a fire. From this time onward many learned papers were written, and the advantages and disadvantages of the various incendiary materials were analysed.

The Ministry of Home Security scientists prepared maps of the principal German cities, carefully classifying each into five areas according to the relative combustibility of each. Zone 1, the city centre, would contain old buildings closely packed together, with narrow streets. Most of the roofs would be penetrated by the 4 lb incendiary bomb, the classic British weapon of the Second World War, which consisted of a magnesium body filled with thermite, although variants would explode to discourage attention from firefighters. Zones 2a and 2b, inner and outer residential areas, were at moderate risk of incineration in Zone 2a, but slight risk in Zone 2b. In Zone 3, the suburban area, the risk of fire was negligible. Zones 4 and 5, industrial areas and communications network, were not considered suitable for incendiary attack.

The mathematics for the destruction of Zones 1 and 2 was formulated, using the estimated number of fire appliances per square mile, the number of bombs falling and the time required to start fires. The relative efficiencies of the 4 lb magnesium/thermite and 30 lb phosphorus gel bombs were calculated for each area, and the number of bombs required determined. This was found to be 'surprisingly small'.[30] About 10 tons per square mile were needed to ignite Zones 1 and 2a. Over 100 tons per square mile were required for Zones 2a and 3, although these figures depended, of course, on the number of appliances and firefighters available.

The real value of incendiary attack had been demonstrated by the Germans in a raid on Southampton. Writing to Harris on 21 March 1942 the Director of Bombing Operations at the Air Ministry quoted from the minutes of a meeting on 6 December 1941, at which Harris had been chairman:

> Before the meeting dispersed, the chairman commented on the recent concentrated attack on Southampton, on which thousands of incendiaries were dropped which effectively ignited and gutted an extensive area. The meeting agreed that in any operations of a similar type which we undertook in Germany (eg the Ruhr) we should also use incendiaries extensively.

The Director went on to comment to Harris that:

> This was the starting point of our investigations into incendiary attacks…Thanks to the decisions taken at your instigation…and to the pressure we have kept up since, there are now ample incendiary bombs, both of the 4 lb and 30 lb types, for continuous operations on a maximum scale at least during the effective life of TR1335 ['Gee'].

Undoubtedly, the two most effective incendiary bombs were the 4 lb magnesium/thermite[31] and the 30 lb phosphorus/rubber/benzol gel bomb. The first had been designed as an incendiary, the second was an improvisation, an old type of gas bomb body now refilled.

The 4 lb incendiary bomb was dropped over Germany in huge quantities. Production had been 200,000 a month in 1940, but after the example given by the German incendiaries, 12 million were ordered for the period 1 April 1941 to the end of December 1941. Later, production was planned to increase to 3 million *per month* by 1942 and 6 million per month by 1943, the only real difficulty being the supply of magnesium. In 1941 2.2 million were produced; in 1942 it rose to 11.8 million, in 1943 to 35.8 million (in addition to 4.5 million from the United States, which were worthless due to a relaxation of the specification) and in 1944 to 35.5 million, which figure did not include further supplies from the United States.

The reader might wonder how it was that 85 million 4 lb incendiaries, cast onto German cities in addition to all the other types and to high explosive bombs, failed to win the war. The answer seems to lie in aerodynamics and in what can only be described as a poor sense of priorities and an infuriating lack of energy from the Air Ministry and the MAP's Directorate of Armament Development.

The 4 lb incendiary bomb was stored in the aircraft and dropped in small bomb containers (SBC), which shed their load immediately. With bombers stacked in layers over the target to make things difficult for the flak, and with thousands upon thousands of 4 lb incendiaries littering the sky, it is small wonder that some bombers were hit and destroyed by incendiaries shed from above. Any real accuracy was impossible. The answer, of course, was to cluster the bombs so that they all fell together to a certain height, and then parted company.

The first 4 lb incendiary cluster was a bundle type, bombs being bundled together and a nose and tail fitted. Later, bombs were packed into cylinders and either ejected through the nose or the tail. The disintegration of the cluster was effected by either a time, or a barometric, fuse. Two conflicting elements were revealed; if the cluster opened high up, the bombs were spread too widely. If it opened too low down, the bombs would have too low a terminal velocity, and might not penetrate a roof. They were also more likely to fail due to the bomb not striking correctly, as at too low a level they had less time to correct any oscillation.

But even without clustering, the 4 lb and the 30 lb incendiary could have a catastrophic effect when dropped from a low level and therefore *concentrated* onto the right target. On 28 March 1942, and between 23 and 26 April 1942, Lubeck and Rostock respectively were devastated by fire raids. At Lubeck some aircraft, because of the light defences, were able to attack from just 2,000 feet.

On 27 April Freeman wrote to Harris, commenting that Lubeck got 45,080 4 lb incendiaries on target, while Rostock got nothing like as much. 'The moral seems to be', he wrote, 'that unless the incendiary attack is on a large scale and concentrated in time it will not achieve any decisive degree of destruction'. Freeman had concluded from the raids that all-incendiary attacks should be carried out. Harris was not convinced. He replied on 29 April that Lubeck was built 'more like a firelighter than a human habitation' 'I feared all along', he went on, 'that the incendiary properties of Lubeck would tend to disappointed reaction by the bloodthirsty on subsequent occasions in other towns'. Not that Harris was less 'bloodthirsty' – he felt that the benefit of one third high explosive was 'to bring the masonry down on the Boche, to kill Boche, and to terrify Boche...'

On 10 May the Director of Bomber Operations disagreed, suggesting that '100,000 incendiaries on Cologne in one night is ten times more effective that 25,000 on four nights'.

With so much belief in, and concentration on, incendiary attack in the Air Ministry, in an offensive which was the British Empire's main war effort for many years, it might therefore be of some surprise to the reader to find Harris, at the end of the war, writing the following to the Vice Chief of the Air Staff (Sir Douglas Evill):

> As you realise, the unaimability of the unclustered 4 lb incendiary has operated very largely in discount of our industrial area attacks. Had they been properly clustered from the start we should have been very much further along our road today. Furthermore, the continued use over so long a period of unclustered 4 lb incendiaries dropped from SBC containers has resulted in serious losses of aircraft, both from direct damage and as casualties in repeat attacks which would not all have been necessary.
>
> For reasons well known to you [Sir Douglas Evill had, it will be remembered, served in Bomber Command before the war] it is not

possible for everybody to bomb on the same level. Aircraft below are in serious jeopardy from showers of loose incendiaries dropped from SBCs. There have been a large number of cases of aircraft returning heavily damaged by such means and in consequence incontrovertible proof that a considerable number of aircraft and crews have been lost, from the same cause. Had the clusters been made available – and nothing will convince me that they could not have been available two years or more ago – the majority of these losses would not have occurred, because the risk from clustered incendiaries as opposed to incendiaries dropped loosely in thousands is negligible.

I consider that the procrastinations and incredible technical incompetence evidenced by the story of the 4 lb incendiary cluster is such as to call for the most serious and immediate action. I hope therefore that you will take steps to have it enquired into.

The urgent necessity now is to get some real drive behind the provision of an adequate supply of efficient clusters and travelling crates and I suggest to examine into whether the existing personnel who dealt with the matter in the past, and thereby show such extraordinary incompetence, are fit to undertake the task and whether they should be changed or strengthened by the addition of other technicians.

I mentioned to you also that we have just discovered that even those clusters which we now have at the stations ...have been found to be very largely unserviceable. Group estimates go up to 75%. This unserviceability is from two causes, firstly damage in transit and during handling on the aircraft, and still more so if the aircraft have to be de-bombed as frequently happens when we get ad-hoc urgent targets or weather necessitates changing the load; secondly, owing to damp getting into the clusters and affecting the fusing and cluster bursting mechanism.[32]

With this letter Harris sent a précis of Bomber Command's correspondence with the Air Ministry on clusters for the 4 lb incendiary, listing fifteen letters from Bomber Command and the replies. His original statement that 'In order to bomb accurately with the 4 lb incendiary bomb it is essential that bombs be clustered' was made on 20 July 1942. The reply from the Air Ministry came on 30 October 1942 and said that 'every effort' was being made. The reader may wonder if $3^1/_2$ years to fail to produce an 'urgent operational requirement' was justified by the relative complexity of the problem and its importance to the planned demolition of German industrial cities.

Fuelling Harris' sense of outrage was the development by the Armament Department of the MAP of the 30 lb 'J' type incendiary bomb, and their persistence despite reports of its poor performance from Bomber Command, and their increasingly obvious favouring of this bomb over the 30 lb phosphorus/petrol incendiary and the 4 lb magnesium/thermite bomb. The 'J' bomb had a steel case containing a mixture of petrol and methane under a pressure of 90–110 psi, and an inner steel tube filled with thermite.[33] The 'J' stood for 'jet', and the bomb was designed to send out a jet of flame some 15 feet in length by 2 feet wide from a nozzle which was intended to be flexible and therefore to sweep around. This proposal was found to be impracticable, and a rigid nozzle necessary.[34] It had already been shown in experiments at Leeds University and at Imperial College London that a butane bomb, which also sent out a jet of flame, had not ignited wood, since 'a powerful jet of flame …prevents a liberal supply of air coming into contact with the wood on which the jet plays, and this is another [with the charring of the wood] factor unfavourable to continuous burning…'[35] The bomb was developed by a private company, Messrs Worssam, in conjunction with the Director of Armament Development. The development of this bomb did not cease until Japan surrendered in August 1945. The cluster worked satisfactorily.[36] In his *Despatch on War Operations*[37] Harris wrote that 'The sorry story of this bomb points a moral anent enthusiastic protagonists of a theoretical weapon being allowed to override the opinion and advice of the operational user'.

Harris was not alone in his criticisms of the Directorate of Armament Development. Air Vice Marshal Bennett wrote to Harris on 29 July 1943.[38]

… My first point is to register a formal protest against the attitude of the officer holding the appointment of DarmD … the PFF [Pathfinder Force] section of RDArm8 was created as a result of an instruction issued by the Secretary of State and Chief of the Air Staff at your request shortly after the creation of the PFF. Its duty was to provide a means of marking aiming points, landmarks and release points in sufficient clarity and variety to overcome the possibility of the enemy copying our marking methods. This section has worked extremely well on the development of suitable markers, and has in fact achieved considerable success. Its work, on the other hand, has at all times been severely handicapped by the attitude of the head of the Directorate. He has failed to give them the support they required either from the administrative point of view or in dealing with others. He is openly derisive of the PFF and the work of the PFF sections. I realise that it may appear in the normal service procedure to be somewhat irregular to name an officer in another Ministry for inefficiency or conduct to the prejudice of the war effort, but I feel certain that in the interests of a early victory no petty qualms or hidebound procedures can be tolerated. I do, therefore, urgently request that the attitude of the officer mentioned towards the requirements of the PFF should be investigated by his superior officer.

These, then, were the systems and weapons with which the highly vulnerable bombers were armed and sent out over Germany. The limitations imposed both by the complete superiority of the fighter and the deficiency of the armament were considerable.[39] They were summed up by Harris in a letter to Sir Charles Portal of 16 June 1943, in an unsolicited comment on why 'particular targets were selected on particular occasions'. First of all, wrote Harris, the short nights and the northern twilight limited his targets to:

Emden, the Ruhr as far as Dortmund, and the Rhine as far as Bonn…

When it comes to the selection of particular targets in any such area this is normally governed by the combination of weather and available navigational aid factors. For instance, on a clear night when one can employ ground marking technique it is best to go for the most valuable target on which the heaviest concentration is required. The ground marking techniques as you know provide great accuracy on a cloudy night where air marking technique has to be employed it is best to go for a scattered area target or a very large town because, owing to the influence of wind, the concentration when using sky-marking technique is never so good. Sometimes, if the wind is, say, upward of 60 mph, it is only worthwhile going over the widest areas wherever a very scattered raid is likely to do worth while damage on a type of target which in any event is not highly profitable for an over concentrated raid…

In addition, within the limitations of the available radius as dictated by the hours of darkness, it is most essential to spread attack over a given area as widely as possible otherwise, as we have found to our cost, the enemy quickly concentrates his defences.

It is also for this reason, to force the enemy to keep his defences spread, that we occasionally bump off such a place as Wuppertal, and I have no doubt that the effect of that attack will have been to set Solingen, Remscheid, Hagen and similar second class targets shouting for protection, because at Wuppertal there were practically no defences…

Harris went on to say that the characteristics of the bombing aids themselves affected the targets chosen. H2S, being never precise, was used against an isolated, compact target, eg against a large city like Berlin the suburbs showed up more clearly then the centre.

Eventually, the debate on Harris and bombing would be haunted by the oil controversy – Portal trying to persuade Harris to accept that oil was a prime target, and Harris saying that he would obey instructions to make it so, but without believing in it. It is presumed by many that Harris only wanted area targets, perhaps because he was simply bloodthirsty! However, Sebastian Cox's comments in his introduction to the *Despatch* exonerate Harris to a large extent. Harris is sometimes thought to have been ignorant of the value of the information sources on oil, and Portal suspected of hiding those sources from him because it 'would not have been the first time when possession of highly classified knowledge gave personal sense of power over others…'[40]

However, on 8 January 1945 Portal wrote to Harris with the comment that '… I am sending you also a dossier of "ultra" information on the same subject covering the period from May to December…' Although, of course, this indicates that Portal thought that Harris had not actually seen these already, and was therefore not automatically 'on the list', it also shows from the fact that Portal launched into his 'ultra' comment without any prior explanation, that Harris knew of 'ultra'. 'Ultra', of course, was the best kept secret of the war, the cracking of the German codes by a team at Bletchley park led by Alan Turing,[41] a mathematical genius and the man who did more then anyone to devise the world's first programmable electronic computer, which was used to decipher the German 'Enigma' codes. To have revealed to the Germans that their codes had been cracked would have perhaps been the biggest disaster possible, since it has been estimated that the possession of this secret shortened the war by eighteen months. It is strange that Harris did not ask for information on the result of his area attacks from this source – perhaps he did. 'Ultra' was top secret for thirty years after the war.

Perhaps Harris also felt that his men were – again – being asked to risk their lives while the Army was being conserved. In a letter to Robert Lovett, United States Secretary of State for Air, on 24 November 1944 he wrote:

> … Do you know that Bomber Command has had more men killed in bombing Germany and enemy occupied countries then the whole of the British, Dutch, French, Belgian, Czech and Polish invasion armies since D-Day, to end October? And more than the whole British Army since the battle of Alamein inclusive, and more than the whole US

Army in France. That does not include the rest of the RAF or the whole *of the US Air Forces*. Who the hell is fighting this war anyway and who in particular fights the 'navy' war in the Pacific? … It was the air which gave the armies their walk over in France – at cost in casualties less than the first day of last war's Battle of the Somme… but above all we have shown the Boche at home for the first time what war is and what it feels like…[42]

The campaign waged by Bomber Command in the Second World War was a transitional stage between the old style clash of armies and navies and the modern 'push button' warfare of scientists and technicians, waged indiscriminately against the state as an entity, and therefore against individuals of all opinions, culpability, sex and age. The aircrew were the link with the past, fighting in the old way with courage and meeting death and facing danger in conjunction with their fellow aircrew in the USAAF on a scale unique in the war in the west, enduring casualties proportionally greater than any other force save the German submarine service. Their so doing saved the Army from a similar effort, an effort which it simply could not have carried out. They were the inheritors of the doctrine, and waged a type of war which their enemy had shown to be a means of victory, if pursued to the limit. They waged it despite a lack of energy or of initiative from those concerned with the minutiae of bomber defence or offence, from the theorists to the Armament Department. Although their shield was always defective, their sword was sharpened by the scientists until it gave the enemy the 'death of a thousand cuts'.

The scientists simply looked at how problems of victory were to be overcome by scientific method. Thus was warfare shorn of all glory and reduced to mathematical calculation. When the time came to plan attacks against Japan, the Research and Experiments Department, unaffected by the cruelties of Japanese soldiers or the innocence of their women and children, could calculate that:[43]

B29 (Super-Fortresses) carrying M69 (6 lb) incendiary bombs…have been successful, that is, have gutted compact areas of several square miles, only when the average density on the ground over the area burnt out has been at least 75 tons per square mile.

It may be hoped that it will be possible on occasion to reduce this density…the most densely built up areas have already been burnt out…75 tons of 4 lb incendiaries per square mile of German cities have, on the average, burnt out 55% of the houses, and serious damage may have extended to 70%. The fire return on Japanese cities has therefore been better…

It is by no means clear that the destruction of dwellings, in Japan or elsewhere, has a serious effect on war production; at the least, it seems desirable to couple it with casualties. We can offer no estimate of casualties in incendiary raids on Japan. Even for high explosive raids, estimates for Japan must be very rough; but they are likely to be of the following order.

Standardized casualty rates (killed and seriously injured) per ton of aluminised blast bombs have been, during this war

17.5 in British houses,
62 in the open;

giving, when 15% of people are in the open (the usual British experience), an overall standardized casualty rate of 24. These casualty rates are calculated at a density of population of 44 to the acre. In the areas of Japanese cities considered, the population density is presumably nearer that of, say, Bethnal Green, i.e. over 100 per acre. A density factor of 2 is therefore probably conservative. Allowing for overhitting, 75 tons of large blast bombs per square mile would then give, per square mile, roughly

1, 500 killed
2,000 seriously injured,
and 4,000 other injured…

The estimates of damage and casualties have been made for bombs fuzed instantaneous. An efficient proximity fuze would be expected to double alike the mean area of effectiveness and the standardized casualty rate: that is, it would be expected to give the same damage and casualties with less than 40 tons per square mile, in place of 75 tons. If such a fuze was available, there is therefore no doubt that high explosive attack would be more profitable than incendiary attack. Certainly this is the ideal opportunity for testing the effect of proximity fuzing in operation…

We conclude that there is a strong case for planning pure high-explosive raids on Japanese cities. At 75 tons per square mile of 4,000 lb or larger H.C. bombs with aluminized fillings, such raids would in effect be as profitable as present incendiary raids, or future raids against a target progressively less fire-vulnerable. Returns in damage and casualties would be high, and little affected by the hazards of incendiary attack – building density, weather etc. With a good proximity fuze, the required density might be reduced to 40 tons per square mile, markedly below the density of successful incendiary attack. This opportunity for testing proximity fuzing in operations should be taken.

The language is one of homely prudence, with its use of 'returns' and 'profitable'; and the 'hazards of incendiary attack' are not the possibility of the incineration of people, but unfavourable weather that might put the fire out, or property that might not burn well. This is the way modern scientific wars are won. Few, however, even among those horrified by such cold terms or enemy civilian casualties, would volunteer to risk being drowned in mud, or blinded, or bayoneted, or shot through the face, or blown to pieces, or made paraplegic, or have their unwilling sons or brothers or fathers or husbands dragged to the slaughter, or die in agony in a prisoner of war camp, in order to attempt to gain a by no means certain military advantage over enemy troops (who rejoiced in combat) which might be better secured by more scientific methods. In Britain, they did not have to suffer so in any great numbers, for the aircrew of Bomber Command suffered for them, in actions mostly hidden and unrecorded, plunging from the dark skies over Hitler's realm 'like glistering Phaethon, wanting the manage of unruly jades...'

But before the cock of victory finally crowed they were denied by Churchill, the chief disciple of the relentless offensive.[44]

Notes

1 In PRO HO/191/203.
2 Avia15/3695.
3 PRO Avia46/285.
4 PRO CAB102/108, *Bombs; Their Design, Development and Production During and In the Years Immediately Preceding the 1939–1945 War* by Miss D McKenna.
5 RAF H51.
6 JBS Haldane, *Callinicus – A Defence of Chemical Weapons*, Kegan Paul, Trench, Trubner & Co. Ltd, London, 1925, 14–15.
7 PRO Avia46/285.
8 GI Brown, *A History of Explosives*, Sutton Publishing, Stroud, 1998, 164.
9 Minol 1 was 48/42/10, Torpex 1 45/37/18, see MOHS file on PRO HO191/191.
10 PRO Air16/302.
11 PRO HO195/13.
12 PRO HO191/191.
13 PRO Air8/811.
14 PRO HO191/203.
15 And yet scientists always seem to presume that creatures more developed and intelligent than our species will greet us with open arms. Perhaps they will, having an even greater capacity for experiment.
16 PRO HO195/13, 'Applications of Mathematical Statistics to the Assessment of the Efficacy of Bombing'.
17 PRO HO192/1695.
18 RAF H68.
19 PRO Air41/39.
20 Ibid.

21 Webster and Frankland, *Official History*, Vol 1, p178.

22 Denis Richards, *The Hardest Victory*, 146.

23 I am greatly indebted to Harry Winter, whom the reader will become more acquainted with later, for among other things giving me a demonstration of the grids, and explaining their function.

24 David Robertson, 'The Radical Who Shaped the Future', *Institute of Electrical Engineers Journal*, May 2002. I am indebted to David Sawyer for sending me a copy of this magazine.

25 Ibid.

26 Ibid.

27 Harris, *Despatch on War Operations*, 69.

28 PRO HO196/26.

29 PRO HO192/1682.

30 PRO HO192/1682.

31 Sometimes an alloy of magnesium and zinc to save magnesium, see Cab102/108.

32 RAF H15.

33 CAB102/108.

34 PRO Avia 44/30.

35 PRO HO192/1682.

36 PRO Avia 44/30.

37 Harris, *Despatch on War Operations*, 94.

38 RAF H57.

39 RAF H83.

40 Wing Commander John Stubbington, *Bletchley Park Air Section – Signals Intelligence Support to RAF Bomber Command*, Minerva Associates, Alton, 2007, 23.

41 After investigations into a burglary at his home, it was discovered that the most defining quality of this unusual and vulnerable mathematical genius was his sexuality, which a magistrate called upon the aid of modern science to remedy so that it conformed more to the usual. Helped by innovative drugs, Alan Turing eventually committed suicide. Few had contributed more to victory.

42 Harris had concluded this letter on a humorous note – 'however, I like Admirals and Generals. One has to have something to raise a laugh on these days...' The letter had mainly concerned the sinking of the *Tirpitz*, and Harris had earlier suggested that Lovett should 'tell [his] sailor friends to go build their new battle wagons of rubber, self-sealing tank principle. That might serve to keep the water out and the gin in ...'

43 PRO HO196/30, R.E.N. 517.

44 To the horror of Harris and Bomber Command, they received only an oblique and passing reference in Churchill's victory address.

CHAPTER NINE

The Offensive

Here dead we lie because we did not choose
To live and shame the land from which we sprung.
Life, to be sure, is nothing much to lose;
But young men think it is, and we were young.
AE Housman

The great offensive, as we have seen, began in a muted way, in attacks on the German Navy, and later, in attempts to make a difference in the land battles in Norway and France. The catastrophic losses incurred in these operations ended all hopes of a daylight bombing of Germany until the new bombers, with their eight .303" gun armament, became available. When Lancasters were used against the MAN works at Augsburg, however, they fared little better than their medium predecessors. What lessons were learnt?

As has been seen, the Augsburg disaster had been blamed on the ineffectiveness of the .303" armament, as the Lancasters had been blasted at a distance by cannon-armed fighters which had stayed out of range of their guns. But what lesson could be learned when the problem had been attributed to one of sighting? Despite the fighters changing rapidly from eight machine guns to two cannon (later four) it was still held that four machine guns were superior to two cannon in a bomber, not just because of additional weight, but mainly because it was held (quite rightly, of course) that more bullets means more hits, despite the fact that the cannon shell hit with twelve times the force, thus greatly increasing the vulnerable area of the target, and that this advantage increased with range. However, it might not be too cynical to suggest that the greatest ingenuity displayed by the Armament Department lay in the identification of difficulties.

And so the virtually defenceless bombers were virtually confined to the night, when they had great difficulty even locating a city, let alone a target within it. The targets themselves were selected by the Air Staff and usually communicated to the Commander in Chief of Bomber Command by a lower ranking officer, perhaps the Deputy Chief of the Air Staff, or the Director of Bombing Operations, or Director of Plans, in letters which always began 'I am directed…' which often aroused Harris' ire. Unlike the ancient commanders, often kings, who might control everything including recruitment and weapons, the Commander in Chief of Bomber Command was told broadly what targets he should go for, although *when* he went for them was under *his* operational direction. The constraints upon exactly when certain targets might be attacked were considerable, as we have seen, for the horribly vulnerable bombers relied primarily upon evasion, but required a fair visibility over the target. It is hard to find an exact analogy in the past to the Commander in Chief's position; it might not be too inexact to compare him with the commander of an ancient army who had only heavy infantry, and who had continually to beg an equal commander of the cavalry and an equal commander of the light infantry for the use of their troops, while the supreme command planned his general advance, took away his troops at will, and controlled his recruitment, his pay and promotions and ranks and arms and clothing and discipline, and while junior officers, secured from his wrath by acting under the aegis of the supreme command, criticised his tactics, and weapons 'experts' derided his requirements.

The targets given to Bomber Command after the fall of France were all specific – the German occupied 'invasion' ports, oil, power, shipyards, aircraft factories, transport – although it was recognised that where these bombs missed their target in a city, they would still demoralise the workers. Saundby, in a memorandum to all Groups of 18 July 1941 on the importance of precise targets,[1] pointed out that the 'special aiming points' given were in fact:

> …precise targets which have been specially chosen not only because their destruction in itself is well worth while but because they are so situated that bombs, distributed around them in a pattern determined by the average aiming error and the law of probabilities, will hit the maximum number of important objectives…

In his reply, Slessor of No. 5 Group pointed out that the aiming points given were often market squares, one with three churches adjoining, and added that Saundby's phrase above, 'distributed around them …objectives' was 'about as good a definition of area bombing as could be written', and pointed out that 'However much you try to impress upon crews that a market place or a cathedral square is a precise and vitally important target, you won't get away with it…'

Saundby replied on 26 July,[2] enclosing a new list of aiming points.

But on 9 July 1941, with Russia now in the war and the Chiefs of Staff deciding that salvation lay in an all out effort to 'destroy the foundations' of the 'German war machine' on 'a scale undreamt of in the last war' by bombing,[3] Air Marshal Peirse was informed that 'the weakest points in …[the enemy's] armour lie in the morale of the civil population and in his inland transport system…'[4] In an appendix to the directive, it was recognised that, since targets could only be identified in 'clear moonlight', it was therefore necessary in the absence of this heavenly aid to make 'heavy, concentrated and continuous area attacks of large working class and industrial areas...' where these could be found. In attacks on railway centres, it was expected that the average aiming error would be 600 yards. 'On the law of probability', and 'supported by practical evidence of results in England and Germany', ran the argument, ninety aircraft finding the target and dropping 675 five hundred pound bombs and 11,250 incendiaries would result in 112 bombs and 1,874 incendiaries finding the target, and fifty-six of the high explosive bombs would hit 'vulnerable points'.

Just forty days after this directive was issued, the Butt Report into the accuracy of British bombing was published. Examining night photographs taken in the previous two months, it concluded that, 'of those aircraft recorded as attacking their target, only one in three got within five miles' (8,800 yards). In a full moon it was two in five. Less than half were within 8,800 yards under ideal night conditions, as opposed to the expected half within 600 yards! In the new moon, the proportion within five miles was one in fifteen. These failures called the whole offensive into question. And losses were beginning to rise significantly, even with the cover of darkness. A particularly ill advised raid on Berlin in foul weather on 7 November 1941 brought 12.4% casualties and the involvement of Churchill. On 13 November, Peirse received a new directive, to conserve his forces for the next spring and the arrival of 'Gee', it being 'undesirable…that attacks should be pressed unduly'. The relentless offensive was again on hold, and under question.

The Air Staff had planned a campaign in which forty-three German towns were marked for destruction by a vast force of 4,000 bombers. Churchill began to falter, wondering in a minute to Portal of 27 September 1941 if bombing would ever represent more than a 'serious and increasing annoyance' to the enemy. But could it simply be abandoned? There were two main driving factors behind the offensive. First, so much had been committed to it, so much effort, so much production, that its abandonment, as John Terraine so rightly points out,[5] would have represented a heavy defeat. When Churchill seemed to waver, Portal made this point to him in a minute of 2 October, and added that if a different kind of war was to be fought, based upon a greater involvement of the Army, a very different type of air force would be required. This would be the air force of 1916–1918. Churchill replied on 7 October that there was no intention of changing policy, but warning against too great a reliance on air attack, using the example of the fear of the air at the time of the Munich crisis in 1938, and the failure of the eventual German air attack to cause destruction on anything like the scale that had been feared and predicted.

The second great factor behind the offensive was the Soviet Union. That vast country had narrowly avoided the occupation of Moscow after the surprise assault of Germany and her allies, and was now starting a counter offensive. It was absolutely vital to keep her in the war by all means available, for her defeat would ensure that not only would Germany possess all the resources she needed to carry her to victory, and the blockade thereby rendered impossible, but her Air Force and Army would be able to strike at the Middle East overland. She could join hands with Japan. Even with the entry of the United States into the war, there would be little more than the prospect of a bloody stalemate between two huge power blocks, with Britain in the front line. Russia simply had to believe, and to see, that Britain was utterly committed to the war. She was engaging – and would continue to engage throughout the war – the major part of the German Army, and inflicting grave casualties on it. Bombing was the only way to assist Russia, for the Army could simply not hope to engage the Germans on any real scale. Indeed, consideration was given to a resumption of daylight bombing in order to draw fighters back from Russia, a loss of 10% of 100 sorties per day for a whole month being considered by Cherwell's aides, although it was acknowledged that 'there might be pilot difficulties but daylight bombing could probably be done by less skilled pilots…' as it was felt that 'the prolongation of Russian resistance is so vital that it seems to justify drastic measures'.[6] Cherwell had minuted Churchill on 30 June 1941 presuming that this, 'facing the risk of heavy losses', had been considered.

On 14 February 1942 came a new directive; feeling that the introduction of 'Gee' gave a six-month window of concentration and destruction, Bomber Command was released into a full offensive onto the morale of the civilian population 'and in particular, of the industrial workers'.[7] The hounds were released untrammelled into the night, and from 21 February were directed by Air Marshal Arthur Travers Harris.

The scientific underpinning of the new policy was provided by the Ministry of Home Security to Lord Cherwell in an analysis of the effects of the German raids on Hull and Birmingham, and was duly passed by Cherwell to the Prime Minister on 30 March 1942.[8] It was described by Cherwell as 'a simple method of estimating what we could do by bombing Germany'. He pointed out that, on 'Birmingham, Hull and elsewhere' a ton of explosive on a built up area demolished twenty to forty dwellings and turned 100–200 people out of their homes. With fourteen operational sorties expected from each bomber with an average bombload of 3 tons, a bomber would drop 40 tons before being lost. On built up areas, these bombs would render 4,000–8,000 people homeless. The forecast production of bombers from March 1942 to April 1943 was 10,000. Attacking the largest fifty-eight German cities, if only half the bombs landed in built up areas, about one third of the German population would be made homeless. In the assaults on the United Kingdom, investigations indicated that being made homeless seemed to damage morale even more than the loss of friends or relatives. And Bomber Command should be able to inflict ten times the damage.

Upon seeing this paper, Tizard wrote to Cherwell, disagreeing with both the facts and the conclusions, and requesting that the two men 'resolve their differences of opinion'.[9] The disagreement was not fundamental, however, but rather over timing.[10] Tizard thought that 10,000 bombers in the period stated was overoptimistic (he was right) and that even 50% of the bombs landing in larger cities was optimistic (he thought only 50% reached Cologne, and that this accuracy would not apply to smaller towns further away). Tizard thought 25% would be more likely.

Tizard wrote:

> My trouble is that I don't see a decisive effect being caused by this wholesale bombing before the middle of 1943. In the meantime, we must preserve command of the seas, and it is difficult for me to see how we are going to do this without strong support of the Navy by long range bombers. However, I may be wrong here. You certainly have more access to the right information than I have…

Tizard indicated that he thought 'we would be very unwise to count on the production of more than 7000 aircraft' over the period. If all the bombers produced were written off over the period, 'we should be left at the end of the period with a front line strength no greater than it is at present, which is surely quite unthinkable…' And further, Tizard made the points that since 'the destruction of houses is roughly proportional to the amount of explosive dropped' and the British general purpose bombs contained less high explosive than the German bombs dropped on Birmingham and Hull (with MC bombs not yet in production) and German towns were not so vulnerable – 'such a policy can only be decisive if carried out on a much bigger scale than is envisaged...'

Cherwell replied on 22 April that the the paper was intended 'to show that we really can do a lot of damage by bombing built up areas with the sort of air force which should be available', and that round figures had been used 'to save the Prime Minister the trouble of making arithmetical calculations'. Even on Tizard's figures, 'the results would be catastrophic'. Cherwell also stated that he believed 'considerably more damage is done in built up areas' than he had assumed, and also pointed out that American bombing had not been taken into account.[11]

Tizard had already argued for a different use of the bomber force. In a letter to Sir Stafford Cripps, the Minister of Aircraft Production, on 18 February 1942, he suggested that:

> ...I say emphatically as a conclusion that a calm dispassionate review of the facts will reveal that the present policy of bombing Germany is wrong; that we must put our maximum effort first into destroying the enemy's sea communications and preserving our own; that we can only do so by operating aircraft over the sea on a much larger scale than we have done hitherto, and that we shall be forced to use much longer range aircraft.
>
> The only advantage I can see in bombing Germany is that it does force the enemy to lock up a good deal of his effort on home defence...The heavy scale [contemplated by the Air Staff] will only be justified and economic at the concluding stages of the war...

There was much in this, of course; victorious Japanese fleets rode vast areas of the Far Eastern seas from Singapore to Wake Island, and the axis, despite a British submarine and aeroplane base in Malta, were supplying a large army in North Africa. Tizard pointed out that in 115 sorties between 4 January and 1 February 1942 in the Mediterranean (and for a loss of three aircraft and five damaged) three submarines, a 20,000-ton liner and two barges had been destroyed; and four merchant ships, two tankers, one submarine one destroyer, one other naval vessel and one flakship severely damaged; and six merchants ships, three submarines, one destroyer and one cruiser 'damaged, but not severely'. During the same period Bomber Command made 2,080 sorties, with fifty-two aircraft missing and nineteen damaged.

Tizard returned to the charge on 2 March, minuting Cripps that:

...It may be said that two extreme schools of thought exist. In the opinion of the one the best, if not the only, chance of defeating Germany decisively, is to concentrate our efforts on the bombing of land targets in order to interfere seriously with productive capacity and to injure the morale of the population. The other school of thought takes the view that this bombing policy is wrong unless it is carried out on an overwhelming scale at the concluding stages of the war when the enemy is seriously weakened by the results of other action and that it is of overriding importance to destroy sea communications of all kinds and generally to interfere with transport as distinct from production in every possible way...

But despite the apparent triumph of the relentless offensive in the highest reaches of the Air Force and Government, in June 1942 Bomber Command possessed roughly 11% of the total RAF force, and this had increased to roughly 17% by the end of the war. The RAF was not only a much larger, but a far better balanced force in 1945 than in 1939. Significantly, however, the American and British strategic bombing offensives distorted the *Luftwaffe* into an unbalanced, mainly defensive force of fighters, which led to a considerable deterioration in air support at the crucially important Russian front, where the German Army was becoming 'de-modernised' in the savage fighting, and where the Russians, already most formidable in courage and endurance, were gaining the advantage in numbers and in equipment, and were becoming the equals of the warlike Germans in fighting skills.

With Harris came the first, spectacular 1,000 bomber raid on Cologne, and furious assaults on the Ruhr and the cities of Germany which saw bomber losses of over 1,200 aircraft by the end of December. Despite his objections to the creation of what he perceived as elites, he was constrained by Freeman and Portal to adopt a special Target Finding Force, a suggestion of Cherwell's, which he then renamed the Pathfinders. This specialist force, aided of course by 'Gee' and H2S and eventually Oboe and 'Gee'-H, using specialist marking techniques, began to effect a considerable increase in accuracy.

On 21 January 1943 came the famous 'Casablanca Directive', which gave as the 'primary object' the 'progressive destruction and dislocation of the German military, industrial and economic system, and the undermining of the morale of the German people to a point where their capacity for armed resistance is fatally weakened'.

Special objectives given were submarine construction yards, the German aircraft industry, transportation, oil plants and 'Berlin, which should be attacked when conditions are suitable for the attainment of specially valuable results unfavourable to the morale of the enemy or favourable to that of Russia'.

The virtually defenceless bombers were committed to their campaign in ever increasing numbers and despite loss rates in excess of 4% per mission because the Germans had to be engaged somehow. Russia was the key to the whole of the war in the west. The scale and bitterness of the fighting completely dwarfed the campaigns in North Africa, in Italy and even, eventually, in France. In the Battle of Stalingrad, the German Army lost more men than the British Army did in the whole of the war. As losses mounted, air power over the battlefront became ever more vital, but more and more air power was diverted to the west, to face the American and British bombers. Casualties grew ever more heavy, pilot training was cut to provide pilots more quickly, and the skill level of the pilots declined rapidly. In 1944 a total of 914 night fighters were destroyed in action, many cut down by day fighter escorts in futile assaults against the American bombers with their heavy machine guns. Yet 674 were destroyed without any enemy action, in accidents which involved flying at night, in fear of intruders, and landing on dimly lit airfields. Over 1,300 night fighters suffered 60% damage, while over the Russian front air superiority passed irrevocably to the Soviets.

The bomber campaign between the Casablanca Directive and D-Day is usually divided into three phases. The first phase, the Battle of the Ruhr, lasted from March to July 1943, and cost 1,038 aircraft, 4.3% of the force.[12] In this period occurred the famous dams raid, in which 'bouncing' torpex-filled bombs specially designed by Barnes Wallis breached the Mohne and Eder dams. The second phase, the Battle of Hamburg, was the most terrible for Germany, 40,000 people dying in the city of Hamburg alone on the night of 27/28 July, and over a million fleeing the city, while the defences were fooled by Window. Yet even on this short offensive, between 24 July and 3 August, despite the relative failure of the defences, 130 aircraft were lost.[13] In the third phase, sometimes called the Battle of Berlin, which lasted from August 1943 to March 1944, 1,778 aircraft were lost. Harris had tried to 'wreck Berlin from end to end' and to finish the war on his own, but had completely failed, with terrible losses. This loss rate could not be sustained, particularly that suffered on the last raid, on Nuremberg, in which ninety-five bombers were destroyed, 11.9% of the force. The raid was conducted in moonlight, the forecast cloud not materialising. If anything proved the vulnerability of the bomber it was the fact that eighty-two bombers were lost on the outward route – on the return, the fighters were landing for fuel. Some 3,000 days had elapsed since the bombers were specified, yet they were still armed with rifle calibre machine guns, still unescorted and still pitifully vulnerable.

The Command was saved by being placed under Eisenhower and his deputy, Tedder, in preparation for Operation *Overlord*, the landing of Anglo-American armies and the creation of a new western front. These operations were on less well defended targets, at shorter range and lower level, often in daylight, and achieved an unexpected accuracy, although occasional forays, as at Schweinfurt on 26 April, produced heavy casualties, and in the period to 5 June 525 aircraft were lost. In July these attacks were extended to the 'V' weapon sites, and to battlefield bombardment, as well as the occasional raid on Germany. Between 5 June and 15 August, 727 aircraft were lost.

Now, with Allied armies streaming eastward for the Rhine, things began to improve for Bomber Command. The German fighters lost their advance warning of attacks. The American drive and initiative in developing fighter escorts (and of course, in developing the heavy armament of the bombers themselves, which became the anvil to the Mustang fighter's hammer) and the American defeat of the German day fighter force made the day safer than the night for the bomber. And 100 Group conducted a literal cloak and dagger operation in the night – giving the bombers electronic cloaks, and ambushing the German night fighters and generally adding to the already considerable dangers of flying by night.

Now Germany's oil plants, deprived of the Rumanian oilfields which were now occupied by Russia, became of vital importance although, as has been seen, this was not recognised by Harris. There seems little doubt that Harris did attack them as ordered, and that the attacks he made were devastating. Much accusation has been levelled at Harris over this, but little attention seems to have been paid to the fact that some 20% of the bombs failed to explode, due to flat strikes and sticking of the vanes which should have spun in the slipstream and armed the bombs. This, added to the incredible failure to develop a workable 4 lb incendiary bomb cluster, to the power of the aluminised explosive which devastated the Messines Ridge in 1917 and which filled torpedoes and mines and Wallis' bouncing bomb being known to seemingly everyone save the Armament Department, and to the simple expedient of putting a greater proportion of high explosive in a bomb to increase the blast effect, are never so attractive to the critic as accusations against the character of a Commander in Chief, for these failures were systemic, were organisational, and were simply not corrected quickly and energetically.

In the end, Bomber Command and the USAAF devastated Germany

from end to end. By 1945 their respective total bombloads were on a par with each other. We have already met a *Luftwaffe* intelligence document which estimated the night fighters lost in 1944 as 1,588 from all causes, with 914 lost to enemy action. Day fighters lost on operations alone totalled 6,039. It was the day offensive by the USAAF which won the war in the air. Many day fighters were lost to the Americam bombers' .5" machine guns, and many more to fighter escorts. The Americans had tried out heavily armed escort bombers, and although they were very difficult to shoot down, they were unable to protect the B17s, for reasons which had been foreseen before the war by the RAF – they were too slow, and unable to keep up with the bombers once their bombs had been dropped. American resources were vastly greater than those available to the RAF, but their greatest resource seems to have been a dynamism which immediately sought ways round obstacles, and did not rest until they were found. This was the American way of war. Eighty years before, their Confederate enemies had ruefully confessed that it was useless to blow up tunnels, as Sherman's engineers always carried a spare.

The desperate urgency felt at the front line for heavier weapons, for better turrets and for better bombs does not seem to have percolated through to the Armament Department or to the Armament Directorates. The need for escort fighters was met by a blank wall of doctrine aided by fallacious logic. The lessons of 1918 were forgotten, and had to be re-learned. It was the military thinking of 1917 which seemed to prevail. The head of the RAF, Sir Charles Portal, when commanding the bombers in July 1940, had drafted notes for a memorandum to his assistant, which contained the following: '…If the operation of sufficient importance, justifies 100% casualties. Rule in Bomber Command should be, have to hold them back rather than urge them on…'[14]

This was to regard war as you might regard chess, with pieces sacrificed without affecting the others. Had the sacrificed pieces shown serious signs of a cracking of morale, the sound of alarm bells might even have penetrated to the recesses of the Air Ministry and the Armament Department.

But the crews did not have to be urged on, and they were not held back until over 55,000 had died, and the war was won, and all save Bomber Command, amid the paeans of the politicians, were crowned with the laurels of victory.

Notes

1 PRO Air14/232.
2 The date on the memo is 26 April.
3 Webster and Frankland, *Official History*, Vol I 'Preparation', 180–81.
4 Webster and Frankland, *Official History*, Vol IV, Appendices and Annexes, 135–140.
5 John Terraine, *The Right of the Line*, 296.
6 CA G181/16.
7 Webster and Frankland, 144.
8 CA G193/1.
9 CA G193/3.
10 CA G193/5.
11 CA G193/9.
12 See Middlebrook and Everitt, *The Bomber Command War Diaries*, 409.
13 Middlebrook and Everitt, 416.
14 PRO Air14/232.

CHAPTER TEN

From Occam's Razor to Cleopatra's Needle

...In reality everything is singular. In other words, concepts
like 'species', 'redness', or even 'man', which name a range of
objects that are united by some common form or feature, are purely
inventions of the human understanding: ways of collecting together
many individual objects for psychological simplicity. In
reality there are only individuals. Universals do not exist....
Philip Stokes, *100 Essential Thinkers – William of Occam*[1]

The doctrine that animated and propelled Bomber Command was a destroyer of cities, of industries, of homes. In those cities and industries and homes, human beings of all ages and beliefs were blasted, asphyxiated or immolated. Was it successful in its aim? Was it wrong morally? Was it wrong militarily? Could it have been otherwise? Before embarking on an analysis of this ruthless method of defeating an enemy state in war, it would be well to have a view of exactly what the division of 'mankind' which we call a state is, and what a nation and a race are, and what is the true nature of the activity of mankind that we call war.

We see the whole world (as we know it) with our brains. But the human brain is a survival mechanism. It is not an essential instrument for distilling philosophical truth from the environment, but a machine which is very costly to run, and which needs to produce behaviour which benefits the survival of the whole organism at the minimum expense in energy. Neuronal activity is so expensive in energy that 'less than one per cent of the neurons in the cortex can be active at any moment'.[2] The brain uses some 20–25% of the body's energy, and weighs some 3 lbs, which has to be carted around with us, which in critical situations of food supply is a great disadvantage. The great compensating advantage is that a wider range of survival strategies and behaviours are enabled. Perhaps the greatest of these strategies is that of an almost infinite capacity to be programmed, to adopt behaviours and thoughts that individually we would have been completely incapable of inventing, to believe in the reality of these programs, and thereby form enduring, but illusory, combinations with other people.

There are perhaps six billion creatures on this planet whom we would recognise as human, but we know only a few hundred of them at most. How, when people know so little of others, do we manage this vast co-operation? It could be done perfectly if we had brains of sufficient size to know everyone else, and to interact personally with them. But this ability would present insuperable problems – we would be simply unable to carry such vast brains around on our shoulders, or to feed them with the requisite energy. Instead, we have evolved a simple strategy of shortcuts to thinking, which is full of injustices and faults, yet has vast advantages. We create entities in our minds, and group individuals into them in our thoughts. Thus all are grouped into 'mankind', and sub-divided into states, races, sexes, classes. We happily create entities out of millions of individuals – negroes, bank clerks, women, motorists, singers, the under fives, animal lovers, Equadorians. To categorise, to group together in our minds, always seems to advance our understanding. When we contemplate the world we do not know, these categorisations flicker across our imaginations and form a cheap and useful substitute for the complete understanding of which we are utterly incapable.

Our political combinations are subject to the same reifications. A citizen of Athens might contemplate the view of his city from the sea, and see the temples and statues, bring to his mind the deeds of the past, see the teeming multitudes from a distance, and laugh at the suggestion that it had no existence in the real world. What, after all, had he just been looking at? Yet, in reality, he had not seen more than individual men and women, houses, temples and ships. The unity which was Athens existed only in the minds of men, not in physical reality. Athens was a program.

All entities created in the minds of men seem to exist, because we can see the individual 'parts'. But the separate, individual creatures, each with its own digestive, reproductive and cognitive systems, each with their own separate viabilities which we categorise as 'mankind', or as 'British' or 'German' or 'Indian' are of a most variable intellect, from genius to stupid. In 'mankind' Newton and Shakespeare, Einstein and Homer, Marie Curie and Helen of Troy are bracketed with the most stupid and bestial of creatures, and the most demonic and savage of rulers. 'Mankind', the

'United Kingdom' and Germany' are not real entities, but concepts, programs of the mind, a film show on a mental screen.

It is not rather the intelligence of 'man', but of a few men and women, and the easy programmability of the mind, which has been responsible for the present triumph of 'mankind'. The truly original mind is very rare indeed, but its creations and inventions may be understood by the many. *Man* did not invent the wheel, but *a* man (or woman) did. Similarly, the bow and arrow, the gun, the steam engine, the aeroplane, the computer, were all invented and developed by a man, or by the co-operation of a very few men, and all had been programmed by the discoveries, creations and inventions of previous ages. All but the very first have 'stood on someone else's shoulders'. But *all* have adopted them into their behaviour. I could never have invented the electronic computer, nor could I ever understand how a series of switches could convey ideas – if indeed they do – yet my mind can accept a program which enables me to benefit from these ideas. I am empowered thereby. We do not all need to be of great intelligence, but we need to be of great programmability to benefit from the inventions and ideas of those other separate creatures who are or who were.

This programmability of the mind is the great strength of nearly all minds, strong and weak alike, for it enables the weak to be strong. In a sense, all individuals are now weak compared to man as a whole, and grow weaker by the day. The sum of the knowledge locked in the brains of all human beings is by now far too great to be absorbed even by the most intelligent. But there is in every age a general body of knowledge common to most of us, which forms the general, human program. Some of it lies unchanging in books and now computers, programs waiting to inhabit minds. We often feel that we understand our own little universes, which is simply the content of our minds, but the sum even of all the little universes is way beyond our individual ken, let alone that stored in paper and metal. Each of us is separate and distinct, and the thing which we possess in common is this program, although it is never exactly the same in any of us. It is this program which gives us whatever degree of unity and commonality we possess, for we are born and die physically separate beings.

The individuals who dwell together in great numbers think it normal that they bustle about their separate ways, all interacting in an organised way yet knowing only a few of the millions who pass by, and they think it abnormal when occasionally an individual kills or robs or rapes or cheats another. We disagree as to the reason for these individuals acting outside the generally accepted program, some thinking that, since all are born good the culprits must be mis-programmed, some thinking them to be of vicious genetic structure and some of varying proportions of both. We think, when we look out on our country with its architecture, its language, its countryside, its rivers, its monarch and its parliament, that it is one whole and real entity. Yet it consists of millions of separate minds, programmed into a certain illusory unity and structure.

When new inhabitants are born, they are born into a program, a set of beliefs. 'Growing up' means a rapid absorption of the general program, as well as developing their own particular version of it.[3] Learning is not a process of acquiring an individual philosophical knowledge of the universe, but of acquiring a program, which itself may or may not be based upon truth. An Aztec would have rapidly learnt, for instance, that the Gods needing propitiating every fifty-two years by the rending out of the hearts of victims on their sacrificial altars, a National Socialist would absorb the information that individuals formed a higher and more noble entity called a race, while the liberal elitist would as easily believe that punishment is more reprehensible than crime, and pretend to punish criminals in order to propitiate the victims. People do not believe in Gods, the state, the race or liberalism because they are demonstrably true – indeed, some are demonstrably false – but because we are programmed to do so. The state itself is a program of the mind, although a very tenacious one if allied to a programmed belief in the race, for these beliefs together form the concept of the nation. Yet if all of us were to be infected with a disease which deprived us of memory, and everyone had to learn anew, Britain, China, Germany, the United States would have ceased to exist, and other phantom entities would take their place.

Thus masses of separate, individual men and women, who (save for conjoined twins) are not *physically* connected in any way, are mentally connected through our programs. Though, if we are fortunate, we are surrounded by family and exultant or weeping friends and relatives, our births and our deaths are physically separate things. We whose hearts and brains and limbs and sexual desires and behaviours defy any classification which will encompass us all – even that of men and women – are joined by some programs, although separated by others. The greatest of the programs which unite us is the concept of 'mankind'.[4] The greatest of those that combine in order to divide us are the programs of race and the state. Yet none have any real existence, save in the mind. Thus do quiet, law abiding, generous hearted women and men, who feel themselves as part of humanity, and of a race or a state, arise and kill others of a separate program in one of the only really common programs that we separate individuals have, the program of war. Wars are therefore conflicts of programs, although all the actions of war, all the killings and captures and injuries, are carried out by individuals. Let us look first at some comments on war by the great Prussian military philosopher Karl von Clausewitz.

Clausewitz wrote:

> War is nothing but a duel on an extensive scale. If we should conceive as a unit the countless number of duels which make up a war, we shall do best by supposing to ourselves two wrestlers. War is therefore an act of violence intended to compel our opponent to do our will.[5]

In personifying the countless number of individual duellists as wrestlers, the war seems to take form and a purpose.

It can be understood, as a million separate conflicts cannot. But how valid is this personification?

The supposed 'wrestlers' themselves are states, which struggle sometimes for advantage, sometimes for survival and sometimes to consume and exterminate another state. Yet the states themselves, the wrestlers, have no real, physical existence. The wrestlers are a mental film show, a projection onto the screen in the minds of individuals, 'created' in order to permit millions of individuals to co-operate without each having a knowledge and understanding of the others. How would millions of men and women co-operate without believing that the sum of all their actions was a real thing? The contending states and armies, the wrestlers, seem to be there, yet when we look closely at their physical existence they dissolve away into the individual human parts, the duellists. All the death and damage of warfare is carried out by individuals. A state may die, and yet no individual perish, as in the demise of the great Soviet Union, the 'wrestler' who, more than any other, brought Hitler down. Clausewitz's own Prussia is no more, save as a reviled memory, destroyed since the war by the bloodless stroke of a pen, an unwanted and reviled program, to be replaced by others, less obnoxious to the modern world.

The state is an organisation. It is created or destroyed by acts of will, and maintained and operated by belief and acceptance in the minds of individuals. It has no other existence. An army, the arm of the state, is similar in construction. It seems to be real; yet it is consists solely of individuals who should perform actions in accordance with instructions, and thereby behave as though they were parts of a whole. Yet the very necessity of military discipline demonstrates that they are not. The army is a program in the minds of the soldiers. Armies dissolve like states when discipline relaxes under the influence of panic, or defeat, or the minds of the individual soldiers are subverted by another program.

To return to Clausewitz, who now speaks of 'friction' in war – the chance happenings, misunderstandings, difficulties of terrain and weather, mistakes, oversights, unwarranted presumptions and differing beliefs which affect the pure plans conceived in the mind of a general:

> Friction is the only conception which in a general way corresponds to that which distinguishes real war from war on paper. The military machine, the Army and all belonging to it, is in fact simple, and appears on this account easy to manage. But let us reflect that no part of it is in one piece, that it is composed entirely of individuals...[6]

'War on paper' is conducted by the wrestlers, the states and the armies, phantom entities with no real existence, save in minds and plans and schemes; 'real war' is conducted by individuals, who act in accordance with their conception of the phantom wrestlers' wishes; or sometimes, especially in retreat, more directly in accordance with their own! But the wrestlers themselves are general ideas, broad mental programs, which differ in detail in the mind of each individual. They are strong when the ideas of the individuals are closer in agreement with the general idea, and become weaker as the ideas differ more. As with the Soviet Union, they disappear when other ideas replace them.

Suppose an observer, of vast mental capacities, were, from deep in space, to observe a war. He would only actually *see* countless acts of individual violence. He would then *infer* that the violence was to a plan, and subject to an attempt at control by certain individuals, whose decisions affected the actions of millions – millions who all seemed to labour under a similar program, a similar set of beliefs. He would see the wrestlers as a necessary creation in our minds, the personifications of a system, reified abstractions which had become our masters. For example, we have to believe that a bank exists in the real world. Yet our deposit is simply a mass of transactions and obligations with people whom we do not know, and who do not know us. Their actions, and ours, have to be, when dealing with the bank's affairs, constrained by certain limits and motivated by certain obligations. Yet we know that our money is not a real thing, and is dependent upon a multitude of factors for its apparent value, which it may lose. Similarly, the state, and the nation, and even the race. The number of man's organisations is almost limitless. Organisations are a form of behaviour, a very much more complicated version of the 'Mexican wave' seen in football crowds, the persons 'belonging' to them each behaving in a particular way, whether by agreement or force, when acting on the organisation's behalf. The Mexican wave vanishes completely when the crowd cease to behave in a particular way – and this is true of all organisations, societies and states. Yet a belief in the reality of these phantom entities simplifies cooperative behaviour enormously.

The philosopher Maeterlinck speculated that ants were not individual creatures, but loosely bound, semi autonomous cells, parts of a nest – a nest which itself represented the real, individual creature. In this philosophy, were we to write a complete history of a species of ants as we would write a human history, it would be a history of the individual nests and their wars, their colonies, their disasters and their triumphs. As with modern histories, this history could well be illuminated by an occasional biography, since each class of ant – soldiers, workers, queens and drones – differ so little one from another that the life of one soldier, queen or worker may illustrate the life of all, and by a simple multiplication, a period in the life of the nest as a whole.

A more complex problem confronts the historian who attempts to describe humanity, because the great difference between ants and men is that human beings are of vast variability in everything which classifies them as 'human'; and the mind of man appears to consist not only of genetic hardware, but also of infinitely programmable software, whereas the minds of ants, or perhaps, the will of their nests, appears to be incapable of forming differing societies. The ants have one unvarying program. Their behaviour seems to be 'hard wired', immutable. But the only *complete* history of a human war or a human state, would need to be a million stories, a biography of every individual whose actions formed the state, and fought the war, and fully understanding the whole war would mean the ability to bring them all to mind at once. The human brain is completely incapable of absorbing, and reflecting upon, this vast knowledge, and so history becomes a shorthand, a story of a broad program and its changes, a story of the few individuals who did most to control or shape it.

The human mind, although influenced by the genetic hardware of the hormones, is a product of the surrounding intellectual environment. Few are the human beings who genuinely think new thoughts, and few can be the intellectual thoughts of a mind uninfluenced by education and the thoughts and discoveries of others. The ancestors of Shakespeare and Newton were alive in 25,000 BC, and perhaps had the same potential for genius, yet their thoughts were stunted compared with the average modern schoolchild, who is aided by the cumulative knowledge of all the generations since the invention of writing.

Because of these vast differences, the relation of the ant to its nest and of man to his state are very different. Only in the idealism of Hitlerian concepts of race can they be similar, for whereas the nest represents a genetic unity, all of its members being the descendants of the queen and her deceased mate, the human state is an organisation, an intellectual structure that has no tangible, physical existence, but which is an entity of the mind, existing only in the minds of individuals of great genetic variability, and acts only through their individual actions. States are formed or dissolved in the minds of men and women, and the earth weighed neither more nor less when Rome was founded, or the Soviet Union fell.

Thus the history of the state is the history not of a real nest, not of a real entity, but of an idea – or rather, of millions of broadly similar, consensual ideas. The continual birth and death of the individual human citizen, and the changes in the experience and outlook of the individual over time, means that a changing idea is constantly being passed from one individual to another, and is accordingly subject to constant further changes of form. The idea of the state, never quite the same even in contemporaneous individuals, gradually changes. Here, perhaps, is the 'principle of decay' which Edward Gibbon, the great historian of the *Decline and Fall of the Roman Empire,* gave as a contributory factor in the fall of that colossus, for although modern historians are more inclined to suggest that the empire changed, rather than decayed, the 'Decline and Fall...' is in reality the change, decay and death of an *idea* in the hearts of men. In *An Enemy of the People* Ibsen has Dr Stockmann declare 'What sort of truths are they that the majority usually supports?...A normally constituted truth lives, let us say, as a rule seventeen or eighteen, or at most twenty years – seldom longer.' The state is just such a truth, an idea, changing both by births and deaths, and by defective communication and understanding. Here, also, lies the wisdom of Ecclesiastes' warning to the old –'Ask not why the former times were better than these – thou dost not enquire wisely concerning this' – for ideas are very rapidly absorbed and embedded by the mind in youth, and they change in those who arrive and are programmed in our later years. The old, of course, may also have a faulty, idealised recollection of the past, from which all change is decay.

Yet if the state is an idea, what is war but a conflict of ideas, or programs? In a state of a million people there exist a million ideas of the state, a million programs, a million views of the surrounding world. In some states and societies, such as Sparta or Israel, these programs, through education or religion, have a strong concurrence with each other, leading to a strong state. Israel survived the loss of all territory for 1,900 years, a remarkable survival of an idea.[7] The written word, especially in religion, presents an idea which seems not to change, although interpretations of it may change. Here, diversity is weakness. In other states, such as the United States of America, liberty itself, enshrined in a written although alterable constitution, ensures strength through an acceptance of diversity – *e pluribus unum!* And here, attempts to secure uniformity through compulsion have a weakening effect.

But the great strength of the idea of the modern state, and the demands which it makes of its citizens, is its ability to identify with another idea – the nation, which is bound around inextricably with ideas of race and language. Austria Hungary was a state, but could never be a nation, and under pressure, split into 'national' states. Yet these 'races' are in themselves ideas, since the average genetic divergence between individuals within a 'race' is always greater than that of the average between 'races'. The idea of race connects strings of similar characteristics into a real entity. No one in Britain complains that fair haired people are treated better than the dark haired, as these are not seen as real groups – yet as groups they are no more unreal than any other string of common characteristics. The human mind, being a survival mechanism, and a drain on the body's resources, is unable to distinguish between thousands of individuals, and so takes the often useful, and often essential, shortcut of classification of individuals into groups, and predicting their qualities from the presumed qualities of the group. Individuals happily and willingly classify themselves into these groups as well. Yet problems and injustices arise, and crimes against individuals are easily rationalised, when these groups are accepted as tangible, real entities, and the supposed qualities of the group distributed among its members. The parable of the good Samaritan[8] dissolves these groups into what they really are – entities of the mind.

The modern state, reinforced and strengthened by these illusory entities, demanded all of its citizens, and war became instantly more terrible. The professional armies of monarchs were swept away by the national armies of Revolutionary France, and these mass armies became national levies, filled with national enthusiasm and willingly submitting to Roman standards of discipline. This would have made war much more terrible even without concurrent increases in the power of weapons. Advances in transport, medicine and agriculture enabled these huge armies to be fielded without epidemics; to be fed, clothed, armed and able to keep the field indefinitely. It is often supposed that Hiram Maxim, the inventor of the machine gun, was responsible for millions of deaths in the Great War, or that artillery innovations or poison gas were responsible. In reality, the modern state, a program which demanded all of its believers, which conscripted mostly willing and enthusiastic soldiers who would fight as long as they believed, was the cause of the mass casualties, aided by medical science and transport innovations, which enabled such vast numbers of men to be fed and to live in close proximity without epidemics of disease. Had the participants been armed with bows and swords, the slaughter would have been as great. In the Great War, Germany, besieged by the superior strength of the Entente powers and defended by the best army in the world, fought for four long, bitter years until, under the pressure of starvation and military defeats, the idea of the Kaiser's state itself began to be deserted by many of his subjects in favour of two seductive ideas – Marxism, now presenting itself as a more just, more scientific, more modern new world order in Russia, and Americanism, with its new world order of 'national' self determination, materialism, individualism and democracy, wrapped up as Fourteen Points in Wilsonian idealism. Individualism, in a real world in which only the individual exists, is the ultimate decayer of states and armies; it is the force which reminds an individual of his or her separate existence, and which causes soldiers to run away when it is threatened.

We see, in history, the rise of the clan, the tribe, the city states, the nation, and the federation or empire. What has really arisen is a mental program of increasing complexity, an advance from an obedience system to a belief system, which is 'shared' in millions of differing forms by millions of differing people. Think of the United States. Some people would think of cities; some mountains or rivers; some would see justice or injustice; liberty or slavery; or areas, states and groups of states; some a coloured shape on a map; most, at times, all of these. No one can ever know the whole United States, or comprehend it. It is a vast collection of individual thoughts, motives, beliefs and programs, and is constantly changing. We can never really understand the state historically; we consult records, accounts, tables, biographies, even eye witnesses; but each mind throws up a vision on the screen of his imagination. What we actually observe is but a tiny fraction of what we infer from our program. We do not know whether Britain was a 'warfare' or 'welfare' state in the 1930s, and brilliant minds project infinitely varying images of each. Yet all are phantoms of the imagination, images projected onto a swirling mist, a mass of relationships and rules and organisations, a wrestler without real substance. Millions of real individuals are born and die, live and work, from age to age, and were deemed parts of the phantom whole. Yet they lie in separate graves. Our bodies are separate. Our brains are separate, although they are *mostly* similar, and *mostly* programmed similarly.

What therefore constitutes the strength of a state? Obviously, the individuals should have resources at their disposal sufficient to carry on their various co-operative enterprises. But the real strength or weakness is the clarity of the idea, the consistency with which a belief in, and love of, the state is held by its citizens. Despite the broad diversity of the United States, it is a strong nation in that there is a broad acceptance of its theme, the program, and its written constitution, by many millions of people, who themselves feel that they belong to sub groups – the individual states, the negro or Irish or Jewish groups, the industrial workers, landowners, farmers etc. Most individual Americans believe themselves to be members of many groups, all of which are ideas or programs. Historically, the American Civil War was a war of ideas and programs and beliefs. From the beginning of the United States, 'Dixie' and the North began to develop as separate ideas. The idea of Dixie was incredibly broad and loose – an accent, a social relationship, a place, a vague feeling of belonging and a song – were sufficient to make a feeling of identity strong enough to provoke a war of separation, although many in the South still believed fervently in the United States. Dixie foundered because it was an idea too vague to unite people under the pressure of blockade and war. As an idea, it was not as strong as the idea of the individual states of the Confederacy, which allowed individual state governors to withhold troops. Bad finance, based on borrowing rather than taxation (thus shielding the rich at the expense of the poor) rotted away the enthusiasm of the soldiers, who deserted in droves to defend their individual homes and their individual wives and children. In addition, some five million of the eleven million Confederate citizens were slaves, with no interest at all in the Confederacy and every interest in the United States, who 'deserted' in droves, 180,000 becoming US soldiers, and thereby saving the Union. When the great Union generals, Grant and Sherman, at Lincoln's behest, applied relentless military pressure to the individuals in the seceding states, the Confederacy dissolved away. The idea of 'Dixie' slumbers on, embracing the courage of its soldiers and the nobility of its general, the romantic appeal of the great lost cause – yet it is not a live issue. But had Britain suppressed American independence in 1776, who could doubt that it would have risen again, stronger, more formidable, eventually invincible in its clarity, because of its all embracing appeal and its grandeur. In the minds of most southerners, the great program, the idea of the United States in all its nobility, still overcomes the Confederacy.

The Great War ended with Germany in a similar collapse, again assisted by bad finance (borrowing from the rich, rather than taxing them), blockade, and an ensuing starvation. Germany split along fault lines which had existed, but had been plastered over with patriotism, before the war began. But Germany, unlike the Confederacy, had existed as an idea for centuries, and the idea had been clothed with a state organisation since 1871. Within that German idea, the Prussian program, with its arrogant militarism and its magnificent army, was strongly intertwined. Resources, particularly human, abounded. But among the industrial workers socialist programs, very different programs from racial Germanism, proliferated. These ideas were largely internationalist, and formed the germ of an alternative system, a replacement program, in the minds of many industrial workers, although the German social security and education systems were strong, and a useful support for the state.

In the war of 1914–18, the millions of individual 'Germans' and the broad consensus of ideas which constituted the German state were subjected to a vast pressure – a merciless starvation-inducing blockade, and a four-year siege by numerically superior armies, in which millions died. The assumption of a form of dictatorship by the aged General Hindenburg, the perceived saviour and winner of the great Battle of Tannenburg in 1914, together with his Chief of Staff General Ludendorff, seemed to narrow the aim of the war into victory or nothing,[9] despite calls from the *Reichstag* for a negotiated peace. The plaster cracked and fell off, revealing that the divisions in the ideas which constituted the German state were increasing rapidly.

What happens when overwhelming pressure is applied to states and armies? They may, rarely, cohere and fight to the death, as the Spartans and Thespians at Thermopylae, the Argives and Spartans at the Battle of the Champions, Newcastle's infantry at Marston Moor, the Paraguayans in the war of 1864–1870 against the Triple Alliance of Brazil, Argentina and Bolivia or the Japanese in numerous isolated islands between 1943 and 1945. Mostly, however, the recognition that the ultimate pressure is available to the enemy, and defeat inevitable, is sufficient to induce surrender. In the Confederacy, the idea of the United States, the Federal program, was always an alternative to the idea of the Confederacy, and was, indeed, maintained by a very significant portion of the population – the state of West Virginia being 'created' out of Virginia by the Unionists in 1863. The Confederacy permanently melted away, its ghost remaining in minds as a tribute to the courage and élan of its soldiers, and a vague cultural idea, rather than as an angry and embittered sense of unfinished business. In Germany the state collapsed, soldiers deserted, workers went on strike sailors refused to sail, and the Kaiser fled. These were both causes and symptoms of inevitable military defeat, given the will and resources of the Allies. However, the collapse was regarded with fury by those who saw the confession of defeat as a betrayal of the dead, and this idea became paramount after 1933, until the second collapse in 1945.

Undoubtedly, the collapse of 1918 was hastened and shaped by the fact that Germany was at war with two unusual and revolutionary states. She had defeated old Russia by March 1918, but the new, Soviet Russia, although nominally at peace with them, was an idea which could never really be at peace with any capitalist state, based as it was on revolutionary, internationalist, Marxist principles, which inevitably conflicted with the old conservative, royalist, militarist, dictatorial Germany. And the Soviet program called for workers to defect and to set up a different state, or worse to the conservatives and nationalists, to join the Soviet Union itself.

The other revolutionary state was the United States. It had been created by a declaration of liberty and human rights, tearing itself away from a state which itself seemed to believe in liberty, if not in democracy. Its inhabitants were politically free. It was anti-colonial (despite the acquisition of the Philippines and Caribbean territories from Spain at the turn of the century), and was perceived as anti-war (despite its vast looting of the territory of Mexico). It offered a different, free, capitalist alternative program. The American idea was as seductive, if not more so, than the Soviet idea, because it not only offered liberty and self determination, but its very lifestyle, the popular culture which it radiated, even before the advent of the cinema, altered the way of life and the values of individuals, especially the young, almost imperceptibly. America was, and is, the modern world. Its leaders may now be reviled for oppressive policies, particularly in the Middle East and Latin America, yet its individual freedom and popular, materialist, individualist culture, rotted and sapped the old order, provoking either collapse, as in the old monarchies and even in the Soviet Union, or bitter reaction, as in Nazi Germany and Islam (this is not to conflate these two utterly different programs). Anyone who doubts the influence of America on popular culture should try singing a modern song in their native accent! Since the end of the civil war, the United States has been a danger to all non democratic governments simply by its existence, although as the rulers of America, in pursuit of power, become yearly less sensitive to the rights of individuals, both American and others, this peculiar strength ebbs away.

The American president Woodrow Wilson's Fourteen Points set out a vision of a new world order of self determination and liberty, which had a great appeal to combatants who saw the war as an endless and self perpetuating disorder consuming the youth of nations. It was to show the west, and America in particular, that Germany was a reformed democracy that the Kaiser was sent into exile. It was on the basis of the Fourteen Points that the new German Government appealed for an armistice. Yet despite all this, German defeat, whether she fought, negotiated or surrendered, was absolutely inevitable. Even her victory over Russia was a defeat, since the punitive terms showed to both Germans and their enemies that her rulers were bent not upon the peace which so many in the nation craved, but outright victory. And the new Russia was more of a threat, since war between states is a conflict of ideas fought out by individuals, and the Soviet idea, like the American, seemingly offered peace and justice in a new world order. The German state found it hard to combat these ideas because the German state, like all states, was itself an idea. Germany had been defeated in the field – but the sudden collapse, the catastrophe, the final splitting and shattering of the metal, came after the British Army had broken through the Hindenburg Line. The fatal crack initiated in the mind of General Ludendorff, and propagated catastrophically through the nation. In the words of Sir Basil Liddell Hart:

> The German supreme command lost its nerve – only for a matter of days, but that was sufficient, and recovery too late. On the afternoon of September 29th Ludendorff was studying the problem in his room at the Hotel Britannique at Spa – an ominously named choice of headquarters! Examination only seemed to make it more insoluble, and in a rising outburst of fear and passion he bemoaned his troubles – especially his lack of tanks – and berated all those whom he considered as having thwarted his efforts – the jealous staffs, the defeatist Reichstag, the too humanitarian Kaiser, and the submarine obsessed navy. Gradually he worked himself into a frenzy, until suddenly, with foam on his lips, he fell to the floor in a fit. And that evening it was a physically as well as mentally shaken man who took the precipitate decision to appeal for an armistice…[10]

This confession of defeat in the mind of the commander was the proximate cause of defeat, the crack in the metal which propagated rapidly through the whole of the German system, shattering and fragmenting the old German program for ever. New programs now came to vie for dominance and control, some looking hopefully forward to a new order, some looking vengefully back in a perception of betrayal.

That German morale had apparently suddenly collapsed was not lost on the leaders in the second war, both German and Allied. To crack and fragment a nation's will promised a quicker end to war than simply killing off enemy soldiers until not enough were left to carry on, presuming your own losses to be more sustainable. No government, no army, could ever propose such a pyrrhic path to victory again. The Great War slowly entered into the realms of western legend as useless and incompetent butchery. As a corollary to this, the maintenance of morale at home became a matter of supreme importance to war governments. But how was the cohesion and national will of the enemy to be unsoldered, whilst preserving your own? Blockade was a very slow and uncertain force, and in the Great War, the remains of ten million soldiers – ten million sons, ten million individuals in the prime of youth – had been buried before the weld of German society had dissolved away.

How could the morale of civilians be *directly* attacked? How could the sinews of the state – its industry and industrial workers – be hit? The huge armies of the Great War, spread as a steel barrier across whole frontiers, had originally prevented a direct attack by raiding bands on industry, or on the civilians who laboured to produce the weapons and ammunition that had been consumed so profusely – although the German fleet had briefly raided Britain's east coast towns, and the German Army would later hit Paris by means of huge guns. Flank attacks could not be made, since all flanks were covered by entrenchments, whether in France, Russia or the Dardanelles. But the war soon saw the flanks turned – for attacks were soon to be made on merchant fleets from below the sea, and from the air above both sea and land. Both flanks became the subject of new tactics against fleets and armies, and new strategies. The strategies were aimed not only at armies or fleets, but at civilians, at the heart of the state itself – the minds of its people.

In seizing the dominion of the air it seemed that a highroad was opened to the very heart of a nation. Bombing raids by Zeppelin airships on London had been followed by raids with bomber aeroplanes, which had been retaliated with by raids on German towns. In 1919, the RAF had planned to attack the German cities with four-engined bombers built specifically for the purpose. These attacks might break the will of the enemy civilians, or they might so hinder production that the enemy armies, forced to carry on the fight with inadequate weapons, themselves collapsed. Hugh Trenchard, the first commander of the RAF, believed that the morale effect of bombardment would be twenty times that of the material.[11] With direct air attack, the Clausewitzian wrestler would not need to be strangled in a titanic struggle – he might gradually disappear, he might slowly fade from view, be atomised, to become what in reality he always had been, millions of individual duellists, now demoralised and terrified. Indeed, in 1941 the 1918 collapse was still quoted to prove that a direct assault on morale might once again provide a shortcut to victory over another superb, if more demonic, German war machine:

Air Vice Marshal Slessor of No. 5 Group wrote to his station officers:

...but the point is that the strength of a chain, however mighty it appears, is the strength of its weakest link, and that link in the German chain is the morale of the German people. At the end of March, 1918, the Germans and their allies were in possession of all central Europe and Turkey, had defeated Russia and looked uncommonly like getting Paris and the channel ports in a huge offensive against us and the French in the West. Six months later they were finished, and the rot had started from within...[12]

Churchill, in his 'finest hour' speech to the House of Commons on 18 June 1940 (later broadcast) mentioned the Great War:

...During that war we repeatedly asked ourselves the question: How are we going to win? And no one was ever to answer it with much precision, until at the end, quite suddenly, quite unexpectedly, our terrible foe collapsed before us...

But states may survive with almost no morale at all. Rome, a state with an army, became like Prussia, an army with a state which, as an idea, as a program which enthused millions, gradually disappeared, leaving just the army, the Emperor, the bureaucrats and the eunuchs. By the later empire, belief in Rome had given way to obedience to the Augusti. The army, disciplined and efficient, was both the salvation and the scourge of the Empire. When it finally gave way, the Western Empire was conquered by pitifully small German armed bands, and few were the examples of popular resistance. Few really believed in Oliver Cromwell's republic, but on being told nine out of every ten men were against him, he replied 'Suppose I put a sword in every tenth man's hand?' A monarchical system may exist, based on obedience without belief, as Cromwell's, as in the oriental monarchies. Hitler's system, however, consisted not only in a deep and fanatical belief in the German nation and state, but was backed by an obedience system of great ferocity and an army second to none in fighting spirit. By 1939 this system had the unflinching support of the great majority of the individual creatures on whom it operated, a system which was grounded in a belief in the solidity of the nation and in the determination never again to suffer the disintegration of 1918. How could you break this system down, without engaging in another grinding struggle with the formidable German Army, and enduring another bloodbath?

After the fall of France, the choices open to the British Government were few. The German Army seemed even more fear inspiring and formidable. It was not possible to invade France again unsupported, nor was it possible even to seize a point in France – the Cotentin peninsula, say – and fortify and hold it as Wellington had held the lines of Torres Vedras in the Peninsula War, even after the Battle of Britain was won. Raiding by elite troops was spectacular, but the inescapable fact was that the British Army could not compete with the German in numbers, in equipment, in efficiency, in training or in morale. The British Army of the Second World War was simply not as capable of engaging the German Army in battle without a crushing air superiority. A society which had generally moved, since the reliefs of victory, in the direction of peaceful individualism or of socialist pacifism and visions of the unity of man, which had aimed at world peace and disarmament while sitting, some felt guiltily and immorally, on a large slice of the world's resources, and which had now suffered a catastrophic and demoralizing military defeat in France, found difficulty in raising an army which could face that of a military society burning with the bitterness and humiliation of defeat, and now unified by victory. This difference remained throughout the Italian and *Overlord* campaigns. The British infantry was further denuded of its best troops by the dubious process of drafting them into specialist units – Marine Commandos, Airborne Forces, special forces – and was held back by the politicians' and generals' fear of another Passchendaele, with great losses for small gains, which they simply could not afford if the Army were to be maintained in any strength. This nervousness communicated itself to the troops, whose morale was further eroded by a lack of replacements. And compared with the German, the British Army was ill-equipped. The best tank in the British Army was the American Sherman, and even this, from the ease with which the petrol-engined version caught fire, was referred to by the Germans as the 'Tommy cooker'.

In the war memoirs of Air Marshal Arthur Tedder, who rose to be Eisenhower's second in command, is a passage detailing the despair felt by Air Commanders at the British Second Army's lack of drive, and giving the German Army's contemptuous view of the British infantry as being '...extraordinarily nervous of close combat. Whenever the enemy infantry is energetically engaged, they mostly retreat or surrender'.[13] The British infantryman, however, could not see the point of risking many lives in tackling a machine gun nest with rifle and grenade when it seemed that an armoured car, a tank or an aeroplane might do the job for no loss at all. It is impossible not to sympathise with the infantry; their weapons were inferior and their numbers were few, both the British and American armies having huge 'tails' with a corresponding shortage of men 'at the sharp end'. And whatever the political system they supported, whatever murderers they sheltered, whatever the monstrous things which were done in the east, the German fighting man, whether army or SS, navy or air force, was generally skilful, brave and in all military respects admirable. The German armed forces took the individuals who joined them, mostly already programmed with patriotic fervour, and cemented them together by discipline and created the most formidable military machine on the planet. In an almost complete absence of air support, with supplies routinely something like a third or a quarter of that of the British and Americans, bombed, strafed and outnumbered, they held out heroically, and remained dangerous. A half century of war films in which individualist British heroes habitually defeat inept and blindly obedient German soldiers who woodenly shout 'Achtung!' at each other and scream 'Schweinhund!' when outwitted by superior fieldcraft seem to have conditioned the public to the view that the Army defeated Germany, while Bomber Command conducted a hugely expensive, largely futile and morally bankrupt campaign against German civilians. If this campaign against morale *were* futile, how many myriads of casualties would be suffered when, driven back by hard fighting against superior numbers, this devoted army came to rest on Germany's borders, and the best army in the world fought for its own beloved homeland?

Strategic bombing had always seemed to hold the answer to modern, scientific war. It could surely destroy the physical system by ruining transport, oil supplies, armament industries and power supplies, or it could just as surely produce such a panic that terrified citizens would force the Government to make peace. Since workers' houses were placed around the factories, both might be had for the price of one, since a near miss would be as good as a hit – some might say better. But the most potent bringer of panic was never used. Poison gas was barred by the Geneva protocols of 1925, and was not used in the European war, although both sides possessed stocks in case the other should start. People in shelters might gain some feeling of security and mutual support from each other; but isolated by a gas mask the effects of terror must have been multiplied, while the persistent nature of some of the agents rendered the 'all clear' of dubious value. Yet even terror can be overcome by counter terror; the feelings of impotence against aerial bombardment can be mitigated by revenge, by a feeling that the enemy are being paid back in their own coin.

It has been observed of rats that upon a man entering a sewer and walking along it, the rats will flee in terror before him; but when they reach the limit of their group territory, they will double back past him, overcoming their acquired fear of the gigantic new creature who invades their territory by the more ancient and hard wired and ever present terror of being hounded by their own kind. So it is with man. In the primitive, undisciplined and conformist 'pop' society of the classroom created by the blind faith of platonic liberalism, school bullies may terrify a child into suicide, despite the seeming availability of the superior power of teachers and parents, because they seem ever present and inescapable and their pressures raise ancient and primitive fears. So it was with the terrible *Gestapo*; you might privately fear that the war is lost, or long for any peace, or wish to form a new society, you may lose all belief in the system. But the ancient hard wired laws of survival mean that you fear most of all the informer, a neighbour who might smile at you today and sell you to the dreaded authorities tomorrow. But with their loss of belief in the Nazi German state came no new belief, no communicable idea like communism to seduce the individual. Any combination of individuals would have been crushed instantly. Instead came a belief in nothing but individual survival, in sticking things out until the end, just keeping alive by whatever means possible. Individual minds became deprogrammed and concerned more with basics. The state was atomised into individuals who wished merely to survive the horror, and those who believed fervently in Hitler's program. And the latter ruled.

In previous times, individuals so atomised might be re-programmed, as some of the Romans were re-programmed with the doctrine of Jesus. But if an enemy was at the gates, they could flee to him, as Romans fled from bureaucracy and grinding taxation to the barbarian invaders. You could be induced by greed to surrender the city to the foe, to open the gates. 'No walls are so high', said Philip the Great, 'that gold cannot surmount them'. But you cannot surrender to aeroplanes. Even if you were not terrified of your government, bombing made you dependent upon it for support. Like the man in the sewer, the aeroplanes are a transitory phenomenon, however terrible when they are there. You are still, after the fires, after the blasts, after the rubble of your home, helpless against the state. You carry on, you produce goods, you hate the enemy, you feel hope in new, secret weapons hurled against him, and above all, you survive – but when the enemy arrives at the gates, you surrender, because then you have a gigantic release. You have someone to surrender to and end the horror.

That bombing did destroy German morale is indubitable. Josef Goebbels, the very clever propagandist who as Minister of Propaganda was in charge of morale throughout Germany, and who had 'created' the Hitler image in Germany in films, in rallies, in brilliantly stage-managed events, acknowledged this to his diaries many times. On 6 October 1940 he noted, with some satisfaction, the inaccuracy of bombing.[14] On 20 October he expressed his admiration for Goering and the *Luftwaffe*. By 26 October, the SD (security service) informed him that the continual air raids were making people nervous. But in November, he was again noting that decoy installations had 'extensively duped' Bomber Command. In December he noted that morale was good despite many air raids during a visit to Hamburg. In February 1941 he wrote that Goering was a 'frank, open man' with whom he could work.[15] In April he noted that, although only ten out of sixty aircraft going to Berlin 'last time' (presumably the raid by eighty aircraft on 9/10 April) got through, one dropped a 'rather terrifying' bomb, which was 'no good omen for the future'. The 4,000 lb high capacity bomb came in at about this time. Goebbels inspected the site of the explosion, on the Kaiserdamm, noting that roofs and windows were shattered 'far and wide', but with no 'really serious' damage. A report from Emden a few days later spoke of morale as being 'not of the best', and that 'the party must go into action'.

But the greatest blow to morale in these months came not from British air raids, but from within. Goebbels needed all his considerable abilities to explain away the defection of the Deputy Leader of the *Reich*, Rudolf Hess, to Britain! It is June before Goebbels mentions the RAF again, and this is to ask why they are not attacking. June is occupied with the greatest event of the century, the huge assault on a vast front against the Soviet Union on the 22nd. In July occurs a comment on German 'Bomb Hoboes' (*Bombenfrischler*) who lived out in the open to escape bombing, and who were ruining morale thereby. Goebbels had unspecified 'vigorous steps' taken against them a few days later.

The arrival of Harris at Bomber Command was not noticed, but the terrible destruction at Lubeck and Rostock[16] were, with Goebbels declaring on 28 April 1942 that community life in Rostock had come to an end. However, the day before he had reported Hitler's opinion that industry could never be interfered with effectively by air raids, using the attacks on Britain as evidence. But from now on, air raids occupy an ever-increasing part in Goebbels' thoughts. He notes the effect on transport, but presumes it is the same for all belligerents; he notes the use of juveniles for anti-aircraft defence. In a heavy raid on Berlin in March 1943 he feels that Goering is 'quite unjustifiably' blamed for the *Luftwaffe*'s loss of popularity with the people of Berlin – although he noted that their morale remained 'exemplary', despite damage which will take six to eight months to repair 'even halfway'. In the Rhineland the people are 'getting somewhat weak in the knees' from the continual raids, thought Goebbels, who saw as a critical factor in this 'the inability to reply in kind', *to retaliate*. This was also what the troops wanted.[17] This need to retaliate in order to maintain morale, led Hitler to the 'V' weapons, the V1 flying bomb and the V2 rocket, which certainly raised morale for a time; but the vast effort and expense in development, particularly of the rocket, which scattered non aluminised explosive and the resources of the hard pressed electrical and electronics industries over south eastern England, can be counted as one of the greatest successes of the bomber offensive.[18]

In May 1943 Goebbels attributed the 'English' air supremacy to the tremendous efforts of the RAF and to the British aircraft industy, adding that a contributory factor had been German negligence. Then, in July, came the Hamburg firestorm, in which some 40,000 people perished – some incinerated, some asphyxiated, some simply blown to pieces. 'Air warfare,' thought Goebbels, 'is our most vulnerable point'; however, he told Hitler in September 1943 that the German people could tolerate air warfare as it was then conducted. Strangely, his diary entry for 21 September seems to echo the thoughts of Sir Arthur Harris, for he recognised that the dislocation to public life from city raids, especially on residential areas, had a worse effect on industry than the direct effect on factories, citing the Lanz works in Mannheim, which had been repaired for a fortnight but to which only 60% of the workers had returned. In November he noted the somewhat unsurprising fact that 'the everlasting grumbling has diminished considerably since death sentences against defeatists have been pronounced, executed and published'.

But by 1945 the diaries convey the true effect of the bombing. The air war is described as a 'crazy orgy' against which they were 'completely defenceless'.[19] Goering is blamed, his stock now having entirely vanished in Goebbels' eyes – and in Hitler's as well. The air war is described as 'the greatest tale of woe'. In Berlin damage to power stations had caused unemployment 'even in the most important armament industries'. Speer had put 800,000 people on to the repair of marshalling yards. Not much armament potential will be lost by retreats in the Rhine area, thought Goebbels – but this small consolation was because the arms potential had already been destroyed by air attacks. The population of the 'Western Districts', 'worn down by air war', were giving the Anglo-American forces a welcome – Goebbels had expected them to fight hard. On 7 March he admitted that the morale of the Army in the West was 'slowly sinking', which he attributed to the uninterrupted fighting. He noted that the German population under Eisenhower west of the Rhine – some three million people – were not allowed to leave their homes and were 'tormented' by regulations – but they were happy, 'now that they were finished with air raids'. The 'fundamental ailment' on all fronts was the 'lack of air defence'. Desertions were blamed on 'air bombardment' and the 'fire weapon' to which the people had been subjected for years. On 11 March Goebbels again pleaded with Hitler to get rid of Goering, whom Goebbels now blamed for 'all our set backs'. But Hitler would not.

'The internal situation in the Reich is governed almost completely by the air war', the 'loathsome Mosquito' achieving the harassing effect which Ludlow-Hewitt had predicted on Goebbels himself. The manufacturing decentralisation made essential by air raids had rendered critical the destruction of the railways by air raids – 'in the West the air war is the alpha and omega', wrote Goebbels in fury and despair. After the Rhine crossings, in 'many places' the German civilians 'opposed the [German] troops' and deliberately hampered the defence. Tank barriers were captured without any fighting at all. Air raid shelters became 'hotbeds of defeatism'(!) Troops, reported Kesselring (in command in the west at the end), were withdrawing or surrendering; women 'welcome and embrace' the Americans. 'The reason for our military decay', wrote Goebbels, 'is to be found in the air terror'. Hamburg, reported Speer, surrendered without a fight to a British ultimatum which threatened to bomb the city unless it surrendered.[20] However, Goebbels, who had proposed the extermination of the European Jews to Hitler, also prophesied, very correctly, that in fifty years time 'European mankind will avert its eyes in disgust' at Eisenhower's praise of Bomber Command's destruction of German cities. It is to be doubted that many of the future critics were Allied soldiers who survived only because of the walk over which the ruin of German morale gave them – or, indeed, survivors of the camps who, left for months longer, would themselves have succumbed. And area bombing of German cities would not necessarily have ended with the war; had the surrender terms been violated, had the 'werewolf' resistance which Goebbels tried to institute taken root in Germany, then SHAEF (Supreme Headquarters Allied Expeditionary Force) proposed to warn the nearest town so that the population could evacuate it, and then destroy it by bombing. 'There is no limit on military operations required by military necessity', ran the argument.[21] But this proved unnecessary – strategic bombing had done its work. There was no resistance movement at all.

That the Germans suffered an industrial collapse is undoubted. Aircraft were grounded for lack of fuel. Tanks were immobilised in vital battles at the Baranov bridgehead and in the Ardennes. Explosives were mixed with common salt to eke out supplies. Criticism is made of the bombing campaign, that production actually increased during 1944, as though the destruction of cities, of transport, of people, with huge numbers diverted to clearing rubble and firing anti-aircraft guns, were actually a useful stimulus. What bombing – and here the efforts of the USAAF and Bomber Command are inextricably bound up with each other – achieved is to put a cap on the German industrial colossus, and finally to destroy it. As we have looked to Josef Goebbels, the head of propaganda, for the effect on morale, we shall seek the slightly more dubious opinion of Albert Speer, the industrial supremo, that Germany had some 10,000 heavy anti-aircraft guns pointing at the German skies. This was roughly equal to the total number of anti-tank guns[22] – not forgetting, of course, that not only these 10,000, but others lost in production by bombing, would have been available. Speer thought that bombing, by 1945, had meant a loss of production amounting to 35% of tanks, 31% of aircraft and 42% of trucks.

Trenchard's great doctrine, implemented with Harris' leadership and persistence, and immensely reinforced by the Americans, had indeed achieved great results. But it had not achieved victory on its own; it had not won the war, and it could have been used more effectively. It is often thought that this was, in part, due to Harris himself: his insistence upon 'area' bombing of cities; his disbelief in the ability of the Command to hit specific targets; his scorning of 'panacea targets' such as oil installations which were later shown to have had such an effect upon Germany's ability to wage war. But these surely pale into insignificance by the side of deeper faults which ran through the whole of Bomber Command's campaign, some caused by what seems to have been an attitude more commonly ascribed in modern times to the Generals of the Great War, and some by too blind an adherence to the doctrine itself.

The defence of the bomber was at the very centre of the whole question of the viability of the bomber offensive, which was itself at the very centre of British grand strategy. Tizard's dictum that the great criterion was the number of bombs on target per bomber casualty, and Ludlow-Hewitt's observation that 'It is the size of the casualty rate in our fighting forces which will lose the war' were not humanitarian attempts to save bomber crews, but essential truths in the bombing campaign. Yet no great sense of urgency can be detected in the Air Ministry or the Armament Department over a subject which was of immense national importance. The huge industrial effort involved in creating, by 1945, a force of some 1,800 four-engined heavy bombers after starting the war with some 400 two-engined mediums hides the fact that roughly 8,000 were lost in roughly 2,000 days of war. It is too simple and crude a comment, but surely indicative of the importance of the loss rate to the bombload, that if the losses had been halved, the total available bombload would have tripled by 1945.

Despite the acknowledgement that all the famous fighter pilots eventually saw the absolutely critical advantages of accurate fire and who accordingly made themselves marksmen, this vital personal factor seems to have been completely ignored in the training of bomber gunners – to which, of course, it applied equally. Even when training was improved, Harris was rightly infuriated by a suggestion that eyesight standards should be lowered. That this measure could be contemplated for a second was an indication of the attitude to the importance of gunnery standards, let alone the supreme importance of keeping a good look out. It is surprising that standards were not raised. That there had been a shortage of good aircrew is undoubtedly true, but what had made the shortage if it was not their slaughter in the air?

Save for a few bombers converted by Bomber Command's own efforts and some aeroplanes supplied by the United States, the bomber force was equipped throughout the war with .303" infantry calibre weapons. It was realised long before the war that this was inadequate, but a combination of factors led to its retention. The first, and the least understandable, that the extra weight of higher calibre guns would reduce the bombload, had been reinforced by the pre-war calculations of British and German hitting power, which had increasingly focussed on this. While this is obviously true in the first instance, the reduction in total bombload steadily erodes as the losses are reduced and more bombers survive to bomb. Given enough time, it will *always* be the case that the total bombload will end up being greater. It is difficult to see how losses would not have reduced with guns that had a better trajectory, longer range and vastly greater hitting power. Another incalculable bonus of more effective defence is the increasing experience of crews, who grow steadily more effective.

But because this *initial* reduction in bombload was unacceptable, the number of higher calibre guns in this theoretical comparison was reduced compared with the .303", and then because of this reduced rate of fire of larger calibre guns the .303" was declared to be more effective at longer ranges because of a higher bullet density, ignoring the far better trajectory of the higher calibre bullets and the fact that the effective area of the target was much greater with larger calibres. A further argument on relative bullet speeds, which suggested that the bomber's fire to the rear was more effective than the fighter's forward fire, gave an almost completely spurious advantage to the bomber, which made it seem that it was unnecessary to arm the bomber with higher calibres. It was felt that the heavier guns in the rear would create problems with the centre of gravity, but this could scarcely have applied to bombers not yet designed, and even after, it was not insuperable – but would again mean reduced bombload by strengthening the aircraft's structure. But the fighter was cannon-armed very quickly, the arguments of range, group size and rate of fire which had burdened the defence of the bomber having been conducted more realistically for the fighter.

Even with the .303" itself, no great energy or urgency was shown in developing a higher velocity gun, or a more rapid rate of fire. The Director of Armament Development, after pointing out that it had taken fifteen years to develop the 'Gebauer' high-speed gun, was given charge of the development of the high-velocity gun. But in the Gebauer type rapid-fire gun itself, the Armament Department ingeniously discovered a disadvantage; after the pilot was killed by these bullets, more would be wasted on his corpse. Cicero might have said, and Harris would certainly have agreed, that 'Non possum' should have been inscribed on the forehead of each and every one of them. With the Armament Department, it assumed the nature of a religious chant. War is conducted by programmed individuals, and the subprogram which unified and sedated the Armament Department was very different from that which animated the bomber crews and their commanders.

It had been recognised that some, at least, of the .303" rounds would need to be armour piercing in order to force the fighters to carry armour plate, but the relationship between extra bomber firepower and an extra burden of frontal armour for the fighters was not pursued. It was accepted without question that an escort fighter carrying the burden of extra fuel could not compete with a short-range fighter, but to force the compensating addition of a burden of frontal armour plate to the short-range fighter (which severely hampered it in dogfighting) by having the bomber armed with heavier calibre weapons, was not pursued. The classical dilemma, that if an escort fights it cannot escort, and if it escorts it cannot fight, was touted as the last word in wisdom; but the answering dilemma, that if a fighter is engaged with another fighter it cannot attack a bomber, was never used. Escort fighters detracted from the offensive, to which all power should be given. Home defence fighters themselves were at first provided more as a sop to the politicians than from any perceived usefulness. But putting fighters into a separate command made the provision of escorts that much more difficult.

And so the bomber was forced to bomb by night, when it could hit nothing with any accuracy, and often could not find the city where the target lay. This really altered Tizard's ratio for the worse, since although the 'bombers lost' declined, the 'bombs on target' declined even more dramatically. And if the bomber were caught by a fighter at night, he stood less chance than in the day, for the fighter could seldom be seen in time. Here the poorly armed turrets, especially the rear turret, acted as look out posts; but even here Harris could describe them as '80% angle iron and 20% scratched perspex'. Night bombing had always been a part of Bomber Command's plan – so why was it that a turret which you could see clearly out of – the only small advantage the bomber had at night – was not produced until 1944, and only then because the Command designed it themselves?

With the speed bomber, it is possible to sympathise with the detractors, although they were completely wrong. The idea of a bomber that could outrun a fighter seemed wild, and the Mosquito was always a prey to a German advance in technology, such as the jet fighter. Unfortunately, the Mosquito, the wooden wonder, could not be produced in huge quantities, although both Canada and Australia made them as well.

Owing to the failure of the armament engineers and administrators, it was therefore evasion upon which the bomber was forced to rely, and this was assisted by men and women of vast intelligence, great dedication and great *energy*. The same brilliant people devised the very clever navigation and bombing aids. By late 1944, after the American victory over the *Luftwaffe* with heavily armed bombers and fighter escorts, Tizard's ratio moved decisively in Bomber Command's favour, and terrible indeed were the consequences for Germany.

When we turn to look at the *offensive* weapons of the bomber, the position seems even less comprehensible. The doctrine itself was one of a relentless offensive, but the young lion had old and decayed teeth, not having had the advantage of a dental check for many years. Firstly, the 4 lb incendiary bomb. This was the most destructive weapon in Bomber Command's armoury, the destroyer of cities, of Rostock and Lubeck, of Hamburg and Dresden. But when released from 20,000 feet at 200 mph, it was sprayed all over the sky, and was very dangerous to the bombers themselves. It obviously needed a cluster apparatus, which would carry the bombs in one case and, aimed with an accuracy impossible with the individual bombs, and opening at a suitable height, would release the bombs with the desired concentration. How simple an apparatus does this seem, yet how difficult to implement! When the clusters finally arrived, they were often defective, and too easily damaged in transit. What would have happened to German cities if these clusters had been available in 1941 or 1942? How many firestorms would have swept through them, lit by the almost *four million* 4 lb incendiaries which fell over them every month?

Yet the high explosive bombs themselves were often defective. Although the Navy had used Torpex, an aluminised explosive, and its effects had been made known to Saundby in 1942, it was not used in RAF bombs because of a shortage of aluminium. Aluminium powder added some 80% to the blast effect of ammonal. A heavy bomber itself contained some 10 tons of aluminium. When the supply eased, its advantages were forgotten, to be remembered only when Cherwell and others were discussing the probable blast effect of the German rocket in September 1943. Not until 1944 were British explosives as effective as the German. This, however, seems more to have arisen from a genuine mistake than from a defective attitude. Added to this, bombs with a higher charge/weight ratio were devised in 1941/2, which again added to the power enormously. Yet almost 20% of British bombs did not explode at all, due mainly to flat strikes. Bombs were the sole reason for the existence of the RAF, yet were almost ignored between the wars, being designed to fit into existing aircraft, rather than the aircraft being designed to carry the bombs.

'Britain' and 'The Royal Air Force' were programs, organisations at war, and their only reality lay in the individual men and women who fought for them. The RAF was an almost amorphous organisation, and some individuals were more in touch with politicians, with civil servants, with manufacturers, with universities and with research stations than they were with the fighting arms. Gone were the days when an Alexander or a Caesar could inspirit and enthuse his men with a pre-battle speech or a daring action, creating and reinforcing the desired program – nor could the Commander even make decisions on weapons or pay, on promotions or on medals. Bomber Command was just a part of the RAF, and was subject to many supervisors beside its Commander in Chief. It could be pulled this way and that by others, and even Ludlow-Hewitt remarked that 'there are too many people trying to run this Command'. The Commander in Chief of Bomber Command had to enthuse his men mostly without seeing them, and had to stamp his impress upon them in these difficult circumstances. He had to bring his Command to great sacrifices, to order them to sacrifice themselves in campaigns that they had a good deal less than even chance of surviving. Day after day, and night after night, men did not return. He had to forget them, forget that they died on his orders, and concentrate on the next night. Churchill said of Jellicoe at Jutland, that he was 'the only man who could have lost the war in an afternoon'; but the Commander in Chief of Bomber Command risked his whole force on very many occasions.

Yet very many individuals of critical importance to the offensive were not under his control. The Commander in Chief of the force which delivered the bombs had continually to press for improvements to the defence of the aeroplanes and the quality of the bombs with individuals in other organisations who seemed to be fighting a different war, if they were fighting a war at all. Before America had entered the war, the North American Aircraft Company had produced a prototype of the Mustang fighter in 119 days – one day earlier than scheduled. This was not just a triumph of industrial organisation, it was an illustration of a dynamism and a '*possumus*' approach. This contrasted starkly with the Armament Department's tired estimate of fifteen years to develop a gun, and virtual failure to develop a cluster for the 4 lb incendiary, which had been shown by ORS to be the most effective weapon, while pushing forward their own idea, the 30 lb 'J' bomb, which was a failure. Albert Speer, the German Armaments Minister, after assessing the effects of the Hamburg firestorm, told Hitler that another six cities destroyed in this way would bring armaments production to a total halt.[23] Harris, in his *Despatch on War Operations*, concluded that the failure to produce a satisfactory cluster before the war's end '*enormously* [italics added] reduced the efficiency of our incendiary attacks'. The clustering of the little 4 lb incendiary bomb could be ranked in importance with the great strategic debates which have followed the war, for used properly, it might have won it. Grand strategic conceptions also need an attention to humble details. Those at the top of an organisation need to ensure that all are imbued with their program, from top to bottom. This becomes increasingly difficult as the proportion of warriors 'at the sharp end' continues to decline. The tail, in Bomber Command's war, was already wagging the dog, and often forgetting it altogether in its own day to day program.

The Air Staff, in their reply to Harris' accusations of incompetence in *Despatch on War Operations*, accepted that 'there were certainly grounds for complaint in this connection', due to 'deep seated organisational imperfections', mainly due to 'an incorrect outlook in the inter war period'. We have seen Tedder's and Tizard's comments on the armament side. Perhaps, as in Parkinson's Law, the solution was an injection of sergeant major's blood, whose elements were 'the best is scarcely good enough' blended with 'there is no excuse for anything'.[24] Harris would have agreed.

An organisation is, like the state, not a real, tangible thing, but a belief, a program, and the individuals who form it can communicate to each other a certain atmosphere, whether of urgency or sloth, of *possumus* or *non possumus*, of positivity or negativity, of enthusiasm or of resignation. It needed a status and personnel to match its *supreme importance* in the RAF and, therefore, in the nation. Yet the slumbers of its acknowledged 'dead heads' were too little disturbed, even in the greatest war in history.

The survival of the RAF between the wars seemed to depend on the great airman Trenchard and the doctrine of the relentless offensive, and in this the defence of the bomber and the actual detail of exactly *how* the destruction was to be caused were lost in his powerful and dreadful vision of panicking crowds and ruined cities. The doctrine was never really thought out in terms of navigation, of bomb aiming, of the bombs themselves, of the guns, escorts and training. Where an adherence to doctrine is the path to success, as it is in most human activities, whether political, military or commercial, few will be found to openly question it, especially if the originator of the doctrine is a revered figure in the organisation.[25]

Most will believe it without question. Perhaps a 'devil's advocate' should sit in all organisations, arguing against accepted doctrine, testing it; and if no precise way can be found to make it work, then forcing its abandonment or modification. Trenchard's doctrine, so treated, might well have been modified, and have worked, and the war might well have been won from the air alone, had it been tested properly in conclaves of airmen and of engineers, of armament engineers and manufacturers and explosives experts, of radio engineers and aerodynamicists, and its exact requirements discovered, and the precise way to find and to destroy a factory or a city, the type and number and quality and application of the bombs required for it worked out, *and the losses due to flak and fighters assessed and new methods of bomber defence tried*. But in those circumstances, with such a huge investment obviously required, it might never have been tried. Men and women might have shrunk from the expense, and the carnage – although, of course, it was presented as a defensive measure.

The *morality* of the bombing campaign faces the modern liberal with a dilemma. Reeling back in horror from hanging even the vilest murderer, imbued with the Platonic belief that no one does ill by choice, but by ignorance of it being wrong, they do not punish the criminals, but rather persuade them to see that what they did was hurtful and wrong – which the gratified criminal readily does. But if the criminal is armed and has accomplices, the matter is referred to the police force, a body of professionals who arrest the offenders, often by shedding the blood of both themselves and the criminals. The criminal, or a member of the criminal's family, or even a bystander, perhaps a child, may be killed or injured. An enquiry is held, to see if the police used excessive force, and if this is found to be the case, to *punish* the police. The more powerful in numbers and arms that the criminals become, the more the force necessary to overcome them, and the greater the likelihood of an enquiry. The force applied, according to the liberal, must be minimal, and closely controlled. But in war, such nice calculations can seldom be made, and if they are made, they are more often made by the losers.

The British liberal establishment, whose proudest achievement has been to create a new Austria-Hungary in their own land, have developed, since the war, an obsession with race. A person must now even declare to which group they'belong'before being considered for public employment, but this is held not to be 'racism', but to enable a group to see that it is equal. This thinking was at the root of Hitler's brutality, thinking in groups instead of individuals.

If the group, the state, the race, are real things, then they are higher things than the individual, and more important. The more people are willing to serve the state, and to advance it by war, the more militarised its citizens become, and the stronger it will be. This tendency has been checked in two ways by more peaceful societies – by the use of technology, and by professional armies (who are starved of funds). Naval technology and expertise were enabled by the wealth of civilised Athens to hold back the military machine of the Spartans, until the wealth of Persia bought the Spartans a fleet. The Romans, in the decline of military virtue, found a professional army to'save the sum of things for pay'. European civilisation, or rather, the monarch's property, was protected by professional armies until the French Revolution swept them away. A 'natural selection' of states, such as Prussia, then led to the gradual militarisation of the world, and this rise of militarism and a rapid rise in military technology led to the disappearance of the militarily inept societies of Africa and Asia, save those, like Japan, which adopted the new technology and adapted it to the old militarism. This was hardly a moral process, for young men were conscripted and gouged, sliced, smashed, poisoned, burnt and shot to death in ever increasing numbers, while mothers and fathers, brothers, sisters, wives and children wept and mourned and frequently starved, their individual lives changed for ever. But the progress of science, which had done so much to forward the process, enabling soldiers to fight in vast numbers without starvation or disease and slowly increasing the power of weapons, finally ended this process by making the weapons so powerful that the heart of the state, its industry and industrial cities and citizens, could be directly assaulted. The Second World War saw the consummation of this process. The rocket and the bomb have provided an umbrella, under which men and women are free to pursue less martial pursuits without the fear of their masters, that they are thereby made soft and incapable of self defence against more warlike societies – always providing, of course, that the ruler is willing to use the ultimate weapon if attacked. Hitler would have said that it had led to the degeneracy of the martial virtues. Who could, or who would now return to the martial virtues and a mass army? The most significant turning point in this process was in 1940, with the fall of the great French Army and the defeat of the British. The bombing of Britain pointed the way forward. A minute analysis of its effects on British cities and industry by the scientists at the Ministry of Home Security had shown it to be a very useful method of waging war, and the catastrophic state of the Army made it the only one, except possibly hedgehogging after the Battle of Britain, with a side show in North Africa, and Tizard's idea of a bomber reinforced blockade of Germany. But this would have been a defensive war, and might have been seen in both Russia and the United States as a jockeying for position before negotiations. It would, of course, have been possible for Britain's leaders to conclude that the example of dead women and children in Britain's cities should not be requited on Germany, so that Britain might retain, in this, a moral superiority. This, given the inaccuracy of bombing, would have meant the complete abandonment of a strategy on which Britain had relied, and the moral victory would have given Germany the option of a virtual abandonment of the war in the West, for the chances of a British Army invading the continent in inferior numbers and morale, with inferior equipment and without air superiority, were nil. The spider is a short sighted, slow and vulnerable creature, but fighting on ground of her own construction and choosing, she defeats more formidable foes. The result of her contests may be grisly and disgusting to the observer, but if she 'fought fair' with the wasp, she would have been extinct long ago.

A thousand years before, England had been ruled by Aethelred (good counsel) Unraed (no counsel), *the ill advised*, known as the 'Unready'. Both epithets fitted him well. In his ill-starred reign a Danish fleet prowled the English shores for plunder. It was bottled up in Northey Island in the River Pant (Blackwater) by the English Earl Brytnoth and his war band. The Danes wanted to cross the causeway which connected the island to the Essex shore in order to plunder, but would have been under a very severe disadvantage if they tried it in the presence of the English Army. They therefore called on Brytnoth to give up his unfair advantage, to give them a chance, and to stand his army back from the water's edge, so that they might fight it out equally, shield to shield. Brytnoth agreed, gaining the moral advantage! It *was* a fair fight. He was killed, and his companions chose to fight and die on the spot, true to the old Germanic warrior code. The Danes, however, were completely victorious. Britain, in a more calculating and scientific search for victory, did not repeat the folly, noble though it was. 'Without victory', said Churchill, 'there is no survival...' Churchill, *the scientifically advised*, however noble in thought, however warlike in spirit, was no Aethelred, and no Brytnoth.

The inaccuracy of bombing was caused by the use of anti-aircraft guns, which forced the bombers to fly high, and made their aim vastly more difficult, so that they hit industrial areas rather than factories. This was a choice made by the defence, since to allow your factories to be destroyed was to invite defeat. There could have been a convention, of course, to clearly mark factories, and to keep fighter aeroplanes and anti-aircraft guns away from cities! But a more serious choice open to the defence was to evacuate women and children from the cities. This was done to a considerable extent. There was a debate on which, and how many, women should be evacuated when an hourly German rocket with a 10 ton warhead was expected to land on London. The IRA during their recent campaigns issued warnings of bombs placed, which forced the authorities to evacuate whole areas with the result that far more dislocation was caused than by simply ignoring the warnings, and thereby avoided the opprobrium of causing carnage, with the inevitable hardening of the public attitude and calls for reprisals, as after the Enniskillen bomb. It left the way open to the issue of correctly code-worded deliberately false alarms, which caused all the disruption without incurring any cost, save for a phone call. If the Government had chosen to 'raise the stakes', avoid some of the disruption and ignored the warnings, who would have been morally at fault, the Government or the IRA? In reacting to the German rocket threat, it was accepted by the Chiefs of Staff that London, a huge industrial centre, was a legitimate target, although Churchill argued otherwise. Evacuation was an option, although it imposed a heavy burden on the morale of those who went and those who remained, and also imposed a heavy burden on supplies and transport, and deprived industry of workers. Bombing forced this dilemma upon an enemy. The bombers were not directed to rove the skies of Germany, searching below for women and children to kill, as Hitler's acolytes scoured Europe for Jews or gypsies or Freemasons. They were after industrial cities, and anyone who worked in them, because their scientists had seen that this method of warfare worked, and could be improved upon. Thomas Cleary, in his introduction to *The Art of War* by Sun Tsu, stated that:

The ancient Taoist masters showed how the man of aggressive violence appears to be ruthless but is really an emotionalist; then they slay the emotionalist with real ruthlessness before revealing the spontaneous nature of free humanity.

It has become normal in the moral argument to take a German city in isolation from Prussian militarism and sordid Nazi cruelties – most often Saxon Dresden – to dwell upon its ancient culture, its buildings, the bridges over its peacefully flowing waters, the performances in its circus and in its theatres, its mothers and its fair haired children happily playing, its whole 'normality'. And then to describe in detail the sudden cruel fall of the incendiaries, its destruction, the charred bodies of the children, the women burned to ashes, and to then say '*This* cannot be moral!' The next step is to say, 'We *both* did things we regret'. This then becomes a very subtle form of holocaust denial, an equation of the child killed in the city by bombing, with the child deliberately searched out, perhaps in an orphan's home, perhaps, as with poor Anne Frank, hiding in a garret, and deliberately and individually killed because they were seen, not as individuals, but members of a group. Indeed, had there been more 'Dresdens', as perhaps with a working 4 lb incendiary cluster in 1942 there might have been, Miss Frank might have been even now a very great living literary light, and many a flower 'born to blush unseen, wasting its sweetness' in the foul air of Buchenwald or Auschwitz, might have lit the world. Harris, who had not initiated the Dresden bombing but had carried it out and has been blamed ever since, warned that it might be a dangerous precedent in the Japanese war to put the lives of enemy civilians before those of your own soldiers – as indeed it would have been. He, unlike Churchill, knew nothing of the very imminent coming of atomic weapons, and the happy concurrence of both the Churchill and Atlee Governments in their use.

That the German people suffered terribly, from bombing, from mistreatment in American prisoner of war camps and under the Russians is undeniable; but in all justice they can hardly have expected garlands of roses,[26] and at least the full scale of their brutalities in Russia were not requited on them by the Russian soldiery, as Goebbels had led them to believe would happen.

We have two main programs, one behaving as the individual creature that we are, and the other behaving as part of a state, or other necessarily imaginary organisation. 'He prayeth well, who loveth well, both man and bird and beast' is Coleridge's conclusion, in the *Ancient Mariner*, as to how we should conduct ourselves. In the first program, this is open to all. Yet in the second, if we could all have been at liberty to live by this code, we would have avoided war only for a time, eventually to succumb to those who were united and motivated by more violent urges, and who trained and prepared for, and gloried in, the pits and arenas of war. Until, that is, city-destroying weapons enabled us to live in peace – or at least, to avoid a major all out war. In an extension of Vegetius' paradox, 'those who would have peace must prepare for war' has become, 'those who would have peace must be prepared for the complete destruction of the enemy'.[27] And if the program of peace and justice finds itself inevitably embroiled with the program of war and savagery, the paradox becomes a clear imperative – you must win *however you can*.

The relentless offensive was an inevitable stage in this shortcut past the bugles and the drums, the mass armies and mass casualties and military programs of the past to the new peace of cold scientific terrors. Paradoxically, the only mass casualties of Britain's war were inflicted on the men who carried out the relentless offensive. They received little recognition and much opprobrium, save from the soldiers and sailors who had been spared by their efforts, although the scientists who had made the relentless offensive possible, who had quietly solved the problems of how to destroy a city, were lauded and recognised. Indeed, Dr Jacob Bronowski of the Ministry of Home Security would later make a television programme entitled 'The Ascent of Man'. It was fitting that he should do this, for his aid to the destruction of the cities of Germany had played a great part in that ascent. It is also fitting that those who carried it out, who descended into the arena to fight when no one else could (or perhaps would), should be associated with that ascent.

If the curious traveller who had pondered the inscriptions by Cleopatra's Needle were to turn his or her back on the river, wander up Villiers Street to the Strand and head eastward, they would come across a small bust of Sir Arthur Travers Harris outside St Clement Dane's church. Its dedication in 1989 was a brave deed for a frail but grateful old woman, the last Empress of India and mother of the Queen, for it was accompanied by the expected catcalls and jeers and criticised in the liberal press. But the greatest monument to the men of Bomber Command lies overseas, beyond the great river Rhine, where some sixty-five million individuals, horrified alike by what they and their forebears had suffered and inflicted, have re-created and elevated the great German nation in a program of peace and justice, and steadfastly refuse the calls of foolish allies to re-enthrone the grey ghosts of the Prussians, and the bloody program of war.

The future will see the evolution, sometimes aided by revolution, of new programs. What the program(s) will be in a thousand years we have no idea at all; as the Aztecs could not conceive of our modern programs, so we cannot conceive the future. We do not even know if human animals will be around at all. All that we may hope is, that if they still exist, whatever their program, it will consider the reality of the individual to be more than the illusions of our organisations or 'races'. We in the present have been made aware that the ultimate, logical conclusion of the idea of a state as an real entity greater than the individual leads inevitably to fascism – indeed, that is precisely what fascism was. That this program was a blind alley in these times owes much to the individuals who carried out, and those who empowered and directed, the relentless offensive.

Notes

1 Philip Stokes, *100 Essential Thinkers – William of Occam*, Arcturus Publishing, London, 2002, 54–55.

2 Carl Zimmer, *Soul Made Flesh*, Arrow Books, London 2005, 276.

3 If many programs operate side by side, as in 'multi cultural' Britain, you simply acquire more than one state on the same soil, and accordingly become unstable.

4 Although 'mankind' itself can become a form of fascism in which only homo sapiens among all creatures matters, and the 'races' and 'peoples' of mankind must be permitted to increase wildly at the expense of all creation, for to criticise this means 'racism'. Thus it is a liberal shibboleth that neither global warming nor food prices nor hunger can owe anything to the vast increase of homo sapiens. If it was Adolf Hitler's final wish to destroy the world, from his niche in hell he would perhaps place the greatest hopes in the liberals' reaction to his first attempt.

5 Karl von Clausewitz, *On War*, Penguin Books, London, 1982, 101.

6 Karl von Clausewitz, 164–5.

7 The history of the Jewish *people* over the corresponding period is perhaps very different. See Arthur Koestler, *The Thirteenth Tribe: The Khazar Empire and its Heritage*, Random House USA Inc, NY, 1999 (reprint). Koestler argued that the Russian and eastern Jews were descended from the Khazars, who converted to Judaism and spread out after the fall of their empire; that the captivities of Israel and Judah in 722 BC and 586 BC respectively involved the removal of the middle classes and ruling classes, leaving the common people behind; and that therefore, to an extent, the original Jewish people, now Palestinians, were sometimes dispossessed by Khazars, now Israelis. I have absolutely no worthwhile knowledge, and therefore no worthwhile opinion on this, save to make the unsurprising observation that the Israeli authorities disagree. No doubt geneticists are furiously occupied in the matter!

8 Luke 10.25-37.

9 See HE Coemans, *War and Punishment: The Causes of War Termination and the First World War*, Princeton University Press, Woodstock, 2000. Coemans argues that certain forms of government find it difficult to make peace without victory, and that 'mixed regimes', such as Hindenburg's and the Kaiser's Germany, will be punished whether they lose moderately or disastrously. I am indebted to Dr W Philpott, of King's College London, for drawing my attention to this most interesting book.

10 Liddell Hart, *History of the First World War*, Pan Books, London, 1972, 377–8.

11 Richard Overy, *Bomber Command 1939–1945*, HarperCollins, London, 1997, 13.

12 PRO75-53, Air Vice Marshal Slessor to station commanders No. 5 Group, 28 October, 1941.

13 Marshal of the Royal Air Force Lord Tedder, *With Prejudice*, Cassell, London, 1966, 570–71.

14 Translated and edited by Fred Taylor, *The Goebbels Diaries, 1939–1941*, Hamish Hamilton, London, 1982, 133. All subsequent notes until July 1941 are from this work.

15 In March he noted with satisfaction reports that Germany had taken a 'good swig from the bottle' of France since the surrender.

16 Translated by Louis P Lochner, *The Goebbels Diaries 1942–3*, Doubleday & Co., New York, 1948. All references to Goebbels' diary from 1942 to November 1943 are from this volume.

17 Goebbels, 499.

18 Roy Irons, *Hitler's Terror Weapons*, HarperCollins, London, 2002.

19 Trans. by Richard Barry, Ed. by Hugh Trevor-Roper, *The Goebbels Diaries*, Book Club Associates, London, 1978, 18.

20 Albert Speer (trans. by Richard and Clara Winston), *Inside the Third Reich*, Orion Books, London, 1995, 658.

21 PRO WO219/2443.

22 Albert Speer (trans. by Richard and Clara Winston), *Inside the Third Reich*, Orion Books, London, 1995, 382.

23 Albert Speer (trans. by Richard and Clara Winston), *Inside the Third Reich*, Orion Books, London, 1995, 389.

24 C Northcote Parkinson, *Parkinson's Law, or The Pursuit of Progress*, John Murray, London, 1959, 106.

25 Perhaps the most sensible attitude to an authoritative military, or any, doctrine was illustrated by the actor, comedian and singer Alfred Marks, who told the story of the Great Rabbi, the greatest Jewish thinker for 500 years, who lay on his deathbed. Hearing that the Great Rabbi had fallen into a coma, the leading Jewish thinkers from all around the world, from Jerusalem and New York, from Paris and Johannesburg and London, congregated at his bedside. They waited patiently for months. Then, one day, his eyes flickering open, they rushed forward and said 'Master, master, please give us some gem of your wisdom, some last thought which will encapsulate all your teaching and your doctrine and which will stay with us when you leave us and this empty world behind'. The Great Rabbi muttered 'Life…is like a glass of wine'. The brilliant Jewish thinkers then hurried back to their universities and synagogues in Jerusalem and New York, in Paris and Johannesburg and London, and in endless conclaves discussed the Rabbi's summary. They dissected it, analysed it, yet none could not quite grasp *how* it was true, and they returned to the Great Rabbi's bedside, hoping for some elucidation should he temporarily recover. They waited for months. One day, his eyelids flickered again. On his reopening his eyes, they rushed forward and told him how they had endlessly discussed his last thought, 'Life is like a glass of wine', but were quite unable to make any real sense of it. The Great Rabbi uplifted his palms with a weary gesture; 'Ok', he said, 'So life is *not* like a glass of wine'. And he died.

This story should accompany all doctrine, particularly that which seems sanctified more by its originator's status than by its inherent value.

26 The British Bombing Survey Unit, however, found some in the Ruhr who expected compensation from the United Kingdom for the bombing.

27 A woman, a wife and mother, in campaigning to be the Democratic Party candidate for the American presidential election, recently proposed that, in the event of an attack on their ally Israel, the seven million individuals of which the Iranian Government threatens to destroy, Iran, a state of some sixty million individuals, should be obliterated. But who would wish for a return to 1914?

APPENDIX

Harry Winter

I have known Harry Winter for a long time, and besides being grateful for his often sought advice in writing this book, have always been fascinated by the story of his personal war. I have included this story for three reasons.

Herodotus wrote his *Histories* 'in the hope of thereby preserving from decay the remembrance of what men have done…' and it seems fitting that Harry's story, including as it does the very different individuals with very different behaviours who are classified and grouped as 'Germans', not only deserves to be preserved but well illlustrates Chapter 10 of this book. The third reason is that I am sure the reader will find the story as fascinating as does the author.

I was born in Cardiff in 1922 and attended school during the years of depression and high unemployment. My father was a skilled tradesman and therefore in permanent employment.

When I left school, I took up employment at the local paper making mill, first as an assistant stock keeper, then through the costing department and then to processing orders for the making machines.

In May 1940, there was a call for volunteers for the Local Defence Volunteers (LDV), later called the Home Guard, so I joined the local force doing guard duties at the BBC and head post office.

As the nights were getting longer, we started getting air raid warnings. This, being a new experience, it acted as a laxative on a large portion of the population until they got accustomed to them.

On 2 January 1941, Cardiff experienced its first blitz and bomb damage was caused to my house, so I decided to retaliate, and volunteered for aircrew in the RAF. I had my ACSB (Aircrew Selection Board) in May and was called up in September.

After eighteen months training I was passed as a Sergeant Wireless Operator Air and posted to an Advanced Flying Unit, then to an OTU (Operational Training Unit) where the crews got together and I did my first operation in a WELLINGTON BOMBER. At this period of the war, the four engine bombers were replacing the twin engine ones, so the crew were posted to a conversion unit where we picked up another air gunner and an engineer, and were then posted to a squadron.

22 October 1943

After breakfast I reported to Bob the Skipper that I was feeling fitter, having reported sick three days earlier with a touch of 'flu. Bob then informed us that we were scheduled for Ops. that night.

Briefing was immediately after lunch and we were informed that the target was Kassel and that a diversionary raid was to be made on Frankfurt. Take-off time was 17.30 (5.30 pm) and as the squadron was to be in the second wave of attack our ETA (Estimated Time of Arrival) was to be set for 21.04 (9.04 pm).

In the afternoon we had our flying supper, ham and eggs and later transported to the dispersal of 'L' for love, this being the aircraft we were allocated for the trip. On arrival at the dispersal we boarded the aircraft, stowed our kit and started checking the equipment. Bob gave the signal to the fitter outside to connect the trolley ACC (a booster to start the engine) and switched on the port inner engine. After a few attempts to start without success, we signalled by Aldis to flight control that the engine was U/S (unserviceable). We were not allowed to use the RT (radio telephone) because the Germans would pick it up on their listening stations. A short while later the CO (Commanding Officer) who was not flying on this Op drove over in his car and we informed him of the problem. The ground staff confirmed the trouble.

It was then established that 'G' George was a spare already bombed up, so we were instructed to transfer. As the transport had returned to the MT (Motor Transport) section, we had to walk everything over to the other aircraft. On entering 'G' we learned that no 'Window' (anti-radar strips) had been loaded on, so we had to do a shuttle between the aircraft with the bundles of Window.

We took off on time and occupied our respective positions. I switched on the WT Receiver and all other equipment but unfortunately the MONICA receiver, which gave warning of aircraft approaching our tail, was not tuned in and was oscillating, so Bob ordered it to be switched off. MONICA could only be tuned in when the aircraft was on the ground. We set course for Cromer which was the rendezvous for all the Bomber force and upon reaching it all aircraft switched off their navigation lights and set course for Holland.

On reaching the Dutch coast we set course for Frankfurt. As we reached the Dutch–German border, Roy the rear gunner alerted us of a night fighter approaching our tail, giving a commentary, whilst at the same time Tiny, the mid upper gunner, confirmed that he had the fighter in his sight. The fighter then commenced his attack, Roy ordered to corkscrew and at the same time, both gunners opened fire on the attacker. Strikes were reported on the fighter which dived into the cloud below. We then resumed course.

Just north of Frankfurt, we changed course for Kassel and as we neared our ETA flares, followed by TIs (Target Indicators) started to burst ahead. Incendiaries then started lighting up the ground. As we approached the built up area, fighter flares started bursting above us right on our track and it felt like driving down a brilliantly lit street. The fighters had been vectored on to us, as the Germans had no doubt concluded, on the attack of the first wave, that this was the main target.

We then commenced our bombing run under the bomb aimer's instructions and felt the aircraft lift as we dropped our load of high explosive cookie and incendiaries. At the end of the bombing run, when the camera had taken the photo of our bombs bursting, we turned to port and steered a course for Hannover, which would be our next turning point for home.

About eight minutes from the target we were suddenly struck in the tail by cannon shells, no doubt a fighter had picked us up under the flares and followed us out. Bob said 'We have been hit' and called the gunners for a report. As there was no response, he requested Stan, the engineer, to go back and investigate. Stan replied that he was checking the petrol gauges for damage to the petrol tanks. Bob then requested me to go back and try to make contact. Reaching the mid upper turret I struck Tiny on the thighs but there was no response. I then hurried to the rear turret, struck the doors and as there was no response I endeavoured to open them at the same time looking through the porthole. The turret doors were jammed and I could see no movement or reaction from Roy. I then made my way forward and as I reached the rest position there was another burst of cannon shells coming through the fuselage. I felt a sharp sting on the inside of my right thigh and the pyrotechnics were starting to blaze. Reaching the pilot's position I indicated to Bob that there was no response from either of the gunners, at the same time I noticed that the whole of the port wing was ablaze. Bob then gave the order to bale out. I went to my position, which was under the pilot's position, clipping on my parachute whilst Harry, the navigator, collapsed his table and chair to open the escape hatch under the chair, at the same time destroying the IFF and GEE sets which had explosive charges in them. The IFF was to distinguish us from enemy aircraft on the radar screens on our return to the UK (Identification Friend or Foe) and the GEE set was a navigational aid.

The escape hatch jammed and Harry had to stamp on it to force it out. I handed him a parachute, then noticed that it had my name on it. I indicated this so we quickly swapped them. I then swung my legs through the hatch and the 200 mph slipstream whipped me out and as I fell away I pulled the 'D' ring to release the parachute.

It was pitch black below and I had no feeling of movement. Suddenly I crashed into the top of a tree and fell through until my parachute got entangled and left me hanging between branches. My left thigh was numb where I had hit a branch so I placed my right foot on a branch and struck my harness release whilst trying to locate the branch with my left foot. Placing my weight on both feet my legs collapsed and I crashed down through the tree striking my head and losing consciousness.

As I came to my senses it was getting daylight. I endeavoured to stand but had no feeling in either leg. I had landed in a small wood on a slope and could see that it was much lighter downhill than up, so I crawled to the edge of the wood.

Upon reaching the edge of the wood, I could see a man and two boys spreading something from a horse drawn cart onto the ground. Being about twenty yards away I shouted to them and when they came over, I asked for water. They lifted me to my feet but I collapsed and when I again came fleetingly to my senses, I was being carried on a cart. I vaguely remember being taken into a building and when I finally came to, I was lying on a bed with a nurse and doctor bending over me. They informed me that my left femur was broken and that I was wounded in the right thigh. Enquiring where I was, the nurse stated that I was in Germany, to which I replied that I had to get back to England. I endeavoured to get off the bed but my left leg was in a splint.

And so my sojourn as a prisoner of war had commenced.

The hospital to which I was taken was run by the Sisters of Mercy in the village of Lugde which is situated approximately 10 km south west of Hamelin.

I spent the night there and the next afternoon a *Luftwaffe* medical orderly arrived to escort me to the *Luftwaffe* interrogation centre at Oberursel, 10 km north of Frankfurt-on-Main. He was about 19 years old and could speak a little English. I was then carried on a stretcher to the local railway station. As I had only one escort, when the train arrived, I had to stand on one leg and be assisted by the orderly into the compartment and he then had to bring in the stretcher.

The journey by train during the night necessitated several changes, which meant a repeat practice of getting on and off the stretcher. Most stations had no platforms, so I had then to sit on the carriage step and be lifted down to ground level. With his help, I hobbled to the station building and lay on the stretcher.

At one station, I was lying quietly while the orderly was checking for the next connection when a very large and very tall man walked up to the stretcher, looked down at me and said in perfect English 'My house in Kassel has been bombed'. He was leaning on a walking stick so I thought it best not to reply. The orderly then returned and the man turned away.

When we arrived at the next changing station the orderly set me down in a small room next to the refreshment hall and brought me some noodle soup. Having no doubt he had to inform them for whom it was required a constant stream of female staff came to view the enemy flyer. Some gave me a hard look, others a kindlier one.

At yet a further stop I was taken into the refreshment hall, which was full of mixed military and a soldier brandishing a machine pistol started raving and pointing the gun at me. The orderly quickly brought over a soldier wearing epaulettes on his shoulder whom I learned later was a sergeant. The sergeant rapped out an order to the soldier who immediately turned away. I was very grateful to the orderly and said that maybe in the future in better circumstances, I could show my appreciation and offered him my home address, which he took a note of.

Furthering our journey: at another change, we met up with four aircrew, who were waiting at the station for the connection. One of them was my bomb aimer, who informed me that when he baled out he had lost both of his flying boots and that when captured the next day, had been taken to the site of our wrecked aircraft to identify the bodies of three of the crew still in their respective positions.

The journey to Frankfurt took about eighteen hours. We finally arrived there at about eleven the following morning. There were quite a lot of people on the station, which had recently been badly damaged, so the orderly and the escort for the other airmen quickly moved us to a side entrance, where a military ambulance eventually arrived to take us to the interrogation centre at Oberursel, where the unwounded POWs debussed and I was taken a further short distance to a hospital called Hohe Mark, which was an interrogation centre for shot down airmen and a convalescent hospital for wounded German soldiers.

I was carried in and set on a single bed in a small room on the ground floor and one of the stretcher bearers speaking in a Liverpudlian accent requested me to undress and get into bed. All of my clothes were then taken away and the door was locked from outside. After a short while, a

Luftwaffe officer entered and stated he was acting on behalf of the Red Cross, handed me a form headed with a red cross, and requested I fill in the details against the questions. Filling in my name, rank and number, next of kin and home address, I handed the form to him. He pointed out that further questions on the form must be answered, which related to my squadron, base and various personnel. I informed him that the details I had given were all that was required. He then stated he would give me my RAF history, which he then detailed correctly, giving the date and town where I volunteered, my various postings together with dates. He then informed me that he only required the completed form to confirm my identity. He then said that medical attention would now be given me and he left. Within a few minutes he returned to say that he had omitted to mention my posting to Bobbington. Later my clothes were returned by the Liverpudlian orderly which upon examination I noticed that my front collar stud and brass button which had been on my tunic were missing; they of course had contained small compasses issued for escape purposes. Within another short time a doctor came in and introduced himself and examined my wounds and when he had finished, two orderlies arrived, placed me on the stretcher and carried me up to the next floor. I was taken to a room containing four beds, three of which were occupied. The two orderlies I was informed were two paratroopers who had been captured in North Africa and were both from South Wales. The occupants of the other beds were aircrew who had recently been shot down and had been operated on for bone injuries.

In the conversation that followed, I learned that the first floor of the building, consisting of six rooms, plus a bath room and a toilet, was used entirely for Allied wounded awaiting surgery, or having been treated, were awaiting transfer to a convalescent hospital prior to their final destination, the POW camp. A German doctor was in charge with a German corporal and two German orderlies. These were assisted by a few Allied personnel, who had been captured earlier in the war. These consisted of the Liverpool man who was a Warrant Officer Front-Gunner, shot down from a Manchester, an American civil pilot, who had been ferrying Catalinas across the Atlantic, and was captured after landing in the Bay of Biscay, with the two paratroopers, who had been captured in North Africa. The German doctor, Dr Ittersaghan, was an orthopaedist, who was experimenting with mending broken bones, by placing a hollow metal pin inside the top half of the broken bone, pushing it up to the nearest joint, placing the broken bones together, then knocking the metal pin which was protruding from the joint down through the broken bone. There was then no necessity for a plaster cast.

The occupants in the various rooms consisted of two Canadians with broken femurs, two Americans with broken upper arms, an English flight engineer with a broken femur, a Scottish mid-upper gunner with a broken upper arm. All had recently been shot down, had had their operations and were under the observation of the doctor to note their progress.

The following day the doctor re-examined my leg and informed me that travel arrangements would be made for me to be transferred to the Herman Goering *Luftwaffe* Lazarette in a few days, where he would perform the operation on my leg and that I would be walking again very soon.

Early in November, I had the operation and spent a week in the hospital then returned to the Hohe Mark. The seven of us, all with similar operations, were placed together in one room, the Polish American gunner, Mike Sweck, the American waist-gunner, Tommy Ford, from Maryland, the Canadian bomb-aimer Bill Grant, from Fort William, the Canadian rear-gunner from Waterford Ted Bowlby, the Scottish mid-upper gunner Jock Little from Edinburgh, the English flight-engineer from Ongar Jim Shelsher and myself a Welshman from Cardiff, Harry Winter.

A week later the stitches were removed and I was presented with a set of crutches and was told to start walking, and, as we were able to hobble about we were given little odd jobs to do, such as keeping the room clean and tidy, and each afternoon, after coffee, we were permitted to walk around the surrounding grounds for exercise for about one hour.

Early in December, the second legless pilot arrived at Hohe Mark for interrogation and medical attention. He was Colin Hodgekinson, a Spitfire pilot. Originally he had flown in the Fleet Air Arm, had been involved in a flying accident and had lost both legs, one above and one below the knee and was subsequently discharged. He then joined the RAF, and whilst flying over France on a weather reconnaissance, had regained consciousness to find himself sitting in the cockpit of the crashed aircraft which had apparently pancaked under full power. His blacking out, he felt, must have been due to the lack of oxygen. He was cut and bruised when he arrived but had no serious injuries. The German orderlies were intrigued with his nightly ritual of balancing on one side of the bed, un-strapping his legs and swinging into bed.

Christmas was spent playing German gramophone records of which we had about six and the Dichter and Bauer (Poet and Peasant) was the most popular. On Christmas evening, the Evangelist Sisters on the ground floor tending the German wounded, came up and joined us in carol singing.

During the early part of 1944, some very badly wounded aircrew arrived; a few unfortunately did not survive. Two who did were Taffy Peel, who came from Newport. Apparently as he baled out, the Lancaster went into a side slip and one of the propellers sliced off his left arm at the elbow and his right leg at the knee. The other was Derek Salt from Birmingham; he had both legs severed below the knee. When he landed in thick snow he cut the lines of his parachute and made a tourniquet until two young girls came to his assistance.

As spring approached the 'Pin Boys', as the doctor termed us, were getting more mobile, having dispensed with crutches and finally walking sticks and Mike Sweck, feeling restricted, decided that he was going for a walk, but nothing had been pre-planned. Having been farming in civilian life, he felt that he could live off the land. He could speak fluent Polish and felt sure that the Polish slave labour on the land would give him assistance.

On one hot afternoon, in early June he told the two Canadians and myself that immediately after our exercise period he would be making a bid for freedom. The room windows were open and the long Venetian blinds had tapes which when the blinds were rolled up would nearly reach the ground. When just we four were in the room, he went hand over hand down and dropped the last five or six feet to the ground, ran across the grass and into the trees surrounding the hospital. As he very often laid on his bed, we made it look as if it was occupied. His disappearance was unobserved for the rest of the day and at breakfast the next morning, but at mid-morning whilst a few were seated at the table in the main central hall, the English W/O hurriedly approached and demanded the whereabouts of Sweck. Glancing around the hall, someone suggested that maybe he had gone back on his bed, to which we were informed that he had not. The W/O then went straight to the administration and reported to the German corporal that Sweck had escaped. An alarm was raised and in a very short time, officers from the interrogation centre arrived and started questioning us and dogs were brought to search the hospital grounds. As we had had a thunderstorm the evening before, no trace could be found.

Immediately after lunch the W/O requested that the two Canadians and myself were to pack our belongings, take off our hospital dress and put on our uniforms and we were escorted on foot to the interrogation and put in separate cells [the cooler]. Two days later one of the German ambulance drivers who had got to know us due to his frequent visits to Hohe Mark came along and requested me to give him my boot laces and braces. He spoke perfect English with an American accent. Apparently, he had lived in America for some years and had come to Germany for a holiday in 1941. Hitler declared war on America and he was detained and put into the *Luftwaffe*. When questioned the reason for these items, he replied that the Allies had landed on the French coast and that our hosts were taking precautions that we would cause no further problems. A few days later I was taken out of the cooler and with the two Canadians was taken by ambulance to Bad Homburg where we met up with the other 'Pin Boys' in a hospital. There we were informed that they had found Sweck who was now in the cooler and that we were all going to have our pins extracted. Whilst waiting on the balcony outside the operating theatre, a young nurse sidled up to us to say that she was Belgian and that the Allies had landed.

With the pins withdrawn, we were returned to Hohe Mark for a short while until the stitches were removed. The two Welsh orderlies, we learned, had been sent to Luft 1. We were also informed that we were being transferred to respective English and American prison camps but that Shelsher and Little were being kept there as medical orderlies. Some days later, the two Canadians, myself and a few other partly recovered wounded were escorted by train to Ober Masfelt, which had a larger convalescent hospital for Allied services except American. Here we were able to walk around the compound from dawn to dusk. There was an area outside the compound where football could be played on a Saturday afternoon for all soldiers but not flyers.

Mid-July saw a small party of RAF escorted by two guards armed with a handgun each entrain for Luft VII in Upper Silesia. The first part of the journey was by passenger train where we were put in a carriage together with civilians who were made up of women and children. We had been issued with a Red Cross food parcel each for travelling so we extracted the chocolate from it and offered it to the children. They were reluctant to take it until their mothers, recognising what it was, permitted them to accept. We then lit up cigarettes showing off the packets of 20 American brands, German civilian men were only allowed three cigarettes a day and women none.

Just before noon there was an air raid alarm and a lot of B17s and B24s passed overhead. Our first change of trains was at Erfut, which unfortunately had just sounded the all clear after being visited by the bombers. Our guards seeing the chaos on and around the station, moved us to the end of the platform where we tried to look inconspicuous, but a civilian with a Swastika on his lapel, had spotted us and started inciting the people around us to hang us 'Terror Fleigers'. Fortunately a goods train with open covered wagons full of German troops had just halted and our guard asked to which town they were next heading. When informed Leipsig, we were ordered to jump aboard which we did very smartly. We learned from the troops that they were heading for the Russian front. We reached Leipsig after dark where again we had to change trains; here we hid behind stacks of rubble until our connection came in.

Our next change was at Dresden, which we reached in the early daylight hours. At that time, Dresden was untouched and the guards found us a room in a platform basement where we were able to refresh ourselves and eat before getting down to sleep. In the afternoon we boarded another train bound for Breslau which we reached at about midnight. We then had to halt. We caught another train to Bankau, which we finally reached in the early daylight hours. The camp was about two miles walk which we arrived at before the administration had arrived, so we had to sit on the grass outside until they arrived to sign for our receipt and receive our documents. We were then taken up to the gates of the camp where the inmates were waiting to welcome us.

The camp was new having been opened a few weeks earlier and only about fifty men were held there. The camp had been very hurriedly built and consisted of a guard room and a cook house which were about normal dimension, but the huts for the prisoner accommodation, were only fourteen feet long, nine feet wide and seven feet high at the apex of the roof and they were to sleep six men. A small two feet square table and a stool was provided for each man but no beds, just a wood shave filled sack for each to sleep on. At night the stools were stacked on the table in a corner. There was no lighting provided so oil lamps had to be made from small fish paste tins filled with margerine and a wick made from string or pyjama cord. One blanket, a horse-hair filled sack for a pillow, a china mug and a spoon to each man. We were photographed and our records updated then passed through the for-larger into the main compound. Here we were met by an Australian Sergeant Pilot who introduced himself as the Camp Commander, Peter Thomson. After taking our details at his office we were allocated our accommodation. The weather was at that time very warm and the only means of keeping fairly clean was by stripping, standing under the only hand water pump and having someone pump the handle. A new compound had just been wired off next to ours and a labour force of Russian POWs were building larger huts which when finished we would move into, which had electric lighting, a heating stove, also shower blocks. They were to be ready by late autumn.

The cook house was staffed by 'Kriegies', POWs, and provided one meal a day supplied by the Germans. This consisted of three one inch diameter frost bitten potatoes, considered unfit for consumption by our captors, and a cup of *ersatz* coffe made from acorns. Anything further was relied upon from Red Cross parcels. Once a week we were allocated a few ounces of pulped stinking fish and soft pulped cheese which would only be eaten if there was a food parcel shortage, which became more often as time went by. We also had a ration of pulped sugar beet, which they termed as jam which most could stomach. Being a new camp buffer stocks of food parcels had not been accumulated so each week we eagerly awaited the arrival of a further consignment. All administration of the camp was done by us and supervised by the Germans. But for the two roll calls per day, we were left very much alone. The next few months were spent with organising sports days and making 'Blowers'. These were used for cooking the food from the parcels. The cans, which came from the meat and the vegetable tins, were made into short pipes, and with a belt driven fan at one end, and a square plate at the other, which had a square inch hole cut in the centre, all encased in wood, which was acquired from the wooden cases in which the food parcels had been packed. These were cut up and distributed to handy men who had DIY skills. Fuel was acquired from the cardboard parcel boxes. Nothing was wasted.

All tins of food were punctured before the parcels were distributed, so things like salmon, fish paste, sardines and meat paste, which deteriorated quickly, had to be eaten first. Generally, we organised ourselves into combinations of six so that by combining the contents of the parcels each day six small tins of powdered egg and the same of bacon could be made into one meal for all six or six tins of sardines shared. Also the bread which was made from sawdust was allocated to perhaps one loaf per hut per day, so this was shared out accordingly.

At the end of October, we were transferred to the adjoining compound where the buildings were about twenty feet high and on stilts, sixty feet long and about twenty feet wide. They were built on stilts to stop us digging tunnels under our rooms. Inside they were sectioned off into rooms each side of a central corridor, with each room containing eight, two-tier bunks. A table was supplied, a round iron stove and a low wattage light bulb. Next to the cook house a room was provided which was turned into a theatre and next to that another room for studies. There was also a shower block which could be used at any time with cold water and we were allowed a hot shower once a week, two minutes each.

At about this time Peter Thomson was notified of his commission being established.

Autumn turned to winter, giving lots of snow. An ice rink was made with packed snow, but very few skates could be obtained from the Red Cross. A gramophone arrived with a few records, so each room borrowed it in turn. Musical instruments began arriving, a piano was acquired and as there were a few musicians now in the camp, a band was made up. Bandstands were made from the tea chests from the Red Cross parcels, and as we had also had a few budding actors, various entertainments were organised. For Christmas a pantomime was organised together with one of Noel Coward's plays called 'The Red Peppers'.

Unfortunately the supply of Red Cross food parcels dried up so each week our allocation diminished first to a parcel between two, then finally by Christmas, one between four.

Various study groups had been formed and classes to learn languages. The Welsh boys had a weekly get together, when various subjects were discussed, and contact was made with some Welsh newspapers to which we made reports of our restricted activities.

Christmas was spent with services in the different religions and the Feast was made up of bits and pieces which had been hoarded for the occasion.

Early in January the rumble of guns could be heard from the East, and with the daily news from the 'Canary', the forbidden radio receiver which had been smuggled into camp, speculation was rife that there was a possibility that the Russians would be arriving in the very near future. But our hopes were dashed by a rumour that we were to be evacuated and marched to the West. The rumour unfortunately proved correct and on 19 January the order came through. To the middle of February we were on a forced march in sub-zero weather through Czechoslovakia into Eastern Germany, finally ending up south of Berlin, where we stayed until being overrun by the Russians in April.

I finally arrived home on 19 May 1945, and was demobilised in April 1946.

Returning to civvy street I went back to my old job and after three years went to the paper coating factory where I spent a further six years.

In 1955, I moved to London and took up a position in the same trade, where I retired after fifty years as a paper technician.

Bibliography

Archival Sources
National Archives (Public Record Office)
Air 1 35/15/1/213, 109/15/17, 462/15/312/12, 515/16/3/83, 2132/207/121/1,
    1160/204/5/25/12, 109/15/17, 2386/228/11/1, 2397/262/1,2387/228/11/50,
    2690
Air 2/2797, 8656, 3193
Air 8/425,427,811
Air 9/82, 121, 149
Air 10/3866
Air 14/12, 60, 76, 98–103, 120, 128, 153–5, 168, 181–2, 203–5, 207–11,
    231–3, 243, 251, 255, 259–64, 284–6, 383, 385, 457–8, 607–8, 631–2, 688,
    733, 735, 739A, 745, 884, 928, 1195, 1225, 1230, 1559, 1915, 2681–2,
    2911, 3012, 3207-8, 3246, 3251, 3932, 3954, 4509, 4535
Air 15/717-8, 742
Air 16/96, 125, 277, 302, 504, 619
Air 19/165, 260–1, 417, 434, 818, 524
Air 20/1568, 3641
Air 23/542
Air 27/1349
Air 41/39–42, 56 (AHB narratives)
Air 75/52–3
Avia 7/93, 96, 241, 242, 1390
Avia 8/592
Avia 9/48
Avia 10/11, 26, 55
Avia 13/722, 879
Avia 15/4
Avia 42/10–12
Avia 44/30, 450, 509, 528
Avia 46/79, 158, 172–3, 285, 303
BT 87/150
Cab 102/108, 207, 102/65, 187, 109/45
HO 186/2774
HO 191/191–3, 203
HO 192/16, 1619, 1678–9, 1682, 1695, 1702
HO 195/9, 16

HO 196/26, 28–30, 1678
HO 199/465
HO 228/1
Prem 3/14/3, 10, 139/1
Supp 6/870, 22/33
WO 195/1825, 1957, 6435, 291/1376

Air Historical Branch
Ludlow-Hewitt papers, papers by B Melville Jones, AHB Armament
Booklet SD737 Vol I Bombs & Bombing Eqt, Vol II Guns, Gunsights,
Turrets, Ammunition & Pyrotechnics.

Imperial College London
Sir Henry Tizard Papers Files B/Tizard/3/3–5, 3/7, 3/9

Nuffield College Oxford
Lord Cherwell (Professor Lindemann) Archives
CSAC80.4.81/A30
D47, 117, 123, 174, 258/9
E36
F10/11, 5/1, 5/3, 6/4, 6/5, 7/1-2, 8/5, 9/5–6, 23/3–8, 19–21, 26–7, 30–2, 34,
    36–7, 65, 72, 88–94, 217–252, 417–8, 395–407
G1, 3, 5, 10, 16, 20, 26, 37, 40, 42, 62, 79, 96, 180, 183, 192–3, 200, 202–4,
    214, 240–1, 306, 315, 330, 331

RAF Museum
Sir Arthur Harris Papers Files H9, 12, 14–20, 23, 26–7, 29, 32, 34–5, 41, 43,
    45–7, 49–51, 53, 56–9, 61, 63–70, 78-86, 90–1

Published Sources

Alanbrooke, Lord, *War Diaries 1939–1945*, Wiedenfeld & Nicholson,
    London, 2001
Barnett, Corelli, *The Audit of War*, Pan Books, London, 2002
Beck, Earl R, *Under the Bombs: The German Home Front 1942–1945*,
    University Press of Kentucky, Lexington, Ky, 1986
Below, Nicolaus Von, (trans. by Geoffrey Brooks), *At Hitler's Side*,
    Greenhill Books, London, 2004
Bialer, Uri, *The Shadow of the Bomber*, Royal Historical Society, London, 1980
Biddle, Tami Davis, *Rhetoric and Reality in Air Warfare*, Princeton
    University Press, Oxford, 2002
Bishop, Patrick, *Bomber Boys*, Harper Perennial, London, 2008

Boiten, Theo, *Nachtjagd: The Night Fighter versus Bomber War over the Third Reich*, The Crowood Press, Marlborough, 1997.

Boyne, Walter J, *The Influence of Air Power upon History*, Pen & Sword, Barnsley, 2005

Braun, Hans Joachim, *The German Economy in the Twentieth Century*, Routledge, London, 1992

Brown, GI, *The Big Bang: A History of Explosives*, Sutton Publishing, Stroud, 1998

Budiansky, Stephen, *Air Power*, Viking, London, 2003

Buttler, Tony, *British Secret Projects: Fighters & Bombers 1935–1950*, Midland Publishing, Hinckley, 2004

Cantwell, John D, *The Second World War: A Guide to Documents in the Public Record Office*, HMSO, London, 1993

Cargill Hall, R (Ed), *Case Studies in Strategic Bombardment*, Air Force Historical and Museums Program, 1998

Carver, Michael (Ed), *The War Lords*, Pen & Sword, Barnsley, 2005 [Contains biographies of 'Trenchard' and 'Dowding' by Gavin Lyall, 'Harris' by Martin Middlebrook, 'Tedder' by Air Chief Marshal Sir Christopher Foxley-Norris and 'Spaatz' by Alfred Goldberg amongst others.]

Chant, Christopher, *Aviation: An Illustrated History*, Book Club Associates, London, 1980

Churchill, Sir Winston, *Great Contemporaries*, Fontana Books, London, 1959

Churchill, Sir Winston, Great War Speeches, Transworld Publications, London, 1957

Ciano, Count Galeazzo, *Ciano's Diary*, Phoenix Press, London, 2002

Clark, Ronald W, *Tizard*, Methuen & Co Ltd, London, 1965

Clark, Ronald W, *JBS: The Life and Work of JBS Haldane*, Hodder and Stoughton, London, 1968

Clausewitz, Karl von, *On War*, Penguin Classics, London, 1982

Coemans, HE, *War and Punishment: The Causes of War Termination and the First World War*, Princeton University Press, London, 1996

Collier, Basil, *The Defence of the United Kingdom*, Imperial War Museum in association with Battery Press Inc., London, 1995

Cornwell, John, *Hitler's Scientists*, Penguin, London, 2003

Cox, Sebastian (intro), *The Strategic Air War Against Germany 1939–1945*, Frank Cass, London, 1998

Cross, Robin, *The Bombers*, Guild Publishing, London, 1987

Davis, Richard G, *Carl A Spaatz and the Air War in Europe*, Smithsonian Institution Press, London, 1992

Douglas, W Sholto (Lord Douglas of Kirtleside), *Years of Combat*, Collins, London, 1963

Douglas, W Sholto (Lord Douglas of Kirtleside), *Years of Command*, Collins, London, 1966

Edgerton, David, *England and the Aeroplane*, Macmillan, London, 1991 (Web edition 2006)

Edgerton, David, *Warfare State: Britain 1920–1970*, Cambridge University Press, Cambridge, 2006

Elmhirst, Air Vice Marshal Sir TW, (foreword) *The Rise and Fall of the German Air Force 1933–1945*, Public Record Office War Histories, Kew, 2001

Falconer, Jonathan, *Bomber Command Handbook 1939–1945*, Sutton Publishing, Strand, 2003

Fest, Joachim (trans. by Ewald Osers & Alexandra Dring), *Speer: The Final Verdict*, Phoenix Press, London, 2002

Flower, Stephen, *A Hell of a Bomb*, Tempus, Stroud, 2002

Frank, Anne (trans. by Susan Massotty), *Diary of a Young Girl*, Penguin Books, London, 2000

Furse, Anthony, *Wilfrid Freeman: The Genius behind Allied Air Supremacy 1939–1945*, Spellmount Ltd, Staplehurst, 1999

Galland, Adolf, *The First and the Last: The German Fighter Forces in World War II*, Methuen, London, 1955

Gibson, Guy, VC, (Intro by Sir Arthur Harris) *Enemy Coast Ahead*, Pan Books, London, 1955

Goebbels, Josef, *The Goebbels Diaries*
1. 1939–1941, trans. by Frank Taylor, Hamish Hamilton, London, 1982
2. 1942–1943, trans. by Louis Lochner, Doubleday & Co., New York, 1948
3. *The Last Days*, trans. by Hugh Trevor-Roper, Book Club Assocs., London, 1978

Gooderson, Ian, *Air Power at the Battlefront*, Frank Cass, London, 1998

Gunston, Bill, *Night Fighters: A Development and Combat History*, Sutton Publishing, Stroud, 2003

Haldane, JBS, *Callinicus: A Defence of Chemical Warfare*, Kegan Paul, Trench, Trubner & Co. Ltd, London, 1925

Haldane, JBS, 'ARP' [Air Raid Precautions], Victor Gollancz, London, 1938

Hammel, Eric, *Air War Europa: America's Air War against Germany in Europe and North Africa – Chronology 1942–1945*, Pacifica Press, Pacifica, California, 1994

Harris, Sir Arthur, *Despatch on War Operations 23rd February 1942 to 8th May 1945*, Frank Cass, London, 1995.

Harris, Sir Arthur, *Bomber Offensive*, Greenhill Books, London, 1998

Hastings, Max, 'Bomber Command' in *On the Offensive*, Pan Books,
London, 1995

Hecks, Karl, *Bombing 1939–1945*, Robert Hale, London, 1990

Hendrie, Andrew WA, *The Cinderella Service: RAF Coastal Command
1939–1945*, Pen & Sword, Barnsley, 2006

Heuser, Beatrice, *Reading Clausewitz*, Pimlico, London, 2002

Hinchliffe, Peter, *The Other Battle: Luftwaffe Night Aces versus Bomber
Command*, Airlife Publishing, Shrewsbury, 1996

Hodges, Andrew, *Alan Turing: The Enigma*, Random House, London, 1992

Hooton, ER, *Eagle in Flames: The Fall of the Luftwaffe*, Brockhampton
Press, London, 1997

Howard, Michael, *Clausewitz*, Oxford University Press, Oxford, 1992

Hyland, Gary & Gill, Anton, *Last Talons of the Eagle*, Headline Book
Publishing, London, 1998

Irons, Roy, *Hitler's Terror Weapons: The Price of Vengeance*, HarperCollins,
London, 2003

Isby, Donald C (Ed), *Fighting the Bombers: The Luftwaffe's Struggle Against
the Allied Bomber Offensive*, Greenhill Books, London, 2003

Jackson, Robert, *Army Wings: A History of Army Air Observation Flying
1914–1960*, Pen & Sword, Barnsley, 2006

Jarrett, Philip (Ed), *Aircraft of the Second World War: The Development of the
Warplane 1939–1945*, Putnam Aeronautical Books, London, 1997

Jones, RV, *Most Secret War*, Coronet Books, London, 1992

Joubert de la Ferte, Air Chief Marshal Sir Philip, *The Third Service: The
Story Behind the Royal Air Force*, Thames & Hudson, London, 1955

Keegan, John, *The Mask of Command*, Pimlico, London, 1999

Killen, John, *The Luftwaffe: A History*, Pen & Sword, Barnsley, 2003

Kitchen, Martin, *Nazi Germany at War*, Longman's, London, 1995

Knell, Hermann, *To Destroy a City: Strategic Bombing and its Human
Consequences in World War II*, Da Capo Press, Cambridge, Mass., 2003

Knoke, Heinz (trans. by John Ewing), *I Flew for the Fuhrer*, Evans Bros,
London, 1953

Kroge, Harry Von, *Gema: Birthplace of German Radar & Sonar*, Inst. Of
Physics Publishing, Bristol, 2000

Levine, Alan J, *D-Day to Berlin*, Stackpole Books, Mechanicburg, PA, 2007

Levine, Alan J, *The Strategic Bombing of Germany 1940–1945*, Praeger,
Westport, 1992

Mason, Herbert Molloy, *The Rise of the Luftwaffe 1918–1940*, Cassell,
London, 1975.

Meilinger, Philip, *Airwar: Theory and Practice*, Frank Cass, London, 2003

Middlebrook, Martin and Everitt, Chris, *The Bomber Command War*

Diaries: An Operational Reference Book 1939–1945, Midland Publishing Limited, Leicester, 1996

Mondey, David, *The Hamlyn Concise Guide to British Aircraft of World War II*, Chancellor Press, London, 1994

Mondey, David, *The Concise Guide to American Aircraft of World War II*, Chancellor Press, London, 1996

Mondey, David, *The Concise Guide to Axis Aircraft of World War II*, Chancellor Press, London, 1997

Moore, William, *The Thin Yellow Line*, Wordsworth Editions, Ware, 1999

Munson, Kenneth, *Bombers 1939–1945*, Blandford Press, Poole, 1975

Murray, Williamson, *The Luftwaffe 1933–1945: Strategy for Defeat*, Brassey's, London, 1996

Murray, Williamson, *War in the Air*, Cassell, London, 1999

Neillands, Robin, *The Bomber War*, John Murray, London, 2001

Neufeld, Michael J, *The Rocket and the Reich*, The Free Press, London, 1995

Neville, Peter, *Neville Chamberlain: A Study in Failure?*, Hodder & Stoughton, London, 1992

Nichol, John and Rennell, Tony, *Tail End Charlies: The Last Battles of the Bomber War 1944–1945*, Viking, London, 2004

Norman, Guy and Wagner, Mark, *Boeing*, MBI Publishing Co., Osceola, WI, 1998

Orange, Vincent, *Tedder: Quietly in Command*, Frank Cass, London, 2004

Orange, Vincent, *Slessor: Bomber Champion*, Grub Street, London, 2006

Overy, Richard, *The Air War 1939–1945*, Europa Publications Ltd, London, 1980

Overy, Richard, *Goering: The Iron Man*, Routledge & Kegan Paul, London, 1984

Overy, Richard, *War and Economy in the Third Reich*, Clarendon Press, Oxford, 1994

Overy, Richard, *Why the Allies Won*, Jonathan Cape, London, 1995

Overy, Richard, *Bomber Command 1939–1945*, HarperCollins, London, 1997

Overy, Richard, *Interrogations: The Nazi Elite in Allied Hands*, Penguin, London, 2001

Philpott, Wing Commander Ian M, *The Royal Air Force: An Encyclopaedia of the Inter War Years Vol 1, The Trenchard Years 1918–1929*, Pen & Sword, Barnsley, 2005

Postan MM, Hay D & Scott JD, *The Design and Development of Weapons: Studies in Governmental and Industrial Organisation*, HMSO, London, 1964

Price, Alfred, *The Last Year of the Luftwaffe, May 1944 to May 1945*, Greenhill Books, London, 2001

Price, Alfred, *Instruments of Darkness: The History of Electronic Warfare 1939–1945*, Greenhill Books, London, 2005.

Probert, Henry, *Bomber Harris*, Greenhill Books, London, 2001

Pugh, Peter, *Barnes Wallis: Dambuster*, Icon Books, Cambridge, 2005

Raleigh, Walter (Vol 1) and Jones, HA (vols 2–7), *The War in the Air*, Naval and Military Press (Uckfield) and Imperial War Museum (London) 2007

Richards, Dennis, *Portal of Hungerford*, Heinemann, London, 1977

Richards, Dennis, *The Hardest Victory*, Coronet Books, London, 1995

Richards, Dennis, with Hilary St John Saunders, *Royal Air Force 1939–1945* (3 vols) HMSO, London, 1975

Ritchie, Sebastian, *Industry and Air Power: The Expansion of British Aircraft Production 1935–1941*, Frank Cass, London, 1997

Rivaz, RC, *Tail Gunner*, Jarrold's Publishing, London (date unknown)

Robertson, Scot, *A Revolution in Military Affairs? The Development of Royal Air Force Strategic Bombing Doctrine Between the Wars*, Aerospace Power journal, Spring 1998 (Web edition)

Shepherd, Ben, *A War of Nerves: Soldiers and Psychiatrists 1914–94*, Jonathan Cape, London, 2000

Sinnott, Colin, *The RAF and Aircraft Design 1923–1939: Air Staff Operational Requirements*, Frank Cass, London, 2001

Smith, Ron, *Rear Gunner Pathfinder*, Goodall Publications Ltd, London, 1987

Speer, Albert, *Inside the Third Reich*, Phoenix, London, 2000

Spoden, Peter (trans. by Peter Hinchliffe) *Enemy in the Dark*, Cerberus Publishing Ltd, Bristol, 2003

Steel, Nigel and Hart, Peter, *Tumult in the Clouds: The British Experience of War in the Air 1914–1918*, Hodder & Stoughton, London, 1997

Sun Tsu (trans. by Thomas Cleary) *The Art of War*, Shambhala, London, 1991

Sutherland, Jonathan and Canwell, Diane, *Battle of Britain 1917*, Pen & Sword, Barnsley, 2006

Sweeting, CG, *Hitler's Personal Pilot: The life and Times of Hans Baur*, Brassey's, Dulles, Virginia, 2000

Taylor, Frederick, *Dresden: Tuesday 13 February 1945*, Bloomsbury, London, 2004

Taylor, John WR, *CFS: Birthplace of Air Power*, Jane's Publishing Co. Ltd, London, 1987

Tedder, Lord, *With Prejudice*, Cassell, London, 1966

Terraine, John, *The Right of the Line*, Wordsworth Editions, Ware, 1997

Vajda, Ferenc A and Dancey, Peter, *German Aircraft Industry and Production 1933–1945*, Airlife Publishing, Shrewsbury, 1998

Webster, Sir Charles, and Frankland, Noble, *The Strategic Air Offensive Against Germany*, The Naval and Military Press Ltd, Uckfield, 2006

Wells, Mark K, *Courage and Air Warfare: The Allied Aircrew Experience in the Second World War*, Frank Cass, London, 2000

Williams, Anthony G, *Cannon or Machine Gun?* 'The Aeroplane', September, 2004

Williams, David P, *Night Fighter*, Tempus, Stroud, 2001

Wilson, Kevin, *Bomber Boys*, Cassell, London, 2005

Wilson, Thomas, *Churchill and the Prof.*, Cassell, London, 1995

Wood, Tony and Gunston, Bill, *Hitler's Luftwaffe*, Salamander Books, London, 1997.

Wragg, David, *Fleet Air Arm Handbook 1939–1945*, Sutton Publishing, Stroud, 2003

Index